Running a Food Truck

for dummies

A Wiley Brand

Running a Food Truck

2nd edition

by Richard Myrick

Running a Food Truck For Dummies®, 2nd Edition

Published by: **John Wiley & Sons, Inc.,** 111 River Street, Hoboken, NJ 07030-5774, www.wiley.com

Copyright © 2016 by John Wiley & Sons, Inc., Hoboken, New Jersey

Published simultaneously in Canada

For general information on our other products and services, please contact our Customer Care Department within the U.S. at 877-762-2974, outside the U.S. at 317-572-3993, or fax 317-572-4002. For technical support, please visit https://hub.wiley.com/community/support/dummies.

Wiley publishes in a variety of print and electronic formats and by print-on-demand. Some material included with standard print versions of this book may not be included in e-books or in print-on-demand. If this book refers to media such as a CD or DVD that is not included in the version you purchased, you may download this material at http://booksupport.wiley.com. For more information about Wiley products, visit www.wiley.com.

Library of Congress Control Number: 2016952684

ISBN 978-1-119-28613-4 (pbk); ISBN 978-1-119-28614-1 (ebk); ISBN 978-1-119-28882-4 (ebk)

Manufactured in the United States of America

10 9 8 7 6 5 4 3 2 1

Contents at a Glance

Table of Contents

Introduction

Years ago, eating out was an event reserved for special occasions or weekends. In today's flourishing food service industry, however, you can find a lot of options for any time of the day or week, and because of a number of factors, the food truck has surfaced as a new and exciting way to bring food to the customer.

A lot of people dream of success in the mobile food industry, but due to the relative freshness of the industry and a lack of experienced mentors, many have entered it with misconceptions. Keep in mind that a food truck business is just that — a business. You must crunch numbers, make sales projections, and watch labor costs just like every business. Ultimately, your success will be judged on your profitability, like any other business.

Whether you're a long-time restaurant operator or a fresh, new culinary school grad, reading this book is a wonderful step in launching your own mobile food business. After reading it, you should know whether you have what you need to be successful.

About This Book

No food truck industry trade organization will test you to determine whether you have what it takes to successfully enter the mobile food industry. But after you read this book, you'll have a good idea whether this business is right for you — and you'll have the knowledge to get started on the right foot. You can devour this book from start to finish (no pun intended), or you can check out only the sections you need — either option works. No matter what your level of experience is, you'll find this task-oriented reference book your step-by-step guide to entering and staying in the food truck industry.

To help you navigate this book, I use the following conventions:

>> I use *italics* for emphasis and to highlight new words or terms followed by a definition.

>> I **boldfaced** text to indicate keywords in bulleted lists or the action part of numbered steps.

>> I use monofont for web addresses.

When this book was printed, some web addresses may have needed to break across two lines of text. If that happened, rest assured that I haven't put in any extra characters (such as hyphens) to indicate the break. So when using one of these web addresses, just type in exactly what you see in this book, pretending as though the line break doesn't exist.

You don't have to read every word in this book if you don't want to. I know your time is valuable and you don't have much time to spare. Therefore, to help you speed things up a little, feel free to skip over anything with a Tech Stuff icon next to it. The information in those paragraphs isn't really necessary for understanding the topic. Also, the sidebars (those shaded gray boxes) are fun and interesting, but they're a bonus for people who have the time to read them. Feel free to skip them if you must.

Foolish Assumptions

Food truck owners have to make assumptions about the customers who will be approaching their service windows, and authors have to do the same thing — we have to make assumptions about our readers. I've come up with the following list of assumptions about why you picked up this book:

>> You're thinking about opening your own food truck, and you want practical, how-to advice to accomplish your goals.

>> You've worked in the food truck industry, and now you're thinking about spreading your wings and getting behind the wheel as an owner.

>> You've never worked in a restaurant, let alone a food truck, but you've been a success in other professional endeavors and possess skills that you can apply to this business.

>> You're fresh out of culinary school and thinking about putting those skills to work in your own truck.

>> You currently own or operate a food truck and seek advice to keep it running smoothly and successfully.

>> You buy every book that sports a yellow and black cover.

Icons Used in This Book

In this book, I use small pictures, called icons, to highlight important information. Here's a guide to what the icons mean and what they look like.

REMEMBER

The Remember icon indicates ideas that you should take away from this book, no matter what.

TIP

This icon points out helpful ideas that can give you the upper hand on your road to food truck success.

WARNING

Whenever you see this icon, watch out! It alerts you to potential pitfalls to avoid. Reach out for advice from a professional on these matters.

TECHNICAL STUFF

I use the Technical Stuff icon to flag information that's interesting but not essential for a food truck rookie to know.

Beyond the Book

This book comes with an online Cheat Sheet that includes additional helpful information. To get the Cheat Sheet, go to `www.dummies.com` and type Running a Food Truck For Dummies Cheat Sheet in the Search box. (No access code required.)

Where to Go from Here

If you want to know everything involved in owning and operating a food truck, start at the beginning of this book and read it straight through. However, if you're looking for certain aspects of running a food truck, you can refer to the table of contents or the index to find the specific topic you want. Each chapter is meant to stand alone, and the information each chapter contains isn't dependent on your reading previous chapters to understand it.

If you're brand-new to the mobile food industry and aren't sure where to start, Chapter 2 helps you understand the different types of vehicle platforms to choose from that best suit your concept. Interested in tips to create or improve your menu? Turn to Chapter 8. Want to find out how to attract more customers to your service window with the help of social media? Chapter 16 has your name all over it.

You can jump around, start wherever you want, and finish when you feel like it, so buckle in and hit the road.

1

Rolling into the Food Truck Industry

Chapter 1

Food on Wheels: The Lowdown on Food Trucks

So you've just finished watching the latest episode of *Eat Street* or *The Great Food Truck Race* and think that owning a food truck looks like fun. Or maybe you stumbled upon a food truck in your area, watched the busy lines, and noticed that the staff appeared to be having a great time. With these observations, it wouldn't be a huge leap for you to think, "Hey, these trucks get huge crowds, and the employees seem to be happy, so maybe I should run my own."

When on the outside looking in, you can easily miss all the hard work that's involved in getting a food truck business started and ready to serve the community. As the owner, you have to manage every detail of the business, including hiring the staff, designing the menu, and even picking up trash left by your customers. A food truck can quickly become more work than fun if you aren't aware of all you'll be required to do.

This chapter serves as your starting point into the mobile food industry. I take you on a quick tour of a day in the life of a food truck owner and then give you a guide to help you look a little deeper at your motivations and expectations for entering the industry. I also walk you through the steps of starting and running your own truck, from deciding what kind to run to getting (and keeping) followers.

Checking Out a Typical Day in the Life of a Food Truck Owner

Running a food truck is no stroll in the park. In fact, operating a food truck can involve downright dirty, draining, and difficult work. When your employees drop the ball, it's up to you to pick it up. When a tire goes flat, often you'll be the one who has to repair it. You'll work the most (and longest) hours. You'll work every job in the business, from line cook to mechanic to accountant. To create a successful food truck business, you'll need to develop a culture of hard work, with you being the one setting the example for your staff.

After weeks (or months) of refining your recipes and spending numerous hours on the phone, waiting in line, and filling out reams of paperwork, you're finally ready Your truck has been outfitted with the perfect kitchen. The sign company has called to inform you that the graphics and menu board are complete. It's time to fire up the grill and open for business. Now comes the easy part, right? Sure, it can be a 9-to-5 job, but not in the way you may expect. The following sections provide you with a look into a day in the life of a food truck owner. (Keep in mind that your schedule will look different if you opt for a different service time, such as breakfast or lunch.)

REMEMBER

When I say a 9-to-5 workday, I bet the following sections aren't quite what you're expecting. I didn't include this information to scare anyone but rather to provide a look into a typical day of a food truck owner. Many truck owners I've spoken with have told me that nothing is glamorous about running a food truck. Why do they do it then? According to most, the feeling they get when they see their customers' laughs and smiles after taking bites of the items they just ordered off the menu makes it all worth it — they do it for a love of cooking and serving the public.

9 a.m. to noon

The alarm goes off, and you crawl out of bed; it's 9 a.m. While the coffee brews, you boot up your computer so you can check any important emails, tweets, Facebook messages, and the like that may have come in overnight. From the time you wake up until approximately two hours later, you're busy going over your calendar of events and planning for your day. After you complete your correspondence, you start planning for upcoming events. With 30 minutes to go before meeting with your team members, it's time to get ready and drive to your meet-up location, the commercial kitchen.

High noon to 12:30 p.m.

You meet with your team to discuss your notes, daily specials, and suggestions from lessons learned the previous day. Your team shares with you what they've heard overnight from local news and from customers and competitors. Sharing this information keeps everyone in the loop, part of the team, and, in most cases, in high spirits.

12:30 p.m. to 5:30 p.m.

During this time, the team goes to the market and bakery or to inventory the food shipments that have been delivered. After getting the food needed for the truck, everyone heads to the commercial kitchen to chop fruits and vegetables, blend the sauces, and grill the meat (if you serve it). Those team members not involved in the food prep will organize the truck to ready it for the work night, fire up their Twitter and Facebook accounts to notify followers of the truck's location(s), and conduct another round of correspondence and phone calls.

5:30 p.m. to 6 p.m.

Time to head to your "office"; you now take the truck from the commercial kitchen's lot to your first stop.

6 p.m. to 2:30 a.m.

It's time! It's time to open the doors, practice your trade, and make your mark on your community. When you reach your destination and a line of people are already at the curb, the sight is both invigorating and terrifying. It's invigorating because you already have loyal followers who have found your location and are waiting to be served a meal from your heart. It's terrifying because you need to park and start cooking quickly so you aren't keeping your customers waiting too long.

REMEMBER

You'll have little to no awareness of what's going on outside the truck during this period. Your eyes will shift from the growing queue of ticket orders to the fryers to the main cooking surface while you're preparing the orders as they come in. Now is when you must enjoy your job; now is the point where you'll know whether you've made the proper choice in opening a food truck. If you're distracted or dislike your environment, you may want to start planning how to sell your investment and head to another career.

2:30 a.m. to 5 a.m.

The night's service is over, and you've made your way back to the commercial kitchen. You clean out the truck and wash it down so it's ready for the next shift. You break down and marinate the meat and, in some cases, even order the bread for tomorrow's pick-up or delivery.

You store the food and lock up the truck. It's finally time to head home.

On the trip home, you reflect back on the day and are very thankful that the oil in the fryer didn't explode or that you were able to start the truck without any issues, and finally, you see it — home sweet home. After a final round of reading emails and listening to phone messages, you go to bed. Your 9-to-5 workday is over, only to start again in a few hours.

Discovering Whether You Have What It Takes to Run a Food Truck

Have you ever wanted to start your own business? If you're self-motivated and have a love of food and people, opening your own food truck can be a great career option for you. Not everyone is cut out for this diverse industry, though. Are you? You can find out with the help of the following sections.

Monitoring your motivations

Owning your own food truck takes a special type of person. A successful food truck owner needs to have some business sense. Patience is an important asset in owning your own mobile food business, as are good people skills.

Before you invest any more time or money in the process of starting up your food truck empire (except for purchasing and reading this book), you need to find out the real reasons you're motivated to do this. Be as honest with yourself as possible; fooling yourself is only going to hurt you and your pocketbook in the long run.

People have many reasons to want to own and operate a food truck; some of my favorites include the following:

>> They like the business aspect of owning a food truck.

>> They have a passion for food.

>> They want to provide a service to their community.

>> They're self-motivated.

>> They like being around other people.

The following list contains some reasons that *shouldn't* be motivation for starting a food truck:

>> Thinking it'll be easy

>> Thinking it'll make you rich

>> Wanting to be a celebrity chef

>> Being tired of having a "real" job

If you happen to be motivated by any of these reasons, don't fret. Just make sure they're not your only (or primary) motivators to enter this industry.

Tracking key traits

A food truck's success isn't based on any magic formula, but most food truck owners who do well share many of the same personality traits. They're a special breed of culinary entrepreneurs who are highly motivated, caring, and curious individuals. They effectively balance their personal and business goals, take advantage of others' expertise, and continually seek to figure out the best practices exhibited by their competition. Some common traits shared by food truck owners include the following:

>> **Hard workers:** Successful food truck owners work hard and play hard, too. They get up early; they rarely complain; they expect high performance from others, but they expect extraordinary performance from themselves.

- >> **Self-reliant and not afraid to take responsibility:** Successful food truck owners don't worry about blame, and they don't waste time complaining. They make decisions and move on.

- >> **Focused on the future:** Food truck owners who have thrived are good at both short and long-term planning. They're as likely to have a well-thought-out plan for the day-to-day running of their business as a road map for how to run the business for years.

- >> **Eager to learn:** Strong food truck owners are always reading, educating themselves, and asking questions. They ask for advice, try things out, consult experts and amateurs, and always look for a better, faster, and cheaper solution.

- >> **Action oriented:** Successful food truck owners are proactive and always differentiate themselves from their competitors. They're less worried than other small business owners about the state of the economy and are more likely to look at adversity as a sign to keep moving forward.

- >> **Tech-savvy:** Perhaps it shouldn't be a surprise that the best food truck owners invest both time and money on improving their website and are likely to rely a great deal on technology, such as social media and point-of-sale systems, to help make their business more efficient.

Doing Some Initial Work to Start Your Food Truck

REMEMBER

Starting a food truck business may not be as expensive as opening a brick-and-mortar restaurant. With that said, it still costs more money than most people have on hand, and it can still be as potentially risky as opening a diner or fine-dining establishment. Because of this, you have to plan ahead and get your ducks in a row. Here's what you need to do so:

- >> The first thing everyone thinks of when discussing the mobile food industry is the vehicles the food is served from. Depending on your area and the laws there that regulate the industry, you need to determine which type of food truck platform best suits your needs. Chapter 2 covers the pros and cons of each type of truck as well as what you need to consider when determining which will be the best for your business.

- >> Even if you have the best truck on the streets and the most delicious menu offerings, without understanding the needs of your marketplace, a food truck business is going to have a tough time surviving for long. Chapter 3 gives you a firm grasp on how to research your market and how to understand the way to provide your customers with a product and service they keep coming back for.

» A business plan is the best tool for figuring out how much money you need to start your business. It describes why, when, and how you're going to start turning a profit. Chapter 4 has the steps to prepare a plan.

» After you create your business plan, you'll need to start using it to help secure capital for your business. Chapter 5 runs you through calculating your start-up costs and who to approach to get the financing you need.

» To assist you with getting your numbers together for your business plan and financing, you should hire an accountant (preferably one with restaurant or food truck experience) early in the process of starting your business. Chapter 6 has tips on hiring a good accounting professional.

An attorney also can help provide a smooth start-up process for your truck. She can help you get through the mountain of paperwork you'll be required to fill out and submit for your operational permits. She can also assist you in reviewing contracts and setting up the business structure of your company. So make sure you're working with a good attorney before you sign your first vendor contract and kitchen lease, or even hire your first employee. You can find these topics and more in Chapter 6.

» Whether they purchase a new or used food truck, most people want to either change up the equipment or at least give it a clean, fresh look to match their truck concept. You also need to plan where to set up shop in your area — what locations are best for parking? To help you sort out these topics, check out Chapter 7.

Preparing to Launch Your Business

Your menu is going to be the tool used to attract your customers, but a lot goes into preparing the items on that menu. This work includes the menu's content and design (see Chapter 8), where the food is going to be stored and prepared (I explore commissary and commercial kitchen options in Chapter 9), the supplies you need to prep your meals (see Chapter 10), and who will actually prepare it (check out Chapter 11 for info on hiring and training your staff).

You may spend much of your day working in your truck, but completing the business aspects, like bookkeeping or calling your suppliers, from inside your truck can be difficult. You need an office to do these tasks, whether it's at your home or in another location. Chapter 12 helps you set up your office.

Keeping Your Food Truck Business Running Well on All Levels

Your truck is going to be where you spend most of your time during the business day, and it's the spot where you'll be preparing your culinary delights for your customers. Just as a restaurant needs to make sure its kitchen is kept up to code, you must make sure your truck's kitchen and the food you're serving are properly maintained to prevent your customers from getting sick. Check out Chapter 13 to find out more about safe food handling practices and other important safety issues, and turn to Chapter 21 for extra tips on passing all your health department inspections.

You may have a highly trained mechanic who maintains your food truck and makes sure you have a finely tuned mobile kitchen, but he can't determine whether the business being generated in the truck is meeting your expectations. To evaluate the financial side of your business, see Chapter 14.

Luring (and Keeping) Crowds

Sure, stating that attracting customers to your service window is how you're going to make a profit for your business may be common sense, but doing so is a little more difficult when dealing with a food truck because, well, you're mobile. You don't have a permanent location, and to get repeat customers, you have to let the people of your community know where you're going to be. Adding to that, you have the task of providing your customers with products, service, and an atmosphere that they enjoy and that gets them coming back for more and spreading the word to their friends and family.

TIP

So how do you bring in these crowds and keep them coming back? Here are a few questions that can help get you headed down the right path:

>> **What about your truck attracts customers?** In other words, what makes your truck different from all the other food vendors or restaurants vying for your customers' attention? Between the food you serve, the atmosphere you provide, and the service your customers receive, you need to get the word out

about what makes your food truck worth the stop. Check out Chapter 15 to find out how to master the marketing of your truck, along with more promotional ideas.

>> **Got Twitter?** An overwhelming majority of food truck followers track their favorite food trucks through social media sites, like Twitter and Facebook. Take a look at Chapter 16 to find out how to use social media platforms to spread the word about your truck and where it'll be.

>> **Now that you have customers showing up, how do you keep them?** Who are your customers, and what do they enjoy about your food and services? Maybe they like knowing what to expect from your service and menu every time they show up, or maybe you've listened to their previous complaints and made the necessary corrections. Chapter 17 shows you how to build and retain your followers.

After you've become a veteran food truck operator, and depending on how the crowds in your market react to your business strategies, you'll need to determine the direction for your mobile business. If business is booming and you think you need to expand, which route will you take? Franchising? Adding trucks to your fleet? Adding catering services? On the other hand, if the market just hasn't welcomed your business the way you thought it would, you may have to consider the options of rebranding your concept or even selling. Whatever the case, I discuss all your options in Chapter 18.

IN THIS CHAPTER

Developing your food truck's concept

Choosing and buying the right vehicle for your business

Selecting the proper name for your business

Considering the possibility of joining a franchise

Chapter 2

Deciding What Kind of Food Truck Is Right for You

S o you think you want to enter the mobile food industry? If you're like many current and previous food truck owners, you have an idea about what type of truck you want to start up. The question I need to ask you is this: Exactly how much time have you really put into this thought?

Before starting up your food truck, the first thing you must do is develop its concept. Your concept describes what your truck will be like in terms of service style, cuisine, and the atmosphere your truck and staff will present. Your concept frames how the public will see your business and defines a general set of expectations the public will have when they walk up to your service window. You have a lot of decisions to make when formulating your food truck concept, and ultimately, you're limited only by your imagination and budget. With so many possibilities, how do you know what kind of food truck to run?

In this chapter, I go over the items you must decide on as you generate a concept for your food truck. I walk you through the various types of vehicles you can use for your business and explain how to get the vehicle you need. I touch on the important steps in giving your truck a name that people will remember. Last but not least, I present another option for starting a food truck (in addition to starting a business from scratch): joining a franchise.

Generating Your Food Truck's Concept

Figuring out the concept for your food truck is one of the most important decisions you'll ever make for your business. After you've made this decision, everything else about your business will fall in line with it, from its specific menu items and truck design to the number of employees you'll hire and their culinary backgrounds.

In the following sections, I list food choices and general considerations to help you come up with a basic concept; then I help you narrow your idea based on your potential customers and the atmosphere you want.

Note: In some cases, you may not need to determine a concept for your food truck. For example, you may be a food truck franchisee of a restaurant that has already worked out all the details of your concept. See the later section "Another Possibility: Joining a Franchise" for details.

Focusing on your food options

At its most basic level, your truck will be most recognized for the food you serve. In the following sections, I note several categories of food that have found food truck success around the United States.

TECHNICAL
STUFF

Due to my experience in organizing some food truck events, I can tell you that one demographic food trucks haven't left out is individuals who own dogs. Although technically not people food trucks, some trucks navigating around dog parks in the country supply canine customers with locally sourced, healthy dog treats that many dog owners can't pass up when they find them.

Savory foods

You have a wide variety of options when it comes to serving savory foods in your food truck:

>> **American cuisine** is capable of making it onto any list of popular food trucks thanks to Americans' love of hamburgers. Other popular American favorites

are grilled cheese sandwiches, hot dogs, French fries, mac 'n' cheese, and various types of barbecued meat.

>> **Mexican cuisine** is known for its varied flavors, colorful decoration, and variety of spices and ingredients, many of which are native to the country. Tacos, burritos, tamales, and tortas are menu favorites of many food truck owners because they're easily massaged to fit into various concepts.

>> **African cuisine** (for example, Ethiopian, Moroccan, or South African) traditionally uses a combination of locally available fruits, cereal grains, and vegetables, as well as milk and meat products.

>> **Italian cuisine** is hard to explain without mentioning pizza and pasta, but these two dishes tell you almost all you need to know about this style of cuisine. Some truck owners vending Italian cuisine regularly serve these dishes along with veal and eggplant parmesan sandwiches.

>> **Asian cuisine** (such as Chinese and Japanese) typically consists of rice or noodles, with a soup. Foods are made from fish, meat, vegetable, tofu, and the like. Food items are typically flavored with dashi, miso, and soy sauce and are generally low in fat and high in salt.

>> **Mediterranean cuisine** is full of fresh vegetables and high in flavor. Options for food trucks choosing Mediterranean cuisine include (but aren't limited to) kabobs, gyros, pita sandwiches (vegetable, shawarma, falafel, and lamb), hummus, and baba ghanoush.

>> **Thai cuisine** is often confused with Chinese cuisine. The primary difference is in its flavoring. Thai food has a balanced mix of sweet, sour, and spice. Bánh mi is by far the most popular of the foods coming from Thai-themed trucks, such as the Bon Me Truck out of Boston.

>> **Indian cuisine** may provide the widest variety of food for your menu even though it's most known for vegetarian fare. The real treats of Indian cuisine are chicken and fish tikkas, naan, and samosas.

Other styles of cuisine to investigate include Caribbean, Cajun, Cuban, German, Philippine, Native American, Spanish, soul food, seafood, Tex–Mex, vegetarian/vegan, and Vietnamese.

Just desserts

While some of the savory trucks provide minimal coverage of various dessert favorites, other food truck owners focus their attention on these sweet delights — everything from ice cream, waffles, cupcakes, shaved ice, whoopie pies, and brownies. You can even find trucks that provide more ethnic styles of dessert on their menus, such as cannoli, tiramisu, crêpes, and baklava.

TIP

You may wonder whether dessert trucks can provide enough income to justify multiple dessert trucks in one area. Don't think twice about it — they can. Dessert trucks provide a wonderful way for customers to enjoy a full meal by simply going to multiple trucks that are parked near each other. In Chapter 7, I discuss in more detail how savory and dessert trucks can work as a team to maximize the sales of both trucks. So if you're looking to provide your customers a sugar rush to jump-start their day, this avenue may be perfect for you.

Tasty beverages

Although food trucks serving alcoholic beverages haven't been approved en masse, nonalcoholic beverage trucks have. Consumers are constantly attempting to improve their health, and food truck owners have latched onto this phenomenon by providing these customers with a mobile option. Trucks that sell nothing but juice or smoothies have made their way onto the streets of some cities with much success.

Starting the selection process

After you know the food choices available to you (see the preceding section), consider these items when you begin the process of selecting a food concept for your truck:

>> **Having a unique concept:** Make sure your idea is different from the ideas behind both food trucks and similar casual brick-and-mortar restaurants in your locality. If ten Mexican cuisine trucks or restaurants already exist in the area, you may want to avoid opening another one. (See Chapter 3 for details on determining what's already in your local food truck market.) However, if you decide to open a truck with a popular concept anyway, make sure you offer something that differentiates you from the others, such as fusing the basic taco with another ethnic cuisine.

REMEMBER

The mobile food industry is on the leading edge of concept development. Food trucks have developed concepts, such as grilled cheese sandwiches or Korean tacos, that hadn't yet been seen in the restaurant industry. So don't be afraid to try something new.

>> **Making sure your concept is easy to understand:** Although differentiating yourself from your competitors is important, you must make sure your idea isn't so different that people don't get it. This type of consumer confusion can lead to your downfall because customers typically avoid eating from establishments that they're completely unfamiliar with.

TECHNICAL STUFF

The logo and decoration of your truck is half the battle. Customers buy with their eyes. Your vehicle's curb appeal will be a key factor in landing customers out in the street. (I discuss how to present and decorate your food truck in Chapter 7.)

>> **Sticking to one basic cuisine:** Don't try to compete directly with local full-sized restaurants that, based on kitchen size and seating capabilities, can offer more extensive menu options. Focus on a specific style of cuisine for your concept. This strategy allows you to fill your menu with crowd-pleasing items that you can consistently produce to a high standard.

>> **Keeping up with current food trends:** Stay up-to-date with the mobile food industry and understand the latest food trends, such as the desire for healthy local meals and ingredients. Don't hold strictly to these trends for your overall concept, though, because trends come and go. However, that doesn't mean you can't create a concept that allows you to update your menu to use trendy items, such as bison or elk. Check out Mobile Cuisine (www.mobile-cuisine.com) and Nation's Restaurant News (www.nrn.com) for food trends making their way into the mobile food and restaurant industries.

>> **Being inspired by others:** Don't be afraid to take someone else's idea and make it better. If you find a great food truck while traveling through different parts of the country and want to create one with a similar concept in your town, don't be shy — go for it!

TIP

General industry etiquette is not to rip off and duplicate exactly. Food truck operators, like great musicians, know how to pay homage to those who have come before them.

>> **Making sure you have the necessary staff or culinary skills:** If you decide to serve Vietnamese cuisine but don't have any experience with Vietnamese cooking, for example, you need to either hire a chef who does or learn how to cook Vietnamese food on your own. Take classes at a nearby culinary school or speak with restaurant owners in your area to see whether you can learn from them. (I provide information on hiring a chef in Chapter 11.) If these options don't appeal to you, find a different concept for your truck.

>> **Thinking about the locations where you'll operate:** If you plan to operate in an area in which the demographics of the population don't fit a specific style of cuisine or concept, you may need to consider another concept. Check out Chapter 3 for information relating to understanding market demographics.

>> **Considering the time of day you plan to operate:** You need to contemplate whether you plan to work morning, lunch, dinner, or late-night hours. If you plan to work only morning shifts, having a concept that centers on heavy greasy food may not be a great fit. However, a truck that sells coffee and tea along with a variety of breakfast sandwiches for early morning commuters may be a fantastic niche to build around.

>> **Being passionate about your idea:** Your food truck will become a huge part of your life; you'll work long hours and deal with every aspect of running it. With all the time, energy, and money you'll be putting into your mobile business, be sure you're passionate about your concept. A few special

signature dishes that you love to make for your friends and family can be a good indicator of where your passion may lie. If the idea of serving burgers and fries doesn't really excite you, for example, your business may not last very long if you choose burgers and fries for your truck's cuisine, and you may end up wasting a lot of your time and money.

Note: No matter how passionate you are about your idea, don't forget to determine whether it's viable. Is there enough demand in your area for your concept? Will people pay for what you plan to offer on your menu? Ask yourself, would you buy this item at this price? Flip to Chapter 3 for details on researching your local food truck market.

Narrowing your concept according to your customer base

REMEMBER

After you have a basic idea of your concept (see the preceding section), you need to determine the type of customers you want to target. You need to find out whether a substantial market for your concept exists in the areas you plan to operate in. Use the following tools to help you further narrow down your concept according to your potential customer base (see Chapter 3 for details on these tools):

>> **Demographic survey:** Use the demographic survey to determine the demographics of the market you're going to be located in. This survey gives you information, such as the ages, occupations, and income levels, of your prospective customers; ethnic groups in the area; and the size of the market to help you see whether your concept is a good fit for the area. You may find that a large ethnic group in the area isn't currently being catered to by existing food trucks or restaurants. You may want to lean your concept toward this demographic.

>> **Competitive analysis:** This tool helps you understand who your local competition will be. You can use this information to compare your menu prices with those of your competitors. Do the prices required to give you a market advantage fit with your concept?

Understanding the importance of atmosphere as you generate your concept

The atmosphere your truck presents may be one of the most important methods for achieving your food truck concept. When considering atmosphere for your truck, think about the experience you want and the senses that will be affected when a customer walks up to your truck. Read on for some important considerations.

Designing the atmosphere or *feel* of your concept involves a lot of work on your part. Can you manage everything on your own? Do you have the expertise to gather all the information you need? Hiring a professional graphic designer or food truck consultant costs some money, but it can save you a lot of time and potential problems in the long run. By farming out this work, you can brainstorm your ideas with experts and get their feedback, and their professional guidance can give you the confidence you need to move forward with your concept.

Here are a few resources for finding the experts you need to help come up with the right atmosphere for your desired food truck concept:

>> Food Fellas: www.foodfellasllc.com

>> Mobi Munch: www.mobimunch.com

>> Vucurevich | Simons Advisory Group (VSAG): www.vsag.com

Sight

What do you want your customers to see? A concept's visual effect encompasses more than just the graphics you wrap your truck in (see Chapter 7 for the scoop). Lighting applies to trucks that work at night, but even if you plan to work only during daylight hours initially, considering lighting upfront is a good idea in case you later decide to start working shifts after the sun goes down. The lighting on the interior of the truck as well as the lighting inside the kitchen can help you achieve different visual effects. Think about the lighting in the area where you plan to park your vehicle in, too, because it can help you achieve a certain mood as well.

Another important aspect to consider regarding your customers' sight is your kitchen. Will customers be able to see into the kitchen of your food truck? The type of vehicle you select will determine this aspect of your conceptual atmosphere: Some give better views into the kitchen than others based on the height and size of the service window.

The lighting in the kitchen is important. You must provide a safe environment for those working inside. The lighting you choose also influences how well your customers can see inside.

Providing a show in which the food is prepared in full view of the customers, as sushi chefs are famous for, or providing the sight of a few flames flying up from the grill may establish a unique and engaging atmosphere.

Sound

The noises coming from your food truck affect the atmosphere. You may want to play a certain type of music to enhance your concept. Playing Hawaiian or Maria-chi music can give an energetic, exotic feel to the atmosphere around your truck, whereas playing hard rock can help a concept intended to attract a crowd with a little heavier music preference.

TIP

Be sure to check with your local municipality about the laws relating to playing music on your food truck. Some don't allow it or put restrictions on how loud the music can be.

Evaluating Different Types of Vehicles

So you've pinpointed the concept for your food truck, with the help of the infor-mation I provide earlier in this chapter, that's a great start. Now you have to figure out what type of vehicle to use to deliver your concept. You can select from a vari-ety of platforms as a means to make a kitchen mobile. I give you the scoop on trucks, carts, trailers, and buses in the following sections.

REMEMBER

The vehicle you choose for your mobile business must meet your local permitting office's requirements as well as your own personal kitchen needs. Before you begin shopping for your vehicle, I suggest you determine the amount and types of kitchen equipment you'll need to prepare your menu items (see Chapter 10 for full details). You need only a general understanding of your necessary equipment at this point so you can determine the types and sizes of vehicles you can choose from. Some of these vehicles can be restricted in their use, depending on the vehicular codes and laws that regulate food trucks in your area. So speak with the heads of your city's health department and permitting offices to make sure you're aware of their requirements.

Trucks

Food trucks are the preferred choice of most vendors in the mobile food industry because of their range in sizes and their mobility. By definition, a food truck is a licensed, motorized vehicle or mobile food unit that's used for selling food items to the general public. This definition is quite vague, but that may be because the definition of a food truck varies from city to city. In some cities, you may find that a food truck is a set of heating units sitting in the back of a pickup truck. In other areas, a food truck is a mobile kitchen built into a truck the size of a standard delivery truck (this definition has become the most common one since the surge in the mobile food industry in 2008). These trucks can range in length from 14 feet all the way up to 30 feet. The kitchens in these trucks are fully functioning kitchens that are regulated just as any other commercial kitchen, with additional inspection requirements to make sure all this equipment is safe to travel in between uses. You can check out an honest-to-goodness food truck in Figure 2-1.

FIGURE 2-1:
A typical food truck is the size of a standard delivery truck.

The pros of using a food truck over a cart or trailer are that a truck is far more mobile and can use parking spaces designated for one or two cars. Food carts are typically dropped off and parked in a single location and, like trailers, require a secondary vehicle to tow them. The kitchens you can have installed in food trucks are nearly the size of those in some trailers, so using a truck instead of a cart also gives you more space.

TECHNICAL STUFF

Some creative conversions of standard vehicles can be found all around the country. Food trucks have been created by retrofitting Mini Coopers and small postal trucks — one creative company even built a food truck in the back of a Smart Car!

Carts

Food carts are different from food trucks in that they don't travel under their own power. These carts are towed by a vehicle and are typically dropped off for the time that they're permitted, in some cases, multiple years. A major downside to food carts is their size. The average food cart ranges in size from 120 to 200 square feet, which severely limits the amount of equipment and staff you'll be able to fit inside. You can see a food cart for yourself in Figure 2-2.

FIGURE 2-2:
A food cart is smaller than a standard food truck.

Photograph courtesy of Derek Coughlin

Food carts are much smaller than their food truck counterparts; yes, you can see this fact as a negative, but it's also their key advantage. With less space, you'll have lower costs in powering your cart (propane and electricity), so with a lower overhead to operate, you'll have the opportunity to keep your prices lower than those of more mobile platforms.

TECHNICAL STUFF

Portland, Oregon, has experienced a boom in the number of food carts licensed in the last decade. A 2001 report by *The Oregonian* stated that Portland was home to 175 carts; that number increased to over 500 carts in 2016, according to Food Carts Portland (www.foodcartsportland.com).

Trailers

Much like food carts, food trailers lack a drivetrain system and thus require a vehicle to tow them to the locations where vendors plan to sell their fare. However, these trailers are much larger than food carts (some reach the size of cross-country semitrailers). The vast amount of space that these trailers have allow their owners to install much larger kitchens, which in turn allows them to cater to much larger crowds than the average food truck or cart can handle. See a food trailer in Figure 2-3.

TECHNICAL STUFF

Chef Jamie Oliver has gone a step further by installing a full culinary school inside a trailer to teach students around the United States how to prepare food in a healthy way. To check out more about Jamie Oliver's Food Revolution and to see what his culinary school trailer is all about, go to www.jamieoliver.com/us/foundation/jamies-food-revolution.

WARNING

The downside to being this large is that in most cities across the country, trailers are unable to park on public streets, so they're either forced to park in a static location or restricted to only serving customers at large events, such as festivals and sports arenas.

Buses

Up to this point in the mobile food industry's history, eating at food trucks in many locations of the country is still a unique dining experience. But diners in the Los Angeles, California, or Sarasota Springs, New York, areas have an opportunity to dine somewhere that's the epitome of unique. Diners in these two cities now have another mobile food option: the *bustaurant,* a restaurant within a bus (see Figure 2-4).

Instead of the typical standing at a curb, ordering, and eating, the customers of these new eateries are given the option to step onboard and be seated at tables inside the bus. Although these buses are outfitted with state-of-the-art kitchens, the ordinances that regulate them prohibit kitchen operation while they're moving. For this reason, most of the food is prepared off-site, or in the kitchen only while the bus is stopped in a designated parking area.

FIGURE 2-4: A bustaurant seats its customers.

Photograph courtesy of Lorraine Murphy

One of the biggest differences between the bustaurant and its land-locked restaurant brethren is that if you get seated with a bad view, you may have a better one shortly. The other big difference is the price involved in purchasing a double-decker bus (prices start in the $250,000 range for a standard bus without a kitchen).

Using a double-decker bus to operate your food truck business will clearly differentiate you from your competitors, but it has its fair share of problems as well. You must have a commercially licensed driver, and the size of the bus alone can cause issues of parking on the streets because most shop owners won't take too kindly to having their entire storefront blocked by the side of your bus.

In other parts of the country, vendors have converted smaller buses for use only as a serving platform as opposed to a place to seat guests. If you choose to go that route, you may still need a driver with a commercial license, but you'll have fewer parking restrictions to deal with; however, you lose the customer seating option that the double-decker bus provides.

Figuring Out How to Get the Vehicle of Your Choice

Your first step in determining what type of vehicle you can afford is based solely on how much capital you have on hand or how much you can be approved to finance. After you've determined your budget and figured out how to finance your business (check out Chapter 5), you'll be ready to look down the various avenues in which you can acquire the platform for your mobile business. The following sections discuss leasing a vehicle, buying or building a brand-new vehicle, and buying a used vehicle.

REMEMBER

Take the time to test-drive any food truck you're interested in. You must determine the maneuvering of the vehicle and how its sightlines are. You don't want to get on the road and find out that you need multiple spotters to be able to park in most areas. Why risk your insurance premiums if you can find a truck that maximizes your visibility?

Leasing a vehicle

If you don't have access to a large amount of start-up capital but know you'll have enough to make payments for your vehicle, you may want to lease a food truck for commercial use.

When buying your truck, you may need more than $50,000 at the time of purchase, depending on the size of the truck and the amount and quality of your equipment. Leasing is a much better upfront value because you can get a similar vehicle for a payment of only $3,000 a month. Also, commercial truck leasing offers a huge advantage over outright purchases or financed truck ownership in that truck lease payments are tax deductible for your business.

WARNING

The downside to leasing your vehicle is that at the end of the term, your truck must be turned back in, and unless you plan to pay it off or can put together a lease agreement that has a purchasing option, you'll basically have to shut down your business until you're able to find a replacement truck.

TIP

Food truck leasing companies exist throughout the United States and Canada. Companies such as Mobi Munch and Road Stoves in the Los Angeles area, 800BuyCart.com in New York, and Miami Trailers in Florida are examples of companies that work specifically within the mobile food industry, and they'll even ship trucks across the country. Truck and automotive manufacturers, such as Nissan, Mercedes, and Utilimaster, also have vehicle platforms that they'll send out to kitchen builders to retrofit your kitchen equipment prior to leasing the vehicle to you. You can get more information at www.nissancommercialvehicles.com, www.mbsprinterusa.com, and http://www.gourmetmobilekitchen.com/gourmet-mobile-kitchen/.

Buying or building a new vehicle

Purchasing a new truck is what most start-up food truckers whom I've spoken with prefer. The high prices of buying new ($75,000 to $300,000) are their only source of hesitation. Being able to set up your truck the way you want with all the right kitchen equipment and options is very desirable. This scenario is similar to buying a new car: You don't have to worry about how the last owner drove it or how they maintained the kitchen.

An additional advantage to buying new is the warranty. Be sure to ask salespeople about the warranties they offer and what each covers. Another question you should ask is whether the dealer supplies a loaner truck should issues arise that take your truck off the road. The longer you're off the road, the longer you'll need to rely on an alternative plan to sell your product.

Finally, if you decide to purchase from a dealer, be sure the asking price is fair. Research similarly equipped vehicles in similar condition. If you don't have any skills in haggling, either learn how to haggle or take someone with you who can. In many cases, sellers are willing to accept offers as low as 15 percent off their asking price. Saving money on the front end can only help you in the long run.

TIP

You can also ask other food truck owners in your area for the names of reliable local vehicle dealers who provide follow-up after a purchase. Here are some websites of national truck manufacturers that give you the option of searching for dealers closest to you:

>> Nissan: www.nissancommercialvehicles.com

>> Sprinter: www.sprintervansusa.com

If you can't find a new truck with the proper equipment configuration, customizing a vehicle is an option. The main advantage, of course, is having the truck setup of your dreams (instead of having to deal with a poor kitchen layout or a kitchen that isn't equipped for the style of cuisine you plan to sell), but this is by far the most expensive route and can take the most time before the truck is ready for delivery. Although most timing quotes are from four to six weeks, be sure to talk with the shop's previous customers to see whether the seller followed through on his promises or whether it took much longer. Missing a proposed opening date because you received your truck one to three months late will make you look quite unprofessional. Reneging on timing can hurt any positive word of mouth you may have already received and can be very difficult to recover from.

TIP

If you decide to have your truck built from scratch, be sure to use a local truck builder who's familiar with all the current local health code requirements. A knowledgeable builder can help speed up the health department's review of your truck's floor plans and your final inspection.

Here are a few companies that can help you build the truck of your dreams (or at least get you started with one that will deliver your concept and cuisine):

>> AA Catering Truck: www.aacatertruck.com

>> Bens Carts: https://store.benscarts.com

>> Creative Mobile Systems: www.cmssystem.com

>> Cruising Kitchens: www.cruisingkitchens.com

>> Food Cart USA: www.foodcartusa.com

>> Northwest Mobile Kitchens: www.northwestmobilekitchens.com

>> Prestige Food Trucks: www.prestigefoodtrucks.com

Purchasing a previously owned vehicle

Buying a used vehicle is by far the most economical way to purchase your rolling kitchen (costs range from $15,000 to $99,000), but at the same time, it carries the most issues. If you decide to purchase a used truck, be sure to have a certified mechanic conduct an inspection. Your vehicle is the largest investment you'll have when starting up your business; you can't afford to purchase one that's consistently in the shop. In addition, even if a vehicle meets the health department codes in one area, it may not meet them elsewhere. When you buy a truck, you're responsible for bringing the vehicle up to all current standards of the cities you plan to be licensed in.

Check out the following for dealers that sell used vehicles:

>> eBay: www.motors.ebay.com

>> craigslist: www.craigslist.com

>> Commercial Truck Trader: www.commercialtrucktrader.com

>> Road Stoves: www.roadstoves.com

>> Used Vending: www.usedvending.com

Although you can find a used vehicle on sites such as eBay or craigslist for under $10,000, your investment price can skyrocket the minute you start installing vending windows, lined walls and floors, electricity, hot running water, and a retail payment system. Also, while online purchases of food trucks and other mobile vending units have increased over the last few years, some people and companies are taking advantage of this trend. More than a dozen consumers were left out in the cold when they spent thousands to order hot dog carts on eBay and received nothing in return. If you're planning to make a purchase of more than $500 from an online auction site, I recommend using an escrow service. The service receives the item from the seller before sending the seller your payment. eBay recommends Escrow.com and warns consumers of many fraudulent escrow companies, so if a seller suggests another company, investigate that company first. Also avoid paying for online auction purchases via wire transfers, which carry few — if any — fraud provisions compared to credit cards.

Naming Your Food Truck

Although your food truck's name may not make or break your business, having the right name can have a huge influence on your success, especially in your business's early stages. Coming up with a memorable name is one of the first steps in branding your mobile business, and a great name is the beginning of a great brand. Your food truck's name should be memorable and create a certain feeling in those who hear it.

The name you choose is truly the first impression people have of your mobile business. If you're new to the area and people don't know anything about you, they may decide whether or not to frequent your service window solely on the basis of the name you select.

In the following sections, I explain how to create a list of name options for your business; you can then research those names to see whether you can use any of them legally. If you find one that works, you can then register it.

Coming up with name options

So how do you choose the right name? Although opinions differ regarding how to come up with the right name for your truck, the following steps steer you in the right direction:

1. **Brainstorm.**

   Think about how you want people to feel when they hear about your truck or cart. Write down these words on a legal pad and then categorize them by primary meaning.

2. **Relate.**

   Think about related words and phrases that evoke the feelings you want. Hit the thesaurus and find all the synonyms for the words and phrases you identified in Step 1.

3. **Relate more.**

   Find out the Greek and Latin translations of your words or translate them into the language of the country your cuisine is based on. Figure out what colors, gemstones, plants, animals, and so forth relate to your words.

4. **Experiment.**

   Start playing with combinations of your various words and partial words. Don't be judgmental now — just make your list.

5. **Reflect.**

   Review your list and give some thought to each name. How does it make you feel when you hear it?

As you sort through the names you created with the help of the preceding list, keep in mind that your business's name should be a reflection of who you are and what you do. It should give your customers an idea of what to expect when they walk up to your service window. For example, don't call your truck "Ocean Breeze" if you don't have any seafood on the menu. Certain names conjure up certain images. You want those images to lead your customer base to you and your rolling bistro.

TIP

One way to test an idea is to tell the name to your family and friends and have them tell you what image comes to mind. If they heard that name, what would they expect when they walked up to your cart or truck? Ask them to visualize everything from mood to menu items to what the employees are wearing. The more details they can give you, the better idea you'll have about the effectiveness of the name. Do this with several names and get rid of the ones that conjure up the wrong image.

You want your name to be easy to remember. Make it as easy as possible for your customers to be able to tell their friends and family about the great new truck they found. Even if they can't remember exactly where you were located, if they can remember the name, they can always look you up online. Your name should stick with them long after their meal has ended. (Likewise, the name should be easy to spell. If it has an unusual spelling, people will have a hard time looking it up.)

Selecting the right name from your list is largely a matter of personal preference. Some people want to include their own name as part of the mobile restaurant name. Others may use the location of the business or even something that reflects the history of the area they usually do business in. No matter what, keep in mind that you're creating a new brand, so make sure the name is memorable and has positive connotations. (And if it contains a foreign word, make sure it doesn't mean something bad in another language!)

One thing to remember when considering trendy names is that trends change. Strive for a business name that will stand the test of time.

Researching and registering your chosen name

Before you fall in love with the name you've chosen and rush out to print business cards and start advertising, you need to do a little research. You need to make sure that name you really like isn't already registered by someone else. Bypassing this step can mean fines for copyright infringement, plus having to spend time and money to change your name. (A U.S. trademark or service mark costs $325 — a drop in the bucket compared to the cost of defending your name in court later.)

Your goal is to answer three questions as you conduct your trademark research:

>> Do any trademark registrations exist that may prohibit you from using your proposed name?

>> Is your proposed name eligible for registration with the United States Patent and Trademark Office (USPTO) so you'll be able to enforce and defend your name?

>> Does your proposed name infringe on any common law trademark rights?

You can start your research on your own by searching online; just type your desired name into your favorite search engine and see what pops up. In addition, some professional search organizations, such as Legal Zoom (www.legalzoom.com), specialize in doing research on company names.

A search of the USPTO's trademark records (www.uspto.gov) is also a good starting point because it helps you identify trademarks that were previously granted or denied registration. If any registered trademark is identical to your proposed name or might lead to consumer confusion, you may be infringing on another's trademark. (Note that the test for trademark infringement doesn't require two names to be identical but only confusingly similar to the consumer; the spelling doesn't have to be the same.)

During your investigation, you may notice that certain descriptive terms and geographic designations aren't eligible for trademark protection; this is because the underlying policy of the USPTO is to allow business owners to use descriptive terms and names to describe their businesses. For example, "Los Angeles Tacos" would likely be refused trademark registration because "Tacos" is descriptive of the food and "Los Angeles" names the location. This issue is prevalent in the food service industry because many restaurant and food truck owners choose names with descriptive terms, such as "Bar and Grill," "Mediterranean Cuisine," "Denver Steakhouse," and so on. Therefore, to increase your chances of obtaining registration through the USPTO (which is a great tool for future expansion because it provides legal protection throughout the United States), use fewer descriptive terms and geographic designations. Instead, consider a unique alternative, such as making up a word.

Be aware that other food trucks or restaurants that haven't secured federal trademark registrations may still acquire common law rights within limited geographic regions through their use of a name. In this case, you may be prohibited from using a similar name within a given region. With this point in mind, search online to find businesses that haven't registered their trademarks through the USPTO but may still have common law rights.

TIP

While you're searching, check online to make sure an appropriate domain name is available. You want YourFoodTruckName.com, if at all possible. If that's not available, you may want to reconsider your name choice.

If the name you've decided on is available, register it with your state's Secretary of State office, then register it with the USPTO. After your trademark is registered, it stays registered to you as long as you file a renewal every ten years.

REMEMBER

Making an educated decision for the name of a new mobile food business isn't an easy task. It can be filled with complicated details and analysis. I suggest that unless you're an attorney yourself, the best way to fully understand the implications of choosing an appropriate and legal food truck name is to consult an attorney who has a firm grasp of U.S. trademark law.

Another Possibility: Joining a Franchise

For many would-be food truck owners who have little to no business background, a food truck franchise can present the perfect opportunity to open their own food truck due to the ease in replicating their menu items and service. Mobile food franchises offer a lot of benefits, such as instant name recognition and built-in marketing. However, buying into a food truck franchise isn't always as easy as you may think. You find out the pros and cons of joining a franchise in the following sections; I also point you toward more information if you decide that franchising is the best option for you.

In a nutshell: If you're comfortable working with a team and being told what to do and how to do it, a franchise may be the right move for you. However, if you're starting your own food truck to get away from people telling you what to do, being independent is probably a better choice.

Picking out the pros

The advantages of running a food truck franchise include the following:

>> **Fewer upfront decisions:** A franchise opportunity offers you an instant business. You don't have to worry about the name, the truck's design, or the menu.

>> **Professional support:** Almost all franchises come with support from the corporate office. You're given a direct conduit to corporate staff who can address any questions or concerns you may have. This support can be very helpful for newcomers to the mobile food industry who may not always know what to do when they encounter certain problems.

>> **Name recognition:** Name recognition is a huge benefit of a food truck franchise. Whereas other food truck start-ups may want to run some advertising before they hit the streets just to get some name recognition, you won't have to worry about this.

Checking out the cons

Be warned that running a food truck franchise comes with the following disadvantages:

>> **A big price tag:** Buying a franchise can be expensive. Larger restaurant chains that offer franchise opportunities for food trucks can require upwards of half a million dollars in assets before they'll consider letting you buy into their company. Of course, the theory is that you'll make all your initial investment money back sooner than if you were to start an independent food truck.

>> **Less say in the concept:** You have no say in the menu or the truck's design. If you have a certain theme or concept in mind, it may not fit the expectations of your franchisor.

>> **Detailed rules to follow:** In order to maintain customer service expectations, franchises have many rules and regulations you must follow. Everything from the uniforms your staff wears to the brands of condiments you use can be subject to their rules. Failure to follow the rules can result in losing your rights to the franchise.

>> **Royalties to pay:** On top of paying for the rights to the franchise, you're expected to pay royalties in some cases. Wonder how these franchisors make money on your food truck venture? Here's your answer.

Getting more information

If franchising sounds like a route you want to investigate further, check out these businesses that are beginning to offer food truck opportunities:

>> Baby's Badass Burgers (www.babysbadassburgers.com)

>> Cousins Maine Lobsters (www.cousinsmainelobsters.com)

>> Gandolfo's New York Delicatessen (www.gandolfosdeli.com)

>> Gourmet Streets (www.gourmetstreets.com)

>> The Grilled Cheese truck (www.thegrilledcheesetruck.com)

>> ZooHoo's Eatery (www.zoohooseatery.com)

REMEMBER

After you get through the initial process of being approved as a franchisee and secure your financing, you'll be required to sign a lengthy contract with the franchisor. Unless you have vast experience as a franchisee, I recommend you review the contract with an attorney before signing on the dotted line.

HISTORICAL HIGHLIGHTS OF MOBILE FOOD IN THE UNITED STATES

Street food has been a part of Americans' dining habits since the late 17th century, when it was found in many of the larger cities on the East Coast. Since then, food trucks have taken a front seat in the world of American street food and are part of an ongoing food revolution. Here's a brief history of the mobile food industry in the United States:

- In 1691, New Amsterdam (now known as New York City) began regulating street vendors selling food from push carts.

- Charles Goodnight invented the *chuck wagon* in 1866 to feed cattlemen and wagon trains traversing the Old West.

- In 1894, sausage vendors sold their wares outside the student dorms at major eastern universities (Yale, Harvard, Princeton, and Cornell), and their carts became known as *dog wagons*.

(continued)

(continued)

- Ice cream trucks began selling frozen treats in the 1950s.

- In 1974, Raul Martinez converted an old ice cream truck into the nation's first taco truck and parked it outside an East Los Angeles bar.

- In 1979, grease trucks began parking on Rutgers University in New Brunswick, New Jersey, selling "Fat Sandwiches" to college students.

- In November 2008, Kogi BBQ hit the streets of Los Angeles selling Asian-infused tacos.

- The Southern California Mobile Food Vendors Association (SoCalMFVA) was created in January 2010, becoming the first organization to protect the rights of gourmet food truck owners.

- In August 2010, *The Great Food Truck Race* marked the first television program centered on the mobile food industry.

- In September 2010, the U.S. government added "Tips for Starting Your Own Street Food Business" to its small business website (www.business.gov).

- In October 2010, the prestigious Zagat guide announced that it'd begin providing reviews of food trucks in 2011.

- In January 2011, President Barack Obama tweeted that his favorite food truck in Washington, D.C., is D.C. Empanadas.

- In February 2012, food trucks serve NFL Super Bowl Fans in Indianapolis. Street food has been available to Americans for several hundred years, and food trucks have been serving up tasty treats for over two decades, so the basic concept is nothing new.

- In June 2014, the National Food Truck Association is formed.

- In August 2014, the movie *Chef* is released. This Jon Favreau film is centered around a chef who loses his restaurant job and starts up a food truck in an effort to reclaim his creative promise, while piecing back together his family.

Chapter 3

Understanding and Researching Your Local Food Truck Market

Economic competition takes place in all markets and industries, no matter how friendly. The mobile food industry happens to be one that garners friendly competition between truck owners. With that said, competition is competition, and as a prospective business owner, you need to understand how to compete not only with other food trucks in your market but also with brick-and-mortar restaurants that have similar concepts and cuisines.

In this chapter, you discover why competition is essential in the food truck industry (with the help of something called the *competitive response cycle*). I help you identify both your target customers and your competitors, and I show you how to determine the competition's strengths and weaknesses. With this information, you can mold your truck concept to take advantage of your competitors' weaknesses and build your standing in your food truck market.

Understanding the Importance of Competition in the Food Truck Industry

REMEMBER

Webster's New World College Dictionary (Wiley) defines *competition* as "rivalry in business, as for customers or markets." Competition in many sectors of the business world is viewed as a negative, and many brick-and-mortar restaurant owners (wrongly) feel that food trucks hold an unfair competitive advantage over them. However, this view isn't shared within the mobile food industry. Instead, competition is often looked at as a good thing for you, your competitors, and, most importantly, your customers. Competition helps with the following:

>> **Preventing you from becoming too confident:** You can easily feel relaxed and confident in business if you happen to offer a unique product that's in high demand, because you don't have any pressure to improve your food or service. However, should another truck start selling similar, and possibly even better, menu items than yours, you'll begin to feel the pressure to perform. To retain your customers, you'll have to constantly improve your food and customer service. You'll have to work harder to convince your customers to stick with you.

>> **Motivating you to be more creative:** When you realize that you're not the only one selling a particular cuisine, the wise thing to do is to develop better and more distinct menu items. You'll come up with unique items that will knock your customers' socks off or, at a minimum, improve on your existing food.

>> **Forcing you to get out of your comfort zone:** Perhaps you have a huge customer following and haven't needed to invest much into the promotion of your food truck. Competition may require you to work harder in order to remain visible. You can advertise special promotions, make donations to a worthy local cause, or get more engaged with your market.

>> **Keeping prices reasonable:** This result may sound negative to you; however, it isn't. Consumers are always looking for good value for their money. Although earning a lot of money from your menu is great, being fair to your customers will keep them coming back. No one likes to feel ripped off or overcharged. You may have to consider different ingredients or suppliers to keep your prices low, but your customers will show their appreciation by continually coming back for more.

Connecting Profitability to the Competitive Response Cycle

You may have decided to enter the mobile food industry for various reasons. Maybe you have a desire to open a food truck that allows you to show off your culinary expertise, or maybe you want a platform that brings you the pleasure of serving your community with a new style of cuisine. Or perhaps you merely want to make a living and provide for your family. The only problem with this last answer is this: You can accomplish that with almost any job; so why are you going into business for yourself?

Oliver Stone's classic movie *Wall Street* introduced a business concept that many have frowned upon. The movie's main character, Gordon Gekko, is often quoted from a long monologue in which he proclaimed that "greed is good." This phrase has riled many into believing that wanting to make money for one's self and one's business is greedy and, thus, a bad thing. And although many business owners feel that measuring their business's success is based on more than money, ultimately, the bottom line to whether their business is successful is solely based on their profitability.

REMEMBER

The ultimate goals of owning and running a food truck must be to create a product that can be sold and to make a profit while doing so. If you can't get past this point, you're doomed to failure. You may have the coolest designed food truck around, a great group of customers, and a trendy menu, but if you aren't able to make a profit, you may as well save yourself the hassle and never leave your commercial kitchen's parking lot. You also must recognize that making a profit isn't merely going to happen as soon as you open your service window. You're going to have to work hard to keep a competitive advantage that will assist in getting those profits rolling.

REMEMBER

Figure 3-1 illustrates the *competitive response cycle* — a process of researching your competition that you can use to continually make sure your food truck is meeting the needs of the customers you're targeting (and, therefore, helping you increase your profits). Here are the steps of this cycle:

1. **Analyze consumers' needs and wants.**

2. **Analyze your competition and their response to consumers' needs and wants.**

3. **Find opportunities to fill gaps between consumers' needs and wants and your competition's response.**

4. **Develop and implement programs to take advantage of opportunities.**

5. **Evaluate consumers' responses to your programs.**

The rest of this chapter covers these steps in more detail.

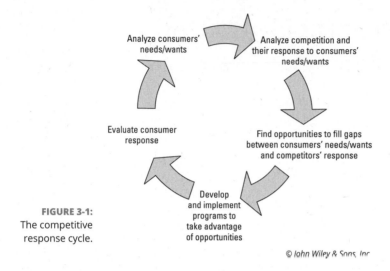

FIGURE 3-1:
The competitive
response cycle.

Identifying and Analyzing Potential Customers

So who are your potential food truck customers? In reality, you may feel that your customers are anyone who wants to pay you money for the food you serve. Although that isn't a bad answer, it isn't a great way to help improve your business and develop a competitive advantage. Because your success depends on your being able to meet customers' needs and wants, you must know who your customers are, what they want, and what they can afford. If you don't know who your customers are, how can you assess whether you're meeting their needs and wants?

In the following sections, you discover how to outline the demographics of your target customers, compile specific customer data, and list the features and benefits of your truck for those customers. After you gather all this information, you can adjust your concept (see Chapter 2), use it in your business plan (check out Chapter 4), or use it to assist you in creating your menu (flip to Chapter 8).

Delving into the demographics of your target customers

Think about the *demographics* of your ideal customer. Demographics are the typical characteristics of the people who will make purchases from your truck. These characteristics include age, income, education, status, type of occupation, and household size.

Certain concepts and cuisines cater to particular segments of your community, so knowing what your customer market consists of will help you tailor your business to those you'll be able to sell to (turn to Chapter 2 for more info on developing your truck's concept). Ask yourself these questions about customer demographics until you feel you have a solid answer for each one:

>> Are your target customers primarily men or women?

>> Exactly how old are they? (Don't aim at the entire population by saying that they're between 18 and 80.)

>> How much education do your ideal customers have?

>> Where do they live?

>> Who else lives in their home?

>> What do they do for a living?

>> How much money do they make?

After you've defined your target customer, you'll be able to adjust your concept to maximize its appeal to these customers and understand what motivates them to make a purchase (I cover this topic in detail in Chapter 2).

After you've determined the traits of your ideal customers, the next step is to gather specific information about them. The most important details are age, gender, income, education, geography, and household size. Knowing how many times a month and which meals a customer eats outside of the home can also be helpful. In the following sections, I provide a few resources for getting the details you need; you can use this info to help determine your food truck's concept, which I cover in detail in Chapter 2.

Consulting the U.S. Census

You can find a lot of good, general information about market demographics at the U.S. Census Bureau website (www.census.gov). All you need to do is go to the People & Households section at the bottom of the home page and search the site by narrowing down the demographic data you want to receive. Using this website can come in handy after focusing your search on a specific market segment (such as males, age 25 to 34) and looking for general statistics, such as regional averages for income, educational background, and household size.

Talking to small business associations

Most college campuses have a Small Business Development Center (SBDC), but if you want to find the closest SBDC in your location, go to the Association of Small

Business Development Centers website at www.asbdc-us.org. Because SBDCs are not-for-profit and community-service-oriented, they can often help you get access to information you wouldn't be able to easily find on your own. SBDC services include, but aren't limited to, assisting small businesses with financial, marketing, production, organization, engineering, and technical problems and feasibility studies. All services given at SBDCs are free and confidential.

Hiring a research firm

Some research companies, like Nielsen (www.nielsen.com), provide demographic information online. They base their fees on the amount of information you request. Although this type of source isn't free, most new food truck operators can still afford it (in the range of $300 to $2,500). You'll receive well-researched data on market demographics or even economic development in your area that's customized to your concept for as little as a few hundred dollars.

Another service a research firm can provide is the moderation of a *focus group*. A focus group is a form of interactive research where a small group of individuals can help you gather information about customer opinions on new ideas, products, or services that are currently either being offered or going through the product development stage. You can form a focus group for information about anything related to your business and your market, from products to service or merely the generation of new ideas for your concept. The research firm asks the focus group participants structured questions about a specific topic and encourages them to discuss their thoughts with the other participants. These open discussions can help generate ideas and can provide you with a wealth of information for your business.

The point of gathering multiple focus group participants is to get as many different perspectives as possible. The ideal size of a focus group is eight to ten people. When a research firm selects focus group participants, it should look at their demographics, familiarity with your products, or their food purchasing history.

A research firm often asks group participants questions based on the objectives of the project. For example, if the focus group objective is to determine why customers in your area would want a food truck selling your style of cuisine, questions may include the following:

>> What is your knowledge of the food truck industry?

>> Would you eat food from a food truck?

>> Do you enjoy *[insert your cuisine here]* style food?

>> Would you be more likely to eat this type of food at lunch or dinner?

>> What is your perception of the cost of this style of food?

>> If you have children, do they like to eat this type of food?

>> If you had the choice between eating this style of food from a truck or from a restaurant, which would you prefer?

TIP

I recommend that you hold at least two different focus groups to ensure that you get a good mix of perspectives for your data.

WARNING

Paying an outside consultant to perform your focus groups will provide the most objective results but can also cost you more than you're originally planning to spend on this data (anywhere between $1,000 and $10,000 unless you're seeking very basic information). I suggest that you pay your group members a small stipend, because people will be more willing to volunteer if they're going to receive, say, $50 for their time and participation.

Listing your truck's features and benefits

To understand what your concept has to offer the public, identify each of your concept's features and benefits. A *feature* is a characteristic that automatically comes with your concept; although features are valuable and can certainly enhance your product, *benefits* (any items or services you provide) motivate people to buy.

For example, kid-friendly menu items may be a feature of your menu, but the benefit to the consumer may be finding food at your truck that her children like. Many customers have children and need to know they can find a truck that provides food that not only they'll enjoy but also their children will want to order.

TIP

Take a piece of paper or create an electronic spreadsheet and make two columns. In one column, list the features of your concept; in the other, list the benefits each feature yields to the consumer. This way, you can know what your concept has to offer and what will attract customers to purchase from you.

Keeping an Eye on the Competition

You've probably heard the old saying, "What you don't know won't hurt you." Guess what? In business, a lack of knowledge can and (in all likelihood) will hurt you. In today's highly competitive mobile food industry, you'll face extreme pressure to outperform the competition. Everything from the items on your menu to the prices you charge (and beyond) is shaped by how your competitors are doing these things.

In the following sections, I explain the differences between your main types of competition, list the information you need about your competition, and tell you where to get that information.

The differences between direct and indirect competitors

REMEMBER

Let's face it: You have business competition all around you. As I mention in the earlier section "Understanding the Importance of Competition in the Food Truck Industry," competition isn't necessarily a bad thing, but that doesn't mean you should ignore it. To delve a little deeper into your competition and how to keep track of it, you should know the differences between your direct and indirect competitors.

» Direct competitors can be businesses that

  • Offer the same products and/or services as you offer your customers

  • Have the same targeted demographic of customers (I discuss these demographics earlier in this chapter)

  A good example of a direct competitor for a food truck is another food truck or fast casual restaurant that sells the same cuisine.

» Indirect competitors are a little more difficult to categorize in the mobile food industry. Although a restaurant may sell the same cuisine that you do, if they're classified as a fine-dining establishment, you likely won't be competing for the same customers. Most of your indirect competitors will be the food trucks that serve different types of cuisine as you do but charge similar prices and operate in the areas you're planning to work.

What you need to know about your competitors

Keeping tabs on your competition is a great strategy for your growing business. By continually monitoring your competitors, you get to know their good and bad behaviors and anticipate what they may be likely to do next, which helps your business gain a competitive advantage over them. Using this data, you can plan a business strategy that helps you keep your current customers and win (not steal) customers away from competitors.

REMEMBER

Before you can identify what your competitive advantage is, you need to obtain answers to the following questions (you can find answers by using the data sources in the next section):

» Who are my top three direct competitors?

» What is the range of the menu items they offer?

» Are my competitors profitable?

- >> Are they expanding? Downsizing?

- >> How long have they been in business?

- >> What are their positive attributes in the eyes of customers?

- >> What are their negative attributes in the eyes of customers?

- >> How can I distinguish my food truck from my competitors?

- >> Do they have a competitive advantage; if so, what is it?

- >> How is their menu priced?

- >> How many customers do they serve each day?

- >> What is their percentage of market share?

- >> What is their total sales volume?

TIP

As you collect the preceding information, write down the name of each food truck or restaurant competitor, its address or typical parking locations, the size of the facility (for restaurants only), and the category it falls into (direct or indirect). This list will become a database of your competitors; if you develop it as a spreadsheet, you'll be able to easily manipulate the data you track so you may compare and evaluate your competition.

Where to find data on your competitors

You can gather information on your competitors in several ways, including the following:

- >> **Direct observation:** Visit all your competitors yourself, or ask one of your staff members to dine from their trucks. Act as a prospective customer and ask questions. You can learn about their menu and service and compare it to your own.

WARNING

Don't use an alias or disguise to gather intelligence about your competitors. Although doing so may seem like a trivial deception, it's dishonest and can come back to haunt you and your business's reputation. In fact, it's best to introduce yourself as a potential new food truck operator. Most operators love to help new vendors.

- >> **Social networks:** Given how food trucks and restaurants are increasingly using social media sites like Twitter and Facebook as marketing tools (see Chapter 16 for details), you may be able to pick up interesting facts about your competition by checking out their social media feeds. Using social media is a cost-effective way to stay in tune with and in the know about the public's sentiment about your competitors. You can also track this information by keeping an eye on review sites, such as Yelp (www.yelp.com). Read your competitors' reviews to find out about events they may be attending, deals they may be offering, or certain service practices you can learn from.

>> **Google search:** Any research project these days should begin with a simple Google search, so start there. You may also want to visit your competitor's web page.

>> **Newspaper and magazine articles:** You can check out articles about your competitors found in newspapers and magazines (as well as those media outlets' websites) to get an idea of what they're planning for the future, how their organization is run, and what new innovations they may be planning. Be on the lookout for company profiles or dining reviews in local newspapers or magazines; they can reveal a competing product's strengths and weaknesses.

>> **Advertising:** Advertising not only gives you a competitor's prices, but it also provides some insight into a competitor's promotional budget. When you find a competitor's advertisement, be sure to note the following: which publication it showed up in, special offers, product features, and benefits highlighted. If a competitor suddenly places an ad in a new restaurant industry publication that neither of you have used, that may be an indication that it's trying to reach a new market segment.

>> **Suppliers:** If you're in an area where you're bound to share the same suppliers as your competitors, asking those suppliers some simple questions, such as what cuts of meat they typically order, can't hurt (at least not too much). Although some suppliers may not tell you what or how much your competitors order, others will, so it's worth a try.

REMEMBER

If these suppliers disclose this type of information about your competitors to you, you can safely assume that they're doing the same thing with your competitors.

>> **Customers:** When it comes to identifying sources of information about your competition, don't skip over your customers. Speaking with your customers is one of the best ways to gather real information on competitors. Even though talking about your competition may be awkward for your customers (and yourself), you can merely ask their thoughts on how your food and service compares to another truck you're attempting to get information on. If you're able to gather enough information, you'll have a good idea of what your competition is offering that customers like or dislike. You'll then be able to adjust menu or service to improve your business.

Building Your Food Truck Battle Plan

You have a fantastic concept (with the help of the guidelines in Chapter 2), you know who your target customers are, and you know who all your competition is. Now what? It's time to take all this information and prepare detailed analyses that you and future investors (see Chapter 5) will be able to use. In the following sections, I explain two different types of analysis tools and how to use them.

Creating a competitive analysis

Competitors in the rapidly developing food truck industry seem to be in a continual race to develop new products for their customers. You can gain a tremendous advantage by learning what your competitors may be developing or improving on their menus. A *competitive analysis* looks at your competitors and how they present a direct or indirect threat to your food truck business. In addition, it provides you with a clear understanding of your local market and how you can refine your strategic business decisions to change the perception or direction of your business. Competitive analysis also can reveal broad trends in the marketplace, again providing you with the advantage of being able to spot opportunities for differentiating your products and service before your competitors can.

The first step in writing a competitive analysis is to list your competitors. Name the companies that you're competing with. (For this exercise, I recommend that you select two direct competitors; if you want to do a more thorough examination later, you can expand this number and include some of your indirect competitors as well.) Explain what they do — are they a truck or a restaurant? List where your competitors operate, or where they're located, and how they provide service to their customers, whether from a food truck service window, a drive-thru, or table seating.

REMEMBER

Be sure to list your competitors' strengths to give yourself an honest analysis.

You'll then list how your business compares on these points and why or how your food truck does it better. This chart shows how your food truck differs from the competition, especially what you provide that others don't or can't do. Creating this list helps you spot gaps in your business, or even in your market.

Table 3-1 is a sample competitive analysis. Note that this table allows you to define your direct competition and their strengths and weaknesses. After gathering this data, you'll need to compare yourself to your competition and determine what areas you need to improve.

TABLE 3-1   **A Sample Competitive Analysis**

Criteria	The Road Grill (You)	Ben's Burger Truck (Direct Competitor #1)	Sports Zone (Direct Competitor #2)
Type of establishment	Food truck	Food truck	Restaurant
Location	Mobile, varies from day to day	Mobile, varies from day to day	Downtown corner; difficult to park
Menu	Wood-fired pizzas, black angus burgers, and wing flights	Burgers, wings, and cheese sticks	Wings, pizzas, and sandwiches
Price/value	Prices based on "quality" costs of premium ingredients	Value priced based on volume and lack of required labor for pre-prepared foods	Price based on national brand and image; portions and quality not in line with price
Efficiency	Personal service and menu cooked fresh to order; 5 minutes average	Quick service for foods due to convenient preparation	Slower service due to staffing levels
Targeted demographic	Affluent foodies and sports fans	Mid-market sports fans	Tourists, convention business
Type/style of service	Food truck service window	Food truck service window	Table service

Drawing up a SWOT analysis

REMEMBER

A SWOT (strengths, weaknesses, opportunities, and threats) analysis, much like a competitive analysis (see the preceding section), is an important part of planning your truck's future. The strengths (S) and weaknesses (W) sections provide a look at your truck's current market position. The opportunities (O) and threats (T) sections help you project possible goals and challenges that may affect business down the road.

>> **Strengths:** In a SWOT analysis, you look at the *strengths* of your business first. Strengths include those things that you do better than others and what makes you stand out from your competition. For example, you may have a permit to operate your truck on weekends in a prime location near a bar that doesn't serve any food past 10 p.m. Whatever your strengths are, use them as a base for future decisions.

>> **Weaknesses:** *Weaknesses* in SWOT refer to those areas in which you can improve that would help better the product or services you provide. That you'd see advantages in assessing your weaknesses may seem counterintuitive, but understanding your weaknesses makes them easier to deal with. For

example, a weakness can be a lack of expertise in preparing popular desserts that are common in the type of cuisine your concept follows.

>> **Opportunities:** The *opportunities* section is critical to your mobile food business's development by helping you discover ways to improve. You use the strengths and weakness you've already listed to identify your opportunities. Opportunities may be internal, such as pointing out that by hiring a pastry chef that has formal training in creating desserts, you'd be able to eliminate one of your weaknesses. Opportunities form the basis of the future goals you adopt.

>> **Threats:** Lastly, SWOT analysis looks at *threats* or possible issues your truck could run into. Examples of threats your food truck business may face include the addition of competition in the market, increased gas prices, and changing consumer trends. Threats may also come from changes in legislation or licensing requirements. Identifying threats can help you prepare and plan for issues that may come up that could throw your goals off course.

Here's a sample SWOT analysis:

>> **Strengths:**

- Strong, experienced food truck staff

- High brand recognition

- Prices are cheaper than competitors'

- Pride in putting forth innovative food with the freshest ingredients

>> **Weaknesses:**

- Limited funds available

- Costs rising due to increases in food costs

>> **Opportunities:**

- In a new, emerging food truck market

- A main brick-and-mortar competitor has closed

- Collaboration with a local bar to start a dinner and a drink package

>> **Threats:**

- A main competitor has lowered its prices

- Municipality reexamining current legislation and may add further restrictions on food trucks

Acting on the data you've compiled

After developing your own competitive and SWOT analyses (as I outline in the preceding sections), it's time to put your battle plan into action. Create a differentiation plan that uses the information you've gathered to maximize the types of customers you're looking to draw to your service window.

>> Use your strengths to focus on the needs of your customers. For example, having a strong, experienced food truck staff allows you to focus on customer service because your staff's cooking abilities keep your products consistently fantastic.

>> If a competitor is stronger in one area, do what you can to either close the gap or create an advantage for yourself. For example, if food prices from your suppliers requires that you increase your menu prices above your competition, use your own and your staff's desire to create innovative dishes to remake your menu. Doing so allows you to either provide a far superior food product or cut the quantity of ingredients you use per item to be able to maintain your prices.

>> If your weaknesses are keeping a segment of customers you hope to serve away from your business, continually work at improving it so you can start taking some of that market share and converting it into profits. For example, if you have a large vegetarian demographic in your market, take one of your current menu items and convert it into a vegetarian option; doing so is likely to attract people who have chosen to keep meat out of their diets.

REMEMBER

As soon as you open your service window, your competition is going to attempt to counter each of your business strategies as often as it can. You can never rest on your laurels as a food truck owner. You can't stop researching your competitors, keeping up on the market, and maintaining your awareness of the latest culinary trends. To stay competitive, you must continually (every three to six months) analyze and reevaluate your strengths and weaknesses and compare them with your competitors'.

2

Getting Your Food Truck Ducks in a Row

Chapter 4

Writing a Food Truck Business Plan

I n the early stages of your career as a food truck vendor, you may need a map to help you navigate the streets of the city you're operating in. Getting lost while looking for your next stop takes away valuable time and can only hurt your sales for the day.

In a similar fashion, before you start your mobile food business, you need a map to keep you on a path toward success. A *business plan* is that map, and it guides you toward starting and running a successful business.

Although the prospect of writing a business plan may be intimidating, the benefits of taking this step far outweigh the time it takes to get the plan on paper. Putting this plan together gives you the opportunity to develop assumptions and consider alternatives before you need to commit any resources. At its core, a business plan is a description of your company and how you'll launch, run, and grow it. In this chapter, I explain why having a food truck business plan is so important, and I provide you with some tips for putting your own together.

TIP

In this chapter, I provide guidelines for writing a business plan specific to the food truck industry, but these guidelines are merely the basics. If you want more detailed information, check out the latest editions of the following books (both published by Wiley):

>> *Business Plans For Dummies,* by Paul Tiffany and Steven D. Peterson

>> *Business Plans Kit For Dummies,* by Steven D. Peterson, Peter E. Jaret, and Barbara Findlay Schenck

Understanding Why a Business Plan Matters

Now you may be asking yourself, "Do I really need to create a business plan for my food truck?" In no uncertain terms, the answer is always, YES!

Some of you may assume that you don't need to prepare a business plan if you're not planning to seek financial aid from lenders or investors to open your food truck (see Chapter 5 for details on financing), but every business should have a business plan. I can't overemphasize the importance of creating a comprehensive business plan for your food truck business.

REMEMBER

By laying everything out on paper, you express your business ideas in a living document that outlines every critical aspect of your business's operation. A thorough, well-written business plan becomes a permanent reference point for you to view when needed and assists you in maintaining your focus for the entire life of your food truck business. Some of the following factors critical to your food truck's success depend on this plan:

>> Resources (time, money, and so on) you'll need to get started

>> What and how long it'll take for your business to make a profit

>> What information potential customers, vendors, and investors will need to know in order for you to market your business effectively

Writing your business plan also forces you to think objectively about your future business. And the process of writing a business plan may lead you to new business strategies that you may not have previously considered.

REMEMBER

Writing a business plan is your opportunity to show that your idea is worth backing. Therefore, your plan should answer the following questions:

>> What problem(s) exists that your business is trying to solve?

>> What is the potential consumer's pain caused by the problem(s)?

>> How deep and compelling is this pain caused by the problem(s)?

>> What solutions does your business have to resolve the problem(s)?

>> What will the customer pay you to solve this problem(s)?

>> How will solving this problem(s) make your company a lot of money?

>> How big can your business grow if given the requested capital?

>> How much cash do you need to find a path to profitability?

>> How will the skills of your business team, their business knowledge, and their track record of execution make this happen?

>> What will the investors' exit strategy be?

TIP

The business plan you write for your future food truck must make sense to those who are reading it, because most of them will know nothing about this industry. I suggest that after you've written your business plan (but prior to passing it on to a lender), ask a friend or relative you trust to read it. Ask him to give you a verbal explanation of how he thinks your new business will work, based on your plan. If he doesn't understand the plan or can't explain the business concept from what you've provided, a good chance exists that a financier won't understand your business concepts, either. If questions arise, be sure you incorporate the answers into your plan or clarify an answer so the question is automatically resolved when the financier reads it.

Looking at the Parts of a Business Plan

Because your food truck business will always be evolving, your business plan will be a constant work in progress, but it should always include the key pieces I describe in the following sections. These parts of your business plan best explain your goals for your business and how you plan to execute them. People will read your business plan at times when you're not available to answer questions or clarify your writing, so be sure to write clearly enough to answer any questions a reader may have.

The executive summary

The executive summary is the most important section of your business plan; it tells your readers why you think your business idea will be successful. In this section, you provide a detailed overview of your plan, along with a history of your company and where you want it to be in the future. It's the first thing your readers will see, so it needs to grab their interest and make them want to keep reading. Be sure you engage the reader; keep your tone positive and upbeat.

A good executive summary is no longer than one to two pages, can be memorized, and is ingrained into your thoughts. It's the core of your business concept on paper.

Within the executive summary, you need to include these subsections:

>> **Overview:** Briefly explain the general purpose for your business plan. Include who you are, the name of your company, as well as the area where you'll operate your food truck business.

>> **Products and Services:** What will you sell from your mobile food business? You need to include only a brief summary of the items or cuisine you'll offer because you cover this topic in more detail in the menu section (which I describe later in this chapter). Let the readers know how you'll sell these products, whether just from your truck or through catering services as well.

>> **Financing:** Here's your first opportunity to share with your readers how much money you need to finance the start-up of your business and what you plan to use it for.

>> **Mission Statement:** Why do you want to start a food truck business? Why do you want to sell the items you're planning to include in your menu? Does a need for this style of cuisine in your area exist? In this section, you first share your foresight and vision for why your business is needed and will succeed.

>> **Management Team:** This brief statement includes who you are (and any partners you have) and what working experience you have that will help your food truck prosper.

>> **Sales Forecasts:** The first questions most investors have revolve around the return on their investment. Providing a short, three-year forecast on your business's future sales keeps your investors' attention and keeps them wanting to learn more. (I talk more about forecasts later in this chapter.)

>> **Expansion Plan:** Your business plan tells the reader a story. This section explains where you see your business in the future. Do you plan to add services (catering, online sales, or selling your food products in local grocery stores), additional vehicles to your inventory, or even a brick-and-mortar restaurant to your growing food service empire?

Figure 4-1 shows an example of an executive summary. As in the example, present all the information in each section in a brief, one- or two-paragraph format. Keep in mind that you'll lay out the details of these topics within the plan itself.

Executive Summary

Overview

The purpose of this business plan is to raise money for the development of a gourmet food truck while forecasting the food truck's expected financial progress and operations over its first three years. Mobile Cuisine, Inc. ("the Company"), is a Chicago-based corporation that will provide mobile sales of food to customers in its targeted market. The Company was founded by Richard Myrick in 2010.

Products and Services

The primary revenue generation for this business will come from the sale and distribution of gourmet street food served from the Company's food truck that will operate throughout the Chicagoland area. The business will specialize in serving gourmet food based on ethnic street food from around the world, including the following:

- Tacos

- Samosas (stuffed pastry)

- Noodles

- Sausages

- Desserts

- Beverages

The menu section of the business plan will further describe the services offered by the Company.

Financing

Mr. Myrick is seeking to raise $65,000 from a bank loan. The interest rate and loan agreement are to be further discussed during negotiation. This business plan assumes that the business will receive a 10-year loan with a 5 percent fixed interest rate. The financing will be used for the following:

- Development of the Company's food truck

- Financing for the first six months of operation

- Capital to purchase a company vehicle

Mr. Myrick will contribute $15,000 to the venture.

© John Wiley & Sons, Inc.

FIGURE 4-1:
A sample executive summary.

Mission Statement

Management's mission is to provide the Chicagoland area (and other areas where the Company expands) with inexpensive, high-quality, gourmet food served from a mobile platform.

Management Team

The Company was founded by Richard Myrick. Mr. Myrick has more than 15 years of experience in the food and beverage industry. Through his expertise, he will be able to bring the operations of the business to profitability within its first year of operations.

Sales Forecasts

Mr. Myrick expects a strong rate of growth at the start of operations. Here are the expected financials over the next three years.

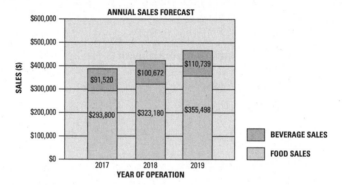

Expansion Plan

As time progresses, the Company will expand its presence throughout Chicago and its surrounding suburbs by attending food truck gatherings, music concerts, trade shows, sporting events, and other venues that feature a large number of people. At typical industry slow times, the Company will provide catering services to businesses and personal events, such as weddings and bar/bat mitzvahs. Additionally, over time, the business will generate a strong repeat customer base from the continual servicing of the routes planned by Management.

In the fourth year of operation, Mr. Myrick intends to acquire a second truck that will operate within selected sections of Chicago. It should also be noted that, after the fifth year of operation, Management may acquire several additional mobile food service trucks in order to greatly expand the revenues of the business.

FIGURE 4-1:
contitnued

The table of contents

To assist the reader in locating specific sections in your business plan, include a table of contents directly following the executive summary. Doing so also helps readers flip to sections that interest them at the moment.

TIP

Be sure your section titles avoid detailed descriptions. Clear, functional titles help get your message across. You can use the titles that I provide in the preceding section as a starting point.

The market analysis

REMEMBER

The market analysis section illustrates your knowledge of the mobile food industry. Here, you present general highlights and conclusions of any marketing research data you've collected (see Chapter 3 for details). This section should include the following:

>> **Industry description and outlook:** In this overview section, include a description of the mobile food industry, the current size of the industry and its growth rate since 2008 (because that's when the gourmet food truck industry exploded onto the American scene), trends and characteristics related to the industry as a whole (that is, show how the mobile food industry is growing exponentially with no signs of slowing), and a description of who the major customer groups are within the industry. You can find national and local mobile food industry growth trends at Mobile Cuisine (`www.mobile-cuisine.com`).

>> **Target market information:** Your target market is simply the group of customers you want to focus selling your food to. When you're defining your target market, narrow it to a manageable size. Overreaching when making these projections will only hurt you in the long run, even if the financial numbers they generate look impressive.

When it comes to target market information, you should gather information that identifies the following:

- **Characteristics of the primary market you're targeting:** These characteristics may include information about the critical needs of your potential customers (the food you serve isn't currently being sold in this area), the degree to which those needs are (or aren't) currently being met, and the demographics of the group. They'd also include the geographic location of your target market and any seasonal trends that may impact the industry or your business (for example, selling ice cream in colder climates tends to slow down in the winter).

- **Size of the primary target market:** Here, you need to know the number of potential customers in your primary market, the number of annual purchases they make from food trucks that have menus similar to your own, the geographic area they reside in, and the forecasted market growth for this group.

- **The extent to which you feel your food truck business will be able to gain market share and the reasons why:** In this research, you determine the market share percentage and number of customers you expect to obtain in your geographic area. You must also outline the logic you used to develop these estimates.

- **Your pricing and gross margin targets:** Here, you define the levels of your pricing and your gross margin levels. (Flip to Chapter 8 for help with these topics.)

- **Resources for finding information related to your target market:** If you have access to a professional market analysis or information you've received from a news article or a trade magazine, explain where you gathered your information from.

- **Media you'll use to reach your target audience:** These sources may include print or online publications, radio or television broadcasts, or any other type of credible source that may have influence with your target market. (Check out Chapters 15, 16, and 17 for more about media.)

- **Market test results:** When you include information about any of the market tests you've completed for your business plan, you must be sure to focus on only the results of these tests (such as the total number of trucks or fast casual restaurants selling the same type of cuisine in the market). You list the specific details in the appendix (I discuss that part of the business plan later in this chapter). Market test results may include, but aren't limited to, the potential customers you contacted, any information or tastings you gave to prospective customers, and the target market's desire to purchase your food at varied prices.

- **Evaluation of your competition:** When you're doing a competitive analysis, you need to identify your competition by researching food trucks with similar menus as your own (savory meals, desserts, or specialty menus such as vegetarian or vegan). Gourmet food trucks all try to attain the same market segment in each geographic region, so knowing how many trucks navigate the streets of your city is key to your analysis. After you have this information, assess the strengths and weaknesses of the top food trucks in your area, and identify any barriers which may hinder you as you're entering the market.

The financials

REMEMBER

If the primary purpose for putting a business plan together is to attain financing, the financials section will be the most important section of your plan, after your executive summary (which I discuss earlier in this chapter). Here, you must explain to prospective lenders how much money your food truck business will need and how you're planning to spend it. For this section, you need the following critical financial information (I detail the process of creating these financials and give you examples later in this chapter):

>> **Forecasted sales:** This area shows the readers of your plan how you predict your sales will grow over the first three years of your food truck business's life. Without knowing how much cash will come in, you'll have a difficult time determining how much you can spend.

>> **Forecasted expenses:** In showing this prediction, you show the reader how you're expecting to spend money on your business. It shows your food truck's start-up expenses as well as the daily expenses (such as food and fuel cost). You can also include forecasting for the unexpected expenses (such as fines and vehicle repairs) to show that you have a thorough understanding of issues you'll face.

>> **Income statement:** The income statement shows your revenues, expenses, and profit for a particular period of time. It's a snapshot of your business that shows whether your business is profitable at that point in time. Remember this formula: Revenue – expenses = profit/loss.

>> **Forecasted cash flow:** Cash flow is, well, the cash that flows through a company over a specific period of time after all cash expenses have been taken out. Cash flow represents the actual amount of cash that your business has left from its operations that can be used to pursue expansion or increase its value.

>> **Balance sheet:** The balance sheet presents a picture of your business's net worth at a particular point in time. It summarizes all the financial data about your business, breaking that data into assets, liabilities, and equity.

- *Assets* are tangible objects of financial value that are owned by the company, such as inventory, receivables (money owed to your business), cash on hand or in any accounts, kitchen equipment, and vehicles (the food truck and any other vehicles used for the business).

- A *liability* is a debt owed to an investor or creditor of the company. For example, salaries you owe employees, interest you owe, taxes you owe, or even your mortgage are liabilities.

- *Equity* is the net difference when the total liabilities are subtracted from the total assets.

Be sure that any projections you make match your plan's funding requests. You don't want a prospective creditor to catch a mistake before you do.

To clearly present your financial information, add graphs and charts where applicable. Pictures speak louder than words.

The management team

In the management team section of the business plan, write a two- to four-paragraph biography about your work experience, education, and skill set. You should also include a brief biography for each owner or key employee. This section is your chance to detail the experience, expertise, and strengths of your team. I recommend placing it up front in your plan if your team is a strong selling point.

Because most business plans are generally boring to read and the people who read them read many each year, interjecting some personality into the plan can be a good idea. This little bit of personality shows readers that you have a good sense of humor and the right disposition to speak to customers you meet on the street. This is your time to shine.

The primary function of a food truck business plan is to create enough interest from investors to make them want to write a check. If your company's management team is a group of friends who know nothing about business or preparing food, the concept may be fantastic, but investors won't find enough reason to part with their cash. If you don't have a culinary background and don't plan to hire any help to cook your food, what value added experience do you have to prove your product is worth investing in or, at the very least, something people will want to purchase?

If you find yourself in this category (having more business skills than food-creating skills), you need to either hire someone to do the cooking for you or take the time to learn how to cook. Numerous culinary programs around the country can teach you the specifics on how to prepare a fine gourmet meal. Also, if you're using a family member's recipes to develop your menu, ask him or others who are familiar with the recipes to teach you how to properly prepare them. After you've mastered these items, you can include this information in your personal biography.

The appendix

You need an appendix section only when specific information isn't included in the main body of the plan. For example, some information in the business section may be too personal to share with every reader; however, creditors may want access to this information in order to make their lending decisions. Therefore, have the appendix available when requested. The appendix can include the following information:

>> Credit history (personal and business)

>> Resumés

>> Letters of reference

>> Details of market studies

The Bottom Line: Looking Deeper at the Financials

Creating financial projections for your food truck business plan is both an art and a science. Although your prospective investors want to see the cold, hard numbers, predicting your financial performance three years down the road is a difficult task, especially because the mobile food industry is so new. Regardless, short- and medium-term financial projections are a required part of your business plan if you want to capture the attention of serious investors.

Your financial projections are critical to the success of your business plan, especially if you're trying to get a bank loan. In the following sections, I delve into the details of all the financial information you need in your business plan.

REMEMBER

Most people don't have a finance background, so preparing a financial plan is a journey into the unknown. Don't give up! If you just can't wrap your head around this financial data, reach out to friends or family who have a financial background or consider hiring an accounting professional to get you through this section.

Beginning with a few basic guidelines

REMEMBER

A few fundamentals can make the task of compiling financial information a little easier:

>> Starting your financial projections with spreadsheet software will make things go a whole lot smoother. Spreadsheets offer you the most flexibility and give you options to quickly change your assumptions or weigh alternate scenarios. Microsoft Excel is the most commonly used software and the one I recommend for your financial forecasting because of the support Microsoft

provides. If you're unfamiliar with Excel, pick up a copy of *Excel For Dummies* (published by Wiley) for the version of Excel that you use.

>> Getting things right the first time is almost impossible. In all business planning, but especially in the financial section, trying different scenarios is important. What if you choose to purchase used equipment instead of buying more expensive new equipment? What if you raise or lower your menu prices? What if you reduce your salary? By exploring different scenarios, you can determine what it'll take to make your business financially viable. Keep trying until you have a result that's both reasonable and achievable.

>> Forecasting is usually easier when you break your forecast down into components. For example, consider a forecast that simply projects $10,000 in food sales for the month, compared to one that projects 1,000 meals at $10 each. In the second case, when the forecast is price times the number of meals served, as soon as you know your prices are going up, you know that the resulting sales should also increase.

>> Get help in the assembly of your financials, but not in your research. The numbers and assumptions you provide in your business plan should be yours, not another food truck owner's; you need to consider far too many variables to rely on someone else's numbers. Ultimately, you're responsible for achieving these objectives, so you should believe in the numbers you provide. With that said, you may want to have a successful food truck operator review your financials for accuracy. He can challenge your assumptions accurately.

>> Be consistent. Make sure your financial plan is consistent with the rest of the business plan. If an investor finds that various sections don't carry from one section to another, this inconsistency will raise an immediate red flag.

Forecasting sales

In your mobile food business, sales are what determine whether you're able to make it through your first year of operation. Forecasting your future sales is a critical step in ensuring that your food truck is profitable. Prospective investors want to know whether your projected sales will support your business needs. Although no set-in-stone formula can project your sales for your truck, making a well-informed guess is critical to planning your future funding. Pulling numbers out of thin air does nothing for you or investors.

You need to show your sales forecast for the first three years in your business plan. Then show your sales growth for the next two years. I walk you through the steps of forecasting sales in the following sections.

Estimating customer numbers

You may already have a few specific locations, or at least a general idea of some, that you plan to use as regular stops or venues. A great way to find out how many walk-up customers you can expect is to compare your potential business to existing mobile kitchens in those areas. Visit trucks of similar size and cuisine type. Although these businesses may turn out to be your competitors, you can obtain valuable information by observing how many *covers* (number of meals) they serve during peak hours. You may even speak with the owner to learn about how many covers he sees in a week. (Chapter 7 provides additional information on how to track traffic at certain locations.)

Another way to project your customer count is to determine how long it'll take to produce a meal for a customer. Start your timing from the moment a customer places an order to the time the transaction is completed. Your projections will depend on the number of staff you have to complete the transaction and the type of cuisine and how it's prepared. For some styles of food, it may take up to ten minutes to turn an order. Other vendors who serve only prepackaged food can turn an order in two to three minutes.

After you've determined how quickly you can serve a single customer, you can estimate how many customers you can serve in an hour, during a full shift, or a full day. For example, if it takes four minutes to prepare a meal for a customer during a rush, you'll be able to serve 15 customers per hour, 45 customers per three-hour shift, or 90 customers a day if you're open for two three-hour shifts.

REMEMBER

Don't base your approximations on the maximum number of people you can serve from your truck with perfect conditions because you'll unlikely be able to hit or maintain these numbers during the first 12 to 24 months of operation. To be conservative in your sales forecasting, calculate how many customers you can serve, and then use only 75 to 80 percent of that number. After you've started your operation, you'll be able to adjust these numbers to match your real sales figures.

Estimating average spending per customer

Using your customer count estimate, the next step is to put together a per-person average based on your menu prices. Make sure you use moderately priced menu items to figure out this average, because you can't expect all your customers to buy the most expensive (or even the cheapest) item on your menu every time.

Also, be sure to consider the number of customers and per-customer spending averages for different meal periods. For example, lunch periods tend to bring in lower average sales than dinner periods, unless you're able to park in central business districts with a lot of foot traffic and hungry workers. Days of the week also bring in different sales numbers; for example, Thursday nights are usually more profitable for food trucks than Monday nights. You'll also want to break out your food sales from your beverage sales because each of these items is broken out separately when you determine the amounts to purchase and keep in your inventory.

For example: Use a $6 menu item as the base price for your mid-level menu entries. If you add in a $2 side item and a $1 beverage, you have an average of $9 of spending per customer (also known as a *check average*). To give yourself an average for your slower times, you can cut out the side or divide it by two to represent the idea that every other customer will choose to purchase a side dish in his order.

TIP

Generate a chart showing estimated number of customers per meal period each day, as well as the per-person spending average. The data generated in these charts help you determine your estimated monthly and annual sales.

Estimating sales for the year

After mapping out weekly sales projections (as I show you in the preceding section), some mobile food vendors merely multiply their weekly sales totals by 52 weeks to get a year's sales projection. Other owners divide the year into seasons to reflect the business they'll receive during different times of the year. Although using the latter method is a little more complicated because seasons vary per region, it can be more accurate because some months are usually busier than others. Think about what an average week's sales may look like, and then ask yourself what your potential earnings are during a slow week and during a busy week.

TIP

Consulting with seasoned food truck employees or owners in your area can help you decide what kind of traffic or sales volume to expect at different times of the year. These estimations vary from truck to truck and depend on your menu and your locations. After even a few months of operating, you'll have a much better idea of what to anticipate as far as sales go, and you can alter your estimations accordingly. You should also evaluate your operations and promotion efforts if sales aren't matching the projections in your business plan (see Chapter 14 for help).

To show your potential investors how your business will grow, you need to show them more than a single year of sales forecasting. Financial professionals consider 10 to 25 percent to be a strong sign of long-term growth. I suggest using 10 percent as your growth factor to apply to your first year's sales forecast to show strong growth potential in your second and third years in business, without setting the bar too high and having investors question your ability to grow your business.

Figure 4-2 shows a one-year sales forecast for a mock food truck business. As you can see, I broke the chart into separate food and beverage sales per day and shift. This forecast shows investors how many covers occur each shift and day as well as the average spending of each cover.

Cover Counts and Check Average

Food

Lunch	Mon	Tues	Wed	Thurs	Fri	Sat	Averages
Covers		50	50	50	60	60	54
C/A		$10	$10	$10	$10	$10	$10
Dinner							
Covers		50	50	60	75	80	63
C/A		$10	$10	$10	$10	$10	$10
Total:	$0	$900	$900	$1,100	$1,350	$1,400	$1,170

Beverage

Lunch	Mon	Tues	Wed	Thurs	Fri	Sat	Averages
Covers		50	50	50	60	60	54
C/A		$2	$2	$2	$2	$2	$2
Dinner							
Covers		50	50	60	75	80	63
C/A		$4	$4	$4	$4	$4	$4
Total:	$0	$300	$300	$340	$400	$420	$360
TOTALS:	$0	$1,200	$1,200	$1,440	$1,750	$1,820	$1,530

Average daily food sales:	$1,170
Average daily beverage sales:	$360
Average daily sales:	$1,530
Total weekly food sales:	$5,650
Total weekly beverage sales:	$1,760
Total weekly sales:	$7,410
Annual food sales:	$293,800
Annual beverage sales:	$91,520
Annual sales:	$385,320

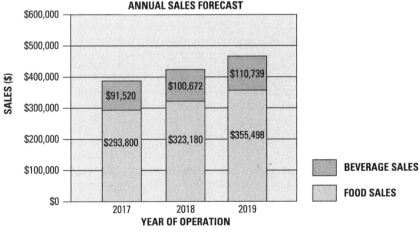

© John Wiley & Sons, Inc.

FIGURE 4-2: A sample food truck sales forecast.

Forecasting expenses

Salaries, food costs, food truck costs, business taxes, commercial kitchen and office rent, equipment leases, phone bills, postage — the expenses associated with running a food truck may seem to never end. However, your ability to get a firm grasp on these cash outflows can play an important role in your business's success or failure. An expense forecast is vital for you and your sales goals; it keeps you on track and helps keep costs down.

You need to show all expenses in your business plan. Not only will they help investors determine whether you've made the proper assumptions, but they'll also assist you in determining what you'll be spending to operate your business.

Accurately forecasting your expenses can benefit your enterprise in myriad ways, including the following:

>> Avoiding cash flow crunches

>> Keeping your company afloat during lean times

>> Assisting you in menu pricing (see Chapter 8)

>> Facilitating your ability to obtain loans and lines of credit

>> Helping you budget properly for growth

Use one year's data for your business plan expense forecast and make sure you include as many expenses as you can come up with. The more detailed you can be in generating your forecasts, the more complete they'll be, which will only be a help to you.

TIP

To help you cover all the possible expenses you'll need to start your food truck business, check out Figure 4-3 for a list of accounting codes the National Restaurant Association (NRA; www.restaurant.org) recommends. Another resource for helping determine what expenses you may run into is your local food truck association or other food truck owners in your area. Incorporating their suggestions into your business plan will give your plan additional credibility if someone asks how you compiled the data.

TIP

Because you're using this book to help you start your business and the cost involved in acquiring this and any other copies is a business expense, be sure to save your receipt so your accountant can deduct it from your taxes.

Income Statement Accounts

3000	**SALES**		**4500**	**MARKETING**	
3010	Food		4510	Selling & Promotion	
3020	Liquor		4520	Advertising	
3030	Beer		4530	Public Relations	
3040	Wine		4540	Research	
			4545	Complimentary Food & Beverages	
4000	**COST OF SALES**		4550	Discounted Food & Beverages	
4001	Food:				
4002		Meat	**4600**	**UTILITIES**	
4003		Seafood	4610	Electrical	
4004		Poultry	4620	Gas	
4005		Produce	4630	Water	
4006		Bakery	4640	Trash Removal	
4007		Dairy			
4008		Grocery & Dry Goods	**4700**	**GENERAL & ADMINISTRATIVE**	
4009		Non-alcoholic Beverages	4705	Office Supplies	
4020	Liquor		4710	Postage & Delivery	
4030	Bar Consumables		4715	Telephone / Communications	
4040	Beer		4720	Payroll Processing	
4050	Wine		4725	Insurance - General	
4060	Paper (QSR)		4730	Dues & Subscriptions	
			4735	Travel Expenses	
4100	**SALARIES & WAGES**		4740	Credit Card Discounts	
4110	Management		4745	Bad Debts	
4120	Dining Room		4750	Cash (Over) / Short	
4130	Bar		4755	Bank Deposit Services	
4140	Kitchen		4760	Bank Charges	
4150	Dishroom		4765	Accounting Services	
4160	Office		4770	Legal & Professional	
			4775	Security / Alarm	
4200	**EMPLOYEE BENEFITS**		4780	Training	
4210	Payroll Taxes		4785	Miscellaneous	
4220	Worker's Compensation Insurance				
4230	Group Insurance		**4800**	**REPAIRS & MAINTENANCE**	
4240	Management Meals		4810	Maintenance Contracts	
4250	Employee Meals		4820	R&M - Equipment	
4260	Awards & Prizes		4830	R&M - Building	
4270	Employee Parties & Sports Activities		4840	Grounds Maintenance	
4280	Medical Expenses		4850	Parking Lot	
4300	**DIRECT OPERATING EXPENSES**		**5000**	**OCCUPANCY COSTS**	
4305	Auto & Truck Expense		5010	Rent	
4310	Uniforms		5020	Equipment Rental	
4315	Laundry & Dry Cleaning		5030	Real Estate Taxes	
4320	Linen		5040	Personal Property Taxes	
4325	Tableware		5050	Insurance-Property & Casualty	
4330	Silverware		5060	Other Municipal Taxes	
4335	Kitchen Utensils				
4340	Paper Supplies		**6000**	**DEPRECIATION & AMORTIZATION**	
4345	Bar Supplies		6010	Buildings	
4350	Restaurant Supplies		6020	Furniture, Fixtures & Equipment	
4355	Cleaning Supplies		6030	Amortization of Leasehold Improvements	
4360	Contract Cleaning				
4365	Menu & Wine List		**7000**	**OTHER (INCOME) EXPENSE**	
4370	Pest Control		7010	Vending Commissions	
4375	Flowers & Decorations		7020	Telephone Commissions	
4380	Licenses & Permits		7030	Waste Sales	
4385	Banquet & Event Expenses		7040	Interest Expense	
4390	Other Operating Expenses		7050	Officers Salaries & Expenses	
			7060	Corporate Office Expenses	
4400	**MUSIC & ENTERTAINMENT**				
4410	Musicians & Entertainers		**8000**	**INCOME TAXES**	
4420	Cable TV/Wire Services		8010	Federal Income Tax	
4430	Royalties to ASCAP, BMI		8020	State Income Tax	

© John Wiley & Sons, Inc.

FIGURE 4-3: Chart of restaurant income and expenses accounts.

In Figure 4-4, I provide a six-month sample of an expense report. Just as you should do when putting your sales forecast together (as I describe earlier in this chapter), use the median cost for your expenses in your business plan. You can easily generate this data by taking your weekly sales forecast and multiplying it by the number of weeks in each month. If you want a complete snapshot of your expenses, produce two more reports in which you use your high and low data. Doing so helps you see how different monthly expenditures can ebb and flow. To prevent any confusion by possible investors, keep these additional reports out of your business plan.

Q1 AND Q2 FY18

	JAN $	FEB $	MAR $	APR $	MAY $	JUN $	TOTAL $
CONTROLLABLE EXPENSES							
Cost of sales							
Food cost	7,889	7,573	8,520	8,204	8,204	8,204	48,594
Beverage cost	2,085	2,002	2,252	2,169	2,169	2,169	12,846
Total COGS	$9,974	$9,575	$10,772	$10,373	$10,373	$10,373	$61,440
Payroll							
Salaries	5,443	5,225	5,879	5,661	5,661	5,661	33,530
Hourly wages	4,082	3,919	4,409	4,246	4,246	4,246	25.148
Benefits	2,177	2,090	2,352	2,265	2,265	2,265	58,678
Total payroll	$11,702	$11,234	$12,640	$12,172	$12,172	$12,172	$72,092
Other controllable expenses							
Direct operating expenses	1,905	1,829	2,057	1,981	1,981	1,981	11,734
Fuel	508	488	549	528	528	528	3,129
General & administrative	826	792	892	859	859	859	14,863
Repairs & maintenance	381	366	412	396	396	396	2,347
TOTAL CONTROLLABLE EXPENSES	$3,620	$3,475	$3,910	$3764	$3764	$3764	$22,297
NON-CONTROLLABLE EXPENSES							
Rent	2,500	2,500	2,500	2,500	2,500	2,500	15,000
Lease expenses	150	150	150	150	150	150	900
Insurance	400	400	400	400	400	400	2,400
TOTAL OTHER EXPENSES	$3,050	$3,050	$3,050	$3,050	$3,050	$3,050	$18,300

FIGURE 4-4: Sample six-month expenses forecast.

© John Wiley & Sons, Inc.

The expenses shown in Figure 4-4 are broken into two categories:

>> **Controllable expenses:** These expenses change with your control. An efficient business can keep food and fuel cost at a minimum, whereas other business owners end up overspending in these areas. Over time, you'll discover how to become much more efficient with these expenses. Although payroll may not seem as controllable as your other operating expenses, it falls into this category because you do determine what you pay your employees and how many hours they work each week. You can adjust the items in the controllable expenses category as needed and can change them from season to season.

Often, this category includes a subcategory called *other controllable expenses* that contains direct operating costs, such as paper and cleaning supplies as well as uniforms if you provide them for your employees. Although many food trucks use social media as their primary source of marketing, you'll have to produce some items, such as business cards and event fliers. In addition to these expenses, this category includes your office utility bills and any truck or kitchen maintenance.

>> **Non-controllable expenses:** In this category, you have all the fixed expenses associated with your business, such as your truck payment, commercial kitchen rent, and insurance. These items are *fixed* because you determine a set price when you negotiate contracts for these items, which may change only at the end of the contract terms.

TIP

Some non-controllable expenses, such as taxes and the depreciation of your vehicle and kitchen equipment, will be difficult to determine yourself, unless you're an accountant. I suggest grabbing a copy of the latest edition of *Accounting For Dummies* by John A. Tracy, CPA (published by John Wiley & Sons) to assist you with these areas, or you can take the more expensive route and speak with an accountant to get realistic numbers for your business plan.

Analyzing your break-even point

If you've accurately forecasted your sales and expenses (as I explain earlier in this chapter), producing a break-even analysis for your business plan is a simple matter of math. I've added all my projected monthly expenses from Figure 4-4 to create the *Monthly Expenses* line in the break-even analysis shown in Figure 4-5. To give myself a way to better monitor my business's efficiency, I've separated the cost of food and beverages (cost of goods sold, or COGS) from my fixed costs. Separating these items allows you to see how changes in rent or your negotiated food and beverage purchase agreements affect your bottom line. Adding the *Monthly Expenses* to the *Monthly COGS* gives you a figure to determine the amount of sales your food truck needs to break even (see the line about required revenue). (*Note:* The chart in Figure 4-5 simply represents the break-even analysis graphically.)

MONTHLY EXPENSES + COGS	$30,074	$28,993	$32,240	$31,158	$31,158	$31,158
REQUIRED REVENUE	$30,074	$28,993	$32,240	$31,158	$31,158	$31,158
MONTHLY EXPENSES	$18,372	$17,759	$19,600	$18,986	$18,986	$18,986
MONTHLY COGS	$11,702	$11,234	$12,640	$12,172	$12,172	$12,172

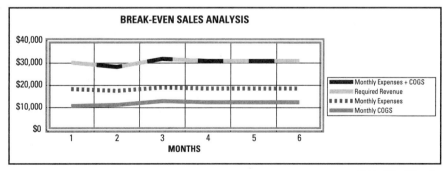

FIGURE 4-5:
Sample break-even analysis.

© John Wiley & Sons, Inc.

Your company will show a break-even point when your total sales are equal to your total expenses. At the break-even point, no profit has been made, nor have any losses been incurred. This calculation is critical because it helps you adjust your sales numbers or expenses as needed. This information lets you show investors how soon you'll be able to begin posting profits and thus able to pay them back on their investment.

Understanding your break-even point is critical to your business. The number of customers you need to serve (say, 15 customers, spending $10 each, or $150 in daily sales) accurately gauges whether you're making money. If you sell prepackaged food, such as cupcakes or other desserts, set aside 15 items so you can physically see them and know that when they've sold, you're now in the black for the day.

Estimating profits

The ultimate goal for your business is to show that it can make a profit. To do this in your business plan, you must create an income statement. Figure 4-6 is a sample six-month income statement (in other words, it shows two quarters of the year — Q1 and Q2).

Basically, I took the forecasted sales from Figure 4-2 and multiplied the weekly sales estimates by the number of weeks in each month then subtracted all the expenses shown in Figure 4-4 to come up with my final net profit/loss figures. Having a good estimate of net profit that accounts for all overhead, wages, and taxes allows investors to judge the probable success of your business. In other words, you use this info to show investors how long it'll take for your books to be in the black (profit). This information also comes in handy when you want to look into various business areas to improve and to test grounds for future or long-term plans.

Projecting cash flow

Cash flow problems can catch some small business owners by surprise; however, putting together an accurate cash flow projection can protect you against this scenario. The cash flow forecast you provide in your business plan shows readers the amount of money you expect your business to receive and pay out each month during a six-month period. If done properly, this forecast allows you to anticipate your cash flow positions over time. It also helps you anticipate cash shortfalls, which gives you time to do something about them. For this reason, I recommend you update this chart every six months for the first two years of your business operation.

Q1 AND Q2 FY18	JAN	FEB	MAR	APR	MAY	JUN	TOTAL
REVENUES	$	$	$	$	$	$	$
Food sales	26,295	25,244	28,400	27,347	27,347	27,347	161,980
Beverage sales	8,341	8,007	9,008	9,002	9,002	9,002	52,362
Other income	0	0	0	0	0	0	0
TOTAL REVENUE	**$34,636**	**$33,251**	**$37,408**	**$36,349**	**$36,349**	**$36,349**	**$214,342**
EXPENSES							
Food cost	7,889	7,573	8,520	8,204	8,204	8,204	48,594
Beverage cost	2,085	2,002	2,252	2,169	2,169	2,169	12,846
Total COGS	**$9,974**	**$9,575**	**$10,772**	**$10,373**	**$10,373**	**$10,373**	**$61,440**
Payroll							
Salaries	5,443	5,225	5,879	5,661	5,661	5,661	33,530
Hourly wages	4,082	3,919	4,409	4,246	4,246	4,246	25.148
Benefits	2,177	2,090	2,352	2,265	2,265	2,265	58,678
Total payroll	**$11,702**	**$11,234**	**$12,640**	**$12,172**	**$12,172**	**$12,172**	**$72,092**
Operating expenses							
Direct operating expenses	1,905	1,829	2,057	1,981	1,981	1,981	11,734
Fuel	508	488	549	528	528	528	3,129
General & administrative	826	792	892	859	859	859	14,863
Repairs & maintenance	381	366	412	396	396	396	2,347
Total operating Expenses	**$3,620**	**$3,475**	**$3,910**	**$3764**	**$3764**	**$3764**	**$22,297**
GROSS OPERATING PROFIT	**$9,340**	**$8,967**	**$10,086**	**$10,040**	**$10,040**	**$10,040**	**$58,513**
OTHER EXPENSES							
Rent	2,500	2,500	2,500	2,500	2,500	2,500	15,000
Lease expenses	150	150	150	150	150	150	900
Insurance	400	400	400	400	400	400	2,400
TOTAL OTHER EXPENSES	**$3,050**	**$3,050**	**$3,050**	**$3,050**	**$3,050**	**$3,050**	**$18,300**
ADJUSTED PROFIT	**$6,290**	**$5,917**	**$7,036**	**$6,990**	**$6,990**	**$6,990**	**$40,213**
NET PROFIT/LOSS	**$6,290**	**$5,917**	**$7,036**	**$6,990**	**$6,990**	**$6,990**	**$40,213**

FIGURE 4-6: Sample income statement.

© John Wiley & Sons, Inc.

See Figure 4-7 for an example of a cash flow forecasting chart. This chart is broken down into the various areas where cash comes in and exits your business. You can use the data you've generated in the previous sections to create your own cash flow projections. You'll also have to come up with your payroll figures by determining how many staff members you have (including yourself) and how much you'll pay them. I discuss the other expenses shown in the chart in more detail in Chapters 5, 6 and 12.

Creating a balance sheet

REMEMBER

The balance sheet is a portion of your financial data that investors use to determine the financial strength or weakness of your business at a specific moment in time. Before you begin creating a balance sheet, look at Figure 4-8. You can see that the balance sheet is broken down into three categories. Each of these categories aims to impart financial information to the reader about a certain aspect of your business.

Q1 AND Q2 FY18

	JAN $	FEB $	MAR $	APR $	MAY $	JUN $	TOTAL $
CASH RECEIPTS							
Food sales	26,295	25,244	28,400	27,347	27,347	27,347	161,980
Beverage sales	8,341	8,007	9,008	9,002	9,002	9,002	52,362
Sales receivables	0	0	0	0	0	0	0
TOTAL CASH RECEIPTS	$34,636	$33,251	$37,408	$36,349	$36,349	$36,349	$214,342
CASH DISBURSEMENTS							
Cost of sales, food	7,889	7,573	8,520	8,204	8,204	8,204	48,594
Cost of sales, beverage	2,085	2,002	2,252	2,169	2,169	2,169	12,846
TOTAL COST OF SALES	$9,974	$9,575	$10,772	$10,373	$10,373	$10,373	$61,440
CONTROLLABLE EXPENSES							
Payroll							
Salaries	5,443	5,225	5,879	5,661	5,661	5,661	33,530
Hourly wages	4,082	3,919	4,409	4,246	4,246	4,246	25.148
Benefits	2,177	2,090	2,352	2,265	2,265	2,265	58,678
TOTAL PAYROLL	$11,702	$11,234	$12,640	$12,172	$12,172	$12,172	$72,092
Operating expenses							
Direct operating expenses	1,905	1,829	2,057	1,981	1,981	1,981	11,734
Fuel	508	488	549	528	528	528	3,129
General & administrative	826	792	892	859	859	859	14,863
Repairs & maintenance	381	366	412	396	396	396	2,347
TOTAL OPERATING EXPENSES	$3,620	$3,475	$3,910	$3764	$3764	$3764	$22,297
OTHER EXPENSES							
Rent	2,500	2,500	2,500	2,500	2,500	2,500	15,000
Lease expenses	150	150	150	150	150	150	900
Insurance	400	400	400	400	400	400	2,400
TOTAL OTHER EXPENSES	$3,050	$3,050	$3,050	$3,050	$3,050	$3,050	$18,300
TOTAL CASH DISBURSEMENTS	$28,346	$27,334	$30,372	$29,359	$29,359	$29,359	$174,129
CASH FLOW FROM OPERATIONS							
Cash receipts	34,636	33,251	37,408	36,349	36,349	36,349	214,342
LESS: cash disbursements	28,346	27,334	30,372	29,359	29,359	29,359	174,129
NET FROM OPERATIONS	$6,290	$5,917	$7,036	$6,990	$6,990	$6,990	$40,213
CASH ON HAND							
OPENING BALANCE	0	5,290	8,207	11,243	13,233	14,223	
PLUS: New loan (debt)	0	0	0	0	0	0	
PLUS: New investment	0	0	0	0	0	0	
PLUS: Sale of fixed assets	0	0	0	0	0	0	
PLUS: Net from operations	6,290	5,917	7,036	6,990	6,990	6,990	
TOTAL CASH AVAILABLE	$6,290	$11,207	$15,243	$18,233	$20,223	$21,231	
LESS: Debt reduction	1,000	1,000	1,000	1,000	1,000	1,000	
LESS: New fixed assets	0	0	0	0	0	0	
LESS: Profit distributions	0	2,000	3,000	4,000	5,000	5,000	
TOTAL CASH PAID OUT	$1,000	$3,000	$4,000	$5,000	$6,000	$6,000	
ENDING CASH POSITION	$5,290	$8,207	$11,243	$13,233	$14,223	$15,213	$15,213

FIGURE 4-7: Sample cash flow chart.

» *Assets* are items, such as cash on hand, receivables, and inventory, that have economic value to your company.

» *Liabilities* are items, such as what your business owes investors or creditors, that cause an economic burden.

» *Equity* consists of all the investments you've made into your food truck business or the funds that you've already earned and then reinvested into the business.

THIS CHAPTER

termining how much capital you
ed

uring out how much you can
ntribute

tting a business loan versus finding
estors

ancing
d Truck

rospective mobile food vendors is figuring
ney they need to get their food trucks onto
as long as you know how much funding
plan to share your vision with investors,
when you're starting up your truck.

n you need to entice investors to assist you
lan features plenty of financial informa-
ut how much money you need to get your
f necessary), and I give you the lowdown
need.

ow Much Money
ar

a less expensive alternative to opening a
costs are still involved in the creation of
the following sections. You need to under-
able to make large purchases, such as your

truck, or smaller purchases, such as your office supplies. To prevent yourself from facing the same problem that some food truck owners have run into, you also need to add operating reserve to your list of start-up costs. All these items add up quickly, but you must have a firm grasp of all your costs before you start reaching out to investors.

Figuring out start-up costs

At each stage of your mobile food business's life, you encounter financial needs that require funding. The funding types for the stages are as follows:

>> **Seed capital:** *Seed capital* is the money you need if your initial research and planning for your business requires substantial sums in cash. In the mobile food industry, this type of capital comes into play if you're initially planning to start a business with more than a single mobile food unit because the research and planning for starting a single truck can be done relatively inexpensively.

>> **Start-up capital:** *Start-up capital,* also known as *working capital,* is the funding that helps you pay for equipment, rent, supplies, and so forth during the first year of operation.

>> **Expansion capital:** *Expansion capital* is funding to help your company grow to the next level, which may entail restaurant owners looking to open a food truck to expand their brand, purchasing better equipment, or adding additional trucks to your fleet.

Each of these funding types may play an important part at various stages of growth in your mobile food business. Most new food truck operators need only start-up capital (because they have only one truck) because your research and planning isn't considered to be large enough to warrant seed money, and expansion capital is used when your business is ready to, well, expand.

The best way to estimate your business start-up costs is to list all of them — the more detailed your list, the better. Begin by brainstorming everything you need, from goods (such as your truck, equipment, and initial food purchases) to professional services (such as accounting, advertising, and legal work). You'll pay some of the costs once, while other costs will be ongoing.

One-time start-up costs include the following:

>> The purchase or lease of your food truck or cart (Chapter 2)

>> The retrofitting and/or bringing of the truck up to code (Chapters 2 and 7)

>> Permits and licensing (Chapter 6)

- ❯❯ Professional, legal, and consulting fees (Chapter 6)

- ❯❯ Initial food purchases (Chapter 10)

- ❯❯ Kitchen supplies (Chapter 10)

- ❯❯ Initial office equipment and supplies (Chapter 12)

- ❯❯ Website design (Chapter 15)

- ❯❯ Initial advertising and public relations (Chapter 15)

Recurring start-up costs include the following:

- ❯❯ Insurance (Chapter 6)

- ❯❯ Commercial kitchen rent (Chapter 9)

- ❯❯ Payroll for you and any employees (Chapter 11)

- ❯❯ Credit-card processing equipment (Chapter 12)

- ❯❯ Truck and equipment maintenance (Chapter 13)

- ❯❯ Miscellaneous (any unforeseen expenses; give yourself 5 to 10 percent in contingency for these costs)

After you complete your list, start researching and calculating how much funding you need to pay for all those goods and services. First, come up with an estimate of one-time costs you need to cover in order to get your doors open, and then develop an operating budget based on your reoccurring costs for the first six months or even the first year of the business.

TIP

You can come up with a good estimate for your start-up costs by researching other food trucks in your region and talking to the owners about how they determined their start-up costs; be sure to ask them specifically about expenses they forgot, too. You can also get an idea of estimated costs by talking to your accountant. If you've chosen an accountant who has food service industry experience, she can help you come up with these figures. Check out Chapter 6 for info on finding the right accountant to assist you.

TIP

When in doubt about your projections, always overestimate your up-front investment cost. To truly play it safe, some experts suggest taking your start-up cost estimate and doubling that number.

Accounting for operating reserve

You need to allow enough money for the true expenses associated with running your mobile business for at least the first 6 to 12 months of its operation. You have no guarantee that your business will immediately start making a profit, so this cushion helps you stay afloat until you do. Make sure you've planned for additional employees, food cost increases, and additional fees and licensing for new locations to sell your gourmet fare at. And don't forget to pay yourself!

TIP

Realistically estimate your financial needs and leave room for the unexpected, or you may unexpectedly find yourself out of business. Take a look at Chapter 4 to help determine what your monthly operating expenses will be; I discuss expense forecasts and cash flow projections there.

Considering the Use of Your Own Funds

Depending on how much funding you need to start your food truck business, you may find that using your own money is your best route. Making this decision can be very scary, but look at it this way: If you're not willing to back up your venture with your own money, why would someone else?

More than 50 percent of small business start-ups are financed with personal funds. The beauty of this approach is that you're financing your business yourself, and having a larger personal investment in your business is a big plus in your favor if you attempt to get a business loan in the future. The downside is that if the business fails, you risk losing all the cash and collateralized assets you used.

If your business plan doesn't require you to hire any employees or pay outrageous sums of cash for your truck's permitting, licenses, and fees, chances are good that you can get away without having much to finance outside of the vehicle. Look at the start-up cost list you put together earlier in this chapter. In almost all cases, prospective food vendors need to purchase a food truck, cart, or trailer, which means you'll be spending some money. This fact alone means that unless you're independently wealthy, you have to dip into your personal savings account, access your 401K, take out a home equity loan, get a personal loan, or tap into your unused credit cards if you can't get a low-priced, used vehicle:

>> **Dipping into your personal savings:** Using your own savings to finance your food truck business is certainly tempting, but before you do, you need to understand the implications: Most importantly, you could lose all the money you put in. Most people have plans for the cash they've saved, so if you lose the money, those plans are no longer viable.

It's a harsh truth, but the reality is that the majority of new businesses fail. Even if you do everything right, bad market conditions may mean that you don't stand a chance. Using your personal savings to fund your food truck business is a risky venture, but doing so can save you from having to pay interest on other forms of financing.

» **Tapping into your 401(k):** If you're considering this route, be aware that you're putting your nest egg in jeopardy. The process of rolling your 401(k) into your new food truck business costs about $5,000 to get started, because you have to pass through significant legal steps to do it properly. The key is to roll over the money into a corporate retirement account that permits you to invest in your business.

You or your financial manager will move your current 401(k) into a profit-sharing plan, which then becomes the retirement plan for your new company. You then use this new plan to buy up the stock of your new corporation. After the funds have transferred, they become tax-free capital for your business. In other words, you're spending the money on your own corporation instead of for stock of another company.

» **Getting a home equity loan:** A home equity loan is a low-risk way to secure funding for your mobile food business. The bank doesn't care what you're using the money for because they have plenty of collateral to get their loan back.

» **Applying for a personal loan:** Taking out a personal loan is also a possibility for funding your business that keeps the business decisions in your hands. With this type of bank loan, you have to let the lender know what you plan to use the money for. The personal loan application process may be the first time you need to provide someone with a copy of your new business plan for review.

» **Using charge cards:** If you're like most Americans, you receive multiple preapproved credit-card offers in the mail every day. Now is the time to take advantage of these credit services. Using personal credit cards can be a risky means of financing your business because they weren't designed for this purpose. However, if you're aware of the costs involved, personal credit cards can temporarily fill the gap between raising start-up capital and getting your company into the black.

TIP

Be sure you investigate the interest rates, annual fees, and late fee charges before you take this step. One way to help prevent paying late fees or being hit with higher interest rates is to pay at least the minimum payment every month and pay off the balance as soon as possible.

WARNING

The downside of using personal assets to fund your food truck is that you have no guarantee of succeeding as a business owner. You could drain all your savings or retirement accounts, take a hit to your credit rating if you fall behind on loan pay-ments, or even lose your home. The key to determining whether self-funding your new business is feasible is to make sure that if your business fails, you haven't sacrificed your family's future.

Consult with an accountant before you begin the process of financing your food truck business. These professionals will help you assess all the risks involved, as well as give you the odds of a loan being successful. Getting a professional's opinion can help you navigate through the risks and even find an alternative source of funding.

Understanding Different Types of Capital Funding

If personally financing your food truck venture is out of your reach (see the preceding section), other means of acquiring capital are available. But with these forms of funding, you need to ask yourself some tough questions. You have two avenues to choose from when deciding the type of capital funding you want for your prospective mobile food service business:

» **Debt capital:** Going in this direction involves getting a business loan that you pay back over a set period of time, with interest and possibly some additional fees. In this scenario, you maintain full control of your company, but you also have a loan to pay back when everything is said and done. To see whether this form of capital funding is for you, ask yourself these questions:

- Can I qualify for debt financing? (Think credit rating here.)

- Will I be able to make the monthly payments to pay off the debt?

- If I need more money in the future, will the lender give it to me?

» **Equity capital:** If you choose this type of financing, funding is provided by individuals or firms who require partial ownership rights to your food truck business to secure a return on their investment.

The big question you must ask yourself with this route of capital acquisition is whether you're willing to give away part of your company in exchange for the cash you need to make it happen.

In most cases, you can get more money from investors than you can from a loan, but one of the top reasons culinary geniuses start up mobile food businesses (as opposed to brick-and-mortar establishments) is because they don't require as much start-up capital.

In the following sections, I go into more detail on these two types of capital and how to obtain each.

Make sure to consult a financial advisor or accountant before making any decision on what type of funding to proceed with. These professionals can give you advice on the form that's most suitable for you and your business.

Debt capital: Getting a business loan

If you decide to get a business loan for your food truck or cart from your local bank or credit union or the government, you have several things to consider. Ask your-self these questions, and be specific in your answers:

>> **How is the loan going to be used?** Are you going to buy your food truck with the loan? Are you going to use it to purchase a kitchen to have installed on a truck you already own? You need to think through these things because you want to make sure you get a loan that best fits the use of the money. You don't want to finance the full funding of your truck with a 12- or 18-month loan unless the payment for that term works with your business plan. Go back to your start-up cost worksheet for help; see the earlier section "Figuring out start-up costs" for details.

>> **How long do you need the terms of the loan to be?** Be sure the type and length of loan fits what you're using the funds for. For example, you don't want to finance your initial food purchases or office supplies for 15 years. I suggest looking at multiple loans with different term lengths to minimize the amount of interest you end up paying.

>> **What assets can you use as collateral?** *Collateral* is any item you pledge against the value of your loan. If you default on the loan, the lender has the right to obtain the collateral from you in lieu of payment. Some items you can use as collateral for a business loan include home equity or your personally owned vehicles.

In the following sections, I explain your main options for finding a business loan: going to a local bank and getting help from the government.

Tapping into your local bank

If you were to sit down and listen to today's television talking heads or some small business owners, you'd get the impression that getting a business loan is nearly impossible. At the same time, if you were to sit down and speak with a banker, you'd be told that small business loan approvals across the country are up. With this contradictory information in hand, the immediate question that comes to mind is "Can I get a loan or not?"

The problem is, although the information is contradictory, both sides of the issue are right. Whereas national banks have drastically cut back small-business lending, smaller community banks — which have traditionally made their living off of loans — have continued with this practice. The good thing for you as a prospective small business owner is that these small local banks make up the vast majority of the country's lending institutions.

Even though the mobile food industry has shown great growth potential since 2008, banks are skeptical about lending money to individuals looking to enter the food truck industry. Not only do banks assume that food trucks have all the risks of starting a restaurant, but they also fear that the food truck industry may be just a fad that may disappear as fast as it began. These lending institutions like to see a couple years of profitability before they dole out cash, but of course, most start-ups have no business history.

Banks aren't interested in the potential of your food truck, only your ability to pay off the loan. To help cover themselves in the event of default, they rely on *asset-backed borrowing,* whereby they require you to back the loan with some form of collateral, such as personal vehicles or real estate. You can actually use many things to back your loan, including the equity in your home or even your children's college fund.

Another option is to have someone cosign the loan for you. You may have a friend or relative who doesn't necessarily have the money to invest in your company but feels comfortable enough to cosign. Just make sure that person has a good credit record.

Every bank or credit union uses slightly different criteria to decide whether to lend you money. What they all do is look at the financial projections from your business plan and credit history. They also look at how you present yourself and your plan. To increase your chances of receiving a loan, you must be able to demonstrate exactly how you plan to use the money and why your business plan makes sense.

When you start visiting local banks, make sure you do the following:

>> **Call for an appointment.** Don't just show up and expect to get a walk-in appointment with a banker. Bankers have busy schedules, so respect their time and set up a formal time to meet.

>> **Dress and groom yourself for success.** Applying for a loan is a business transaction; show that you understand that by wearing a suit and running a brush through your hair.

>> **Take multiple copies of your business plan and financial documents with you.** You never know how many people will be involved in reviewing your financials. Instead of requiring people to pass your documents around the

room, bring enough (three or four copies) for everyone to have a copy during the meeting. (See Chapter 4.)

>> **Be professional.** Again, you're conducting a business transaction with the bank to begin your business. Show your respect for the process as much as you expect the banker to.

>> **Be prepared to answer questions.** Bankers may ask about anything and everything related to your business, your credit history, and your financial status. Make sure you can answer these questions. If you can't answer a question, make sure you come straight out and tell the banker that you need to get back to her with the answer, and then follow through and get her the answer that same day if at all possible.

>> **Show confidence in your plan.** If you don't have confidence in your plan, how can you expect someone else to?

>> **Don't appear desperate for the money.** Act as though this bank is just one of the banks on your list of many. Banks make money by giving loans; make them work for your business.

>> **Be truthful about everything.** You never want to be caught in a lie, no matter how small you may think it is. Being dishonest is the quickest way to receive a "rejected" stamp on your loan application.

>> **Keep in mind that bankers only want to know how they're going to get their money back.** Give them only the information they ask for, and don't get into long, drawn-out explanations that do everything but provide the answer to their question.

TIP

You may have to visit many banks before you actually find one that's willing to take a chance on you and your food truck business. Don't get discouraged; if you're turned down, follow up with the individual you spoke with to find out the specific reasons your application was rejected. By addressing these concerns, you increase your chances of being approved next time.

Finding government assistance

The Small Business Administration (SBA) can help you get a loan for your new mobile food business. The SBA is a government agency that guarantees the loans that banks make to you. This backing gives your local lender a higher level of confidence in the likelihood of collecting on your loan. With less risk, a lender is more likely to approve a loan for your business.

If you happen to default on your loan, the SBA guarantees your bank that it will pay off a percentage of the loan even if you can't. The guaranteed percentage depends on the amount of the loan. With a standard SBA guaranteed loan, you can borrow up to $2 million; however, most prospective mobile food vendors don't need this huge amount of capital to start up their operations. If your loan is for $150,000 or less, the SBA will guarantee 85 percent. If the loan is for more than $150,000, they'll guarantee 75 percent.

REMEMBER

The guarantee that the SBA provides doesn't eliminate your responsibility to repay a loan. The guarantee is put into place only to reduce the risk to a bank, making it easier for the bank to lend you money.

Microloans are another option backed by the SBA. These loans are small, maxing out at $35,000 with a maximum term of six years. The SBA forwards your loan application to your local SBA-approved lender, and the final credit decision is made by the bank or credit union.

WARNING

Some drawbacks of going through the SBA are the large amounts of paperwork and time delays that the approval process usually involves. You can expect the process to take several months. If you choose to apply for SBA backing, be sure you start this process quickly to avoid any additional delays.

TIP

You can find more information on the various programs the SBA offers at www. sba.gov.

Equity capital: Finding investors

Since the dot-com boom of the 1990s, a larger number of high-tech companies have been started. Many of these companies have been created with outside funding from individuals and groups of *venture capitalists* who provide financial backing to early-stage, high-potential, high-risk, start-up companies. Unfortunately, most food truck owners can't approach these investors because they have a higher appetite for risk and are looking at companies that need well over $250,000 to start their operations. With that said, in the following sections, I discuss the other forms of investors you can work with to get your mobile business rolling.

REMEMBER

When working with investors, make sure you have a clear investment agreement that defines the interest rate and when payment is to be made. There's no right or wrong way to structure this agreement. Some investors don't want an open-ended deal that doesn't define an end to the term of their investment, whereas others want to be involved in the business as it grows. No matter how you put your plan to paper, be sure that both parties have it reviewed by their own separate attorneys.

Partnering up

A partnership is a business association of two or more persons who act as co-owners of a business and operate it for profit. You have a number of different types of partnerships to look at to find the one that best fits your plans:

>> **General partners** invest in the business, take part in running it, and share in its profits. Each general partner is fully liable for any debts that the partnership may have. This arrangement means that they can lose more than their initial investment in the business if it runs into trouble, and their personal assets may be at risk. Every partnership must have at least one general partner.

>> **Limited partners** aren't permitted to participate in the day-to-day running of the business. Their debt is limited to the amount of their initial investment.

>> **Silent partners** invest money in the business and share in its profits but don't take part in running it. Like general partners, they're fully liable for the partnership's debts.

Although most partnerships are formed due to lack of funding, some partnerships don't involve cash being invested at all. For example, you may have a funding source but lack financial skills, such as accounting or financial planning, so you may decide to partner with someone who has expertise in these areas. Likewise, not all food truck owners start their trucks with a culinary background; instead, they go out and find partners who can provide the culinary skills they lack. Be sure you choose people who complement your skills as opposed to mirroring them.

When choosing partners, it's important to confirm that you and your partner share the same vision for your food truck. For instance, if you have dreams of expanding your fleet or opening a brick-and-mortar storefront within five years and your partner is happy with running a single truck, you're bound to run into some conflict down the road.

REMEMBER

Complementary skills and a shared vision are a good starting point, but never underestimate the importance of actually liking your partner. You may know and respect your partner professionally, but if you don't have a personal rapport, you may find that working with this individual every day becomes the downfall of your business.

TIP

A partnership is like a marriage in important ways. It requires compromise on different issues and a high level of trust among all parties involved. But just as in marriages, divorce is common. Unfortunately, these business breakups are often unpleasant and expensive. Each state has specific laws on partnership formation as well as laws regarding the legal responsibilities of each partner. (Check out Chapter 6 for the legal details of setting up your business as a partnership.) Before you start a partnership, I suggest you consult with an attorney and an accountant to fully understand the laws specific to your area.

Asking family and friends to chip in

Have you asked your parents or siblings for a loan? Do your grandparents have a few thousand dollars that they may want to use to invest in your future? Has that high school buddy really been as successful as he said he was at your last class reunion? Tapping into the pockets of friends and family has some benefits, such as your family members may give you the money as a gift and not expect it back or the terms of their loan will likely be more flexible than going to a bank.

WARNING

Asking friends and family also has its share of disadvantages. Number one, you have to approach them to ask for the money. Make sure you present the business to them just like you would pitch it to a bank. Let them decide whether they want to take the risk. Make sure you have a written agreement or promissory note that specifies the details of the loan. And don't get upset when they pester you with questions about how their investment is doing. This minor annoyance is another drawback of tapping into this particular money source.

Overall, borrowing from friends or family is probably not your best choice, simply because of the strain it may put on relationships. This option is only viable if you're confident you can repay the loan. However, it does work for many people and may even strengthen your relationship if your business takes off and is successful.

Seeking online investors

If you don't want to potentially tarnish your close relationships, you may want to consider person-to-person lending through websites. Here are a couple of options:

>> **Prosper.com:** This site allows you take out loans from individuals who are looking to invest some of their excess money. As a prospective borrower, you can request from $1,000 to $25,000 in an unsecured loan and specify an upper limit of interest that you're willing to pay. The investing users investigate your profile, which tells them about your project and shows your site-given credit rating. The lenders can bid as little as $50 on people looking for financing and fund multiple borrowers, spreading out their risk. Depending on the type of loan, lenders can earn upwards of 9 percent interest on their investment. The loans are for three years, and there's no prepayment penalty.

>> **GoFundMe.com:** This site allows users to create their own website to describe what they are raising money for. During this process, members can describe their fundraising cause, disclose the amount they hope to raise, and upload photos or video. Once the website is created, GoFundMe allows users to share their project with people through social media and email. People can then donate to a user's cause through the website using a debit or credit card and track the progress of their funding. Those who donate can also leave

comments on the website in support of the project. GoFundMe generates revenue by automatically deducting a 5-percent fee from each donation users receive. If the user receives no donations, then no charge is made.

>> **Kickstarter.com:** This site represents a new online way to fund your creative culinary idea and has become a means by which numerous food trucks have been able to get start-up capital over the last couple years. Kickstarter runs on a crowd funding concept that allows you to accept donations to reach a monetary goal you set (up to $25,000) in return for rewards you determine. You have the freedom to set up your food truck program for however long you think you'll need to raise the money.

You can make a pitch video (the video isn't a strict requirement, but almost all funded projects have a video). You come up with a set of "rewards" for different pledge levels on the site. You set a funding goal and a time frame for your project. The Kickstarter staff look at your proposed project and provide you with any necessary feedback. If they approve your project, they list it on the site and your timer begins.

Donors become "backers" and pledge whatever amount they choose (as little as $1). This payment is securely authorized through Amazon. If you reach your goal, the payments are processed and you get paid. If you don't reach your goal, your only loss is the time you invested; you don't lose any money.

WARNING

Sounds simple enough, right? So what's the catch? Using Kickstarter does have some hidden drawbacks and costs. You're not permitted to "pledge" toward your own project. All backers must make their donations online; you can't have local fundraising efforts converted into online donations unless you have each of your local donors create an account. Finally, Kickstarter doesn't provide this service for nothing. They take a 5 percent cut of your pledges, and Amazon takes an additional 2 percent on top of that.

Compensating your investors

Most experienced investors have learned over time that businesses need a grace period to get their business off the ground before they're able to start making payments. Investor payment schedules tend to be flexible and are easier to negotiate than the schedules banks or other lending institutions set. You can change or update your terms as needed.

Chapter 6

Understanding Business Structures, Licenses, and Other Legal Stuff

S tarting a food truck means you get to plan the truck's concept and theme, the type of food you serve, and even where you'll operate, but you also have several legal concerns to address before you can serve your first customer. No matter what country you plan to operate, most of your legal requirements will come from a state or local level. State laws vary, and being informed on your state's guidelines is critical to your success. Properly handling these legal issues helps reduce your risk for additional expenses, fines, or legal action.

During the process of opening a food truck business, you'll have a lot on your plate, and you'll likely need assistance to complete some tasks, specifically business and legal tasks. Most food truck owners consider their core business advisors or partners to be their attorney, accountant, and insurance provider. These professionals can help you navigate through the legal aspects of your business while giving you the time to operate the other business facets that you're more familiar with.

In this chapter, you start the process centered around the legal matters related to your mobile food business. These legal matters include hiring help, setting up the structure of the business, and being aware of legal requirements, such as licenses, permits, and insurance.

Identifying the Help You Need

Nearly every food truck entrepreneur — especially those who are new to the industry — needs the assistance of an attorney, accountant, and insurance provider at one time or another. Finding good ones should be one of your first steps when you start planning your food truck business. I provide guidelines on finding, selecting, and working with these folks in the following sections.

Cross-examining attorneys

Although many people never think to hire a lawyer until they have a legal problem, the time to hire a lawyer is *before* you run into trouble. Preventing legal problems is not only easier but also more cost-effective than solving them. An attorney can help with the following:

>> **Evaluating the potential liability associated with operating a food truck in your area:** This liability has implications for what type of business structure you'll ultimately choose to form. (Check out the later section "Surveying Different Structures for Your Food Truck Business" for details.)

>> **Making sure you stay in compliance with any federal, state or local laws applicable to the food truck industry:** As a business owner, you need to comply with laws on everything from business filings to employment practices. Without a lawyer, you may not even be aware that a particular law affects your business, until someone complains that you're in violation of the law.

>> **Creating and maintaining employee applications and documents:** A lawyer will make sure your employment application doesn't ask any discriminatory questions, and he can advise you on how to comply with anti-discrimination laws. A lawyer can also draft any necessary employment

agreements, including non-compete agreements. If you provide employees with an employee handbook, a lawyer can look it over to make sure you don't inadvertently create an employment contract. You can find more information on this topic in Chapter 11.

In the next sections, I walk you through the process of finding, selecting, and working with an attorney.

Finding qualified attorneys

TIP

The best way to find an attorney who has experience in the mobile food or food service industry is to ask other food truck or restaurant owners in your area for a referral. Or if you're lucky enough to have a local food truck organization, you can speak with one of its representatives to get a recommendation. Another option is to ask your accountant and/or insurance provider, if you already have one.

You can also look at an online attorney listing service, like Martindale-Hubbell (www.martindale.com). Search by state first, then type of attorney. You can also search on areas of practice, bar admissions (ability to practice in certain states), years in practice, and languages spoken. You may use this service to generate an initial list, and then you can interview the top candidates.

Choosing and working with your attorney

TIP

Finding a good lawyer (and avoiding a bad one) can be as difficult as finding a great cook for your truck, but it can mean even more to your business. When searching for and selecting an attorney to represent you on legal matters, here are some tips to assist you:

>> Try to find an attorney who's a good business lawyer and has either food truck or food service industry experience. If you live in a small community, finding a lawyer with these credentials can be difficult, but don't get discouraged. Also, don't be afraid to seek counsel out of your immediate area because you may be able to find a lawyer who doesn't have a conflict of interest with any of your competitors.

>> Do some due diligence on lawyers' fees before you contact a lawyer, and consider how much time and money you're willing to spend on one. Don't sign any type of binding agreement unless you're completely comfortable with the fee arrangement and relationship. Make sure an attorney is worth what you're spending and only agree to a fee structure that suits you. Don't sign a blank check for open-ended retainer fees, but insist on a written fee agreement that specifies all anticipated costs and fees.

>> When you feel like you've found a lawyer you're comfortable with, ask him for references from similar business owners. Call the references and ask them about their experience with this lawyer.

REMEMBER

When you hire a lawyer to represent your business, you should have confidence that he'll provide competent, diligent representation. With the many legal issues that can come up while operating a business, establishing a partnership and insisting on a good system of communication with your lawyer is important. A lawyer can help you address your concerns and keep legal problems from getting out of control; however, if you have to wait days or weeks to hear back from your lawyer, either you didn't relate your expectations well enough or you have a lawyer who's too busy to take on your business. If that's the case, any problem you have will take more time and more of your hard-earned money to resolve. In this situation, consider finding a new lawyer as soon as you can.

Auditing accountants

Having the right accountant is critical for your food truck. Accountants provide important advice for your business, and they help you manage your all-important bottom line. Even if you plan to do your books or taxes on your own, you may consider hiring an accountant instead of going it alone for the following tasks:

>> During the planning and start-up phases of your business, an accountant can advise you on a number of practical matters, including what type of business entity to create (see the later section "Surveying Different Structures for Your Food Truck Business") and the tax implications of each. If you're seeking a loan or outside funding to start your food truck business, having an accountant prepare your financial statements and projections for your business plan is a good idea. (See Chapters 4 and 5 for details on business plans and securing financing.) An accountant can also explain loan terms and conditions, help you comparison shop for the best rates, and help you plan for growth.

>> An accountant can create and analyze your financial statements, which help you make important decisions, such as menu pricing and inventory management. Accountants can also provide you with tax planning advice on exemptions that you may not be aware are available to you as a business owner.

>> Adding a single employee or entire staff comes with the tasks of record keeping and financial and tax considerations. An accountant can advise you on payroll, taxes, insurance needs, benefits, staffing costs, and other responsibilities that come with being an employer.

Choosing an accountant isn't as easy as typing *accountant* into an Internet search engine and selecting the first listed in the results. Just as I suggest when searching for an attorney (see the preceding section), ask local food truck or restaurant owners for their recommendations.

For most accounting tasks, such as bookkeeping and preparing your tax returns, you just need a general accountant; for tasks such as IRS audits, you need a Certified Public Accountant (CPA). An accountant with a CPA designation means that he's met a minimum level of education and experience and has successfully completed state-run tests to prove his accounting proficiency.

You need to choose your accountant carefully by conducting research and interviewing different accountants to find the right one for your business. Here are some guidelines on what to look for:

>> **Certifications:** Do they have a CPA or are they a general accountant? Determine the needs of your business and make sure their training will meet those needs.

>> **Industry expertise:** In addition to certifications, you should look for some type of expertise in the food service industry. Some accounting firms partner with networks of other firms and can turn to specialists to resolve certain issues if needed.

>> **Size of firm:** You'll have a vast array of accountants and accounting firms to choose from — from solo accountants to national firms. Unless you don't think you'll be comfortable without hiring a large firm, I suggest you look for a small firm or sole practitioner to do the accounting work for your food truck business.

Investigating insurance providers

Insurance coverage is important to any business owner, but it's even more important to a food truck owner. Not only will you need standard liability insurance and workers' compensation for your staff, but as a food truck owner, you'll also need complete coverage for your kitchen on wheels — the lifeblood of your business. (See the later section "Buying the Insurance You Need" for the full scoop.)

A good insurance provider is as valuable an asset to your business as any other professional consultant you hire. An experienced insurance provider can reduce your exposure to risk and keep your insurance costs to a minimum. Both insurance agents and brokers can help you sort through the vast array of insurance plans available and find one that fits your needs and budget.

When looking for an insurance provider, choose a professional with a good reputation in the industry. You can ask for referrals from other food truck owners in your area or speak with a local food truck organization. Because of the increase of food trucks across the country, a number of insurance sellers have also started specializing in the mobile food industry. Some of these providers are

>> Risk Strategies Company (www.risk-strategies.com)

>> Food Liability Insurance Program (www.fliprogram.com/food-truck-insurance)

>> Insure My Food Trailer (www.insuremyfoodtrailer.com/)

>> Insure My Food Truck (www.insuremyfoodtruck.com/)

>> Stratum Insurance (www.stratumins.com)

>> Whorton Insurance Services (www.mobilefoodvendorsinsurance.com)

TIP

After you've put together a list of preferred insurance providers, be sure to check their references and find out each state they're licensed and registered in. You can also check a provider's disciplinary record by calling your state's insurance commissioner's consumer hotline.

So should you hire an insurance agent or an insurance broker? Here are the primary differences and a couple of guidelines for choosing one over the other for your food truck:

>> Consider using an *agent* if your business has a single truck and only a few employees. Agents typically sell from only one insurance carrier. They're typically paid by the insurers, so your business isn't charged extra for their services. If you decide to work with an agent, talk with more than one to find out what type of coverage each agent carries.

>> Generally, the larger your business is, the more important it is for you to use a broker rather than an agent. Use a *broker* if you have a large number of employees or have a large number of vehicles in your food truck fleet. Brokers are independent, selling for multiple insurance companies. They're often paid on a commission basis by each insurance company, which may be reflected in your business's premiums.

TIP

Designate one person on your staff as the point of contact for all your food truck business insurance issues. This person can be you if you're a one-man show or your truck manager or office manager if you have additional employees who handle truck issues. Having one person deal with the insurance provider helps eliminate any confusion and the possibility of coverage being missed because someone else was going to call.

Surveying Different Structures for Your Food Truck Business

Long before you open your truck's service window, you need to decide which type of business structure best suits your needs. Your options range from sole proprietorships to partnerships and corporations. In the following sections, I discuss some of these common business structures.

REMEMBER

At the end of the day, choosing the right business structure for your food truck comes down to several factors, such as your risk of liability, tax obligations, business objectives, and so on. Your lawyer can help you choose the correct form of business structure, based on factors such as the number of people involved, tax issues, liability concerns, and the business's financial requirements. Your accountant can also discuss with you the tax implications of the form of business structure you choose. See the earlier section "Identifying the Help You Need" for details on finding and working with attorneys and accountants.

Sole proprietorships

A *sole proprietorship* is an unincorporated business owned by one person — in this case, you — known as a *sole proprietor.* The most important feature of a sole proprietorship is that the law makes no distinction between the sole proprietor and your business. Virtually, all the legal and tax consequences associated with sole proprietorships are based around this principle, meaning you keep everything you make; however, you also owe taxes on all your income. A disadvantage to this form of business structure is that if any sort of trouble arises —legal, financial, and so on — your personal property is also up for grabs, including your home, car, personal savings, and so forth.

As a sole proprietor, you're able to conduct business under your own name or under a trade name associated to your food truck (see Chapter 2 for details). You can hire any number of employees or independent contractors. Because the law makes no distinction between you and your business, you're not considered an employee of the business.

Partnerships

A *partnership* is an unincorporated business owned by more than one person. The two most common types of partnerships are general partnerships and limited partnerships:

> » *General partnerships* are made up of two or more partners who manage and are responsible for the business's debts and operations. Each partner

contributes skills, money, and time, and each shares in the company's profits as well as its losses. The biggest advantage of a general partnership is the tax benefit; businesses structured as partnerships don't pay income tax. Instead, all profits and losses are passed through to the individual partners.

» A *limited partnership* may have both general partners and limited partners. The limited partners in the relationship are investors, and they're not liable for the same responsibilities as the general partners. The advantage of a limited partnership is that some partners will be silent partners who only invest in the business, allowing you to run the business as you deem necessary. (Check out Chapter 5 for information on finding financing through partners.)

The disadvantages of both of these partnerships are that because you're not structuring your business as a corporation, these partnerships bring personal liability for all the business's obligations and debts.

REMEMBER

Partnerships are often formed among friends or colleagues, which can make matters even more delicate. To avoid problems down the road, each partner should consult a separate attorney at the outset, and all partners should agree on set terms and conditions of the partnership, including but not limited to the following:

» **Percentages of ownership:** Whether partners are contributing money, time, or both, they're making an investment in the company. In return for this investment, each partner is awarded a percentage of the business.

» **Distribution of profits and losses:** Make sure everyone knows how the profits will be divided. If the partners are to receive a separate salary, be sure to define that in the agreement.

» **Description of management powers and duties of each partner:** Simple enough; spell out each partner's duties and powers. Who makes the final decisions? Who runs the day-to-day operations of the truck?

» **Termination options:** Although having one or more partners leave isn't something you want to think about before the business even gets started, you still need to set the conditions in writing before it happens. These types of options can include one partner buying out another or what to do should one partner pass away.

REMEMBER

Have an attorney prepare the partnership agreement (and let each partner's legal counsel review it); the agreement should include all the important what-if questions in order to avoid problems should the partnership end. If the partnership does go sour, picking up the pieces can severely tax your company's resources and financial health.

Corporations

Incorporating is the forming of a new corporation under the law. The corporation can be a business, a nonprofit organization, a sports club, or a government of a new city or town. In the eyes of the law, a corporation is a person and thus can bring lawsuits, buy, sell, be taxed, and even commit crimes. Just as in a sole proprietorship, a corporation can be created by an individual without partners. The primary difference between the two is that a corporation is a legal entity that separates your personal liability from the corporation's debts and obligations.

Here are some of the benefits you can realize if you decide to incorporate your food truck business:

>> **Personal liability protection:** An incorporated company affords protection from any personal liability for your business debts and obligations. For example, if someone sues your company, he can go after only your company's assets, not your own.

>> **Tax benefits:** If you incorporate, you may gain tax benefits. Be sure to discuss this area with an accountant because the marginal tax rates for corporations with taxable incomes in some cases can be higher than those for an individual in the same scale.

>> **Raising capital:** If your business is incorporated, you have the ability to raise capital through the sale of stock.

WARNING

Some of the disadvantages of incorporation, particularly for those in the mobile food industry, include the following:

>> **Additional paperwork:** Depending on the structure you choose, you may need to file two tax returns — one for you and one for the business — and keep good records.

>> **Cost:** The fees associated with initial incorporation and ongoing maintenance can put a strain on start-ups.

REMEMBER

Because the needs of every business are different and the laws of incorporation vary from state to state, spending an hour or two with an attorney to investigate all the issues that may affect your decision is worth the time. You may also want to consult with other food truck owners you know who have gone through the process and get their referrals and recommendations. You can then choose to pursue incorporating your business with an attorney or through an online legal service, such as LegalZoom (`www.legalzoom.com`). Note that you must also file your incorporation with your state government.

CREATING A FOOD TRUCK ORGANIZATION FOR YOUR LOCALE

With the rapid expansion of the food truck industry, many cities in the country now have more than a dozen food trucks roaming their streets. Because of this trending growth, numerous food truck organizations have been started to give owners in these areas a single, focused voice to discuss their local issues. If you're in a city that lacks this form of organization, perhaps you've considered starting a new, nonprofit, tax-exempt organization specifically centered on the mobile food vendors in your region. If so, have you been trying to decide whether you should organize as a 501(c)(3) or (c)(6), or are you still struggling to figure out the difference between the two?

Before you can narrow down which 501(c) classification meets your organization's needs, you need to understand the distinction between a *nonprofit* and a *tax-exempt* entity. The term *nonprofit* refers to an entity's organizational status as governed by state law; *tax-exempt* refers to federal income tax exemption governed by the IRS. The 501(c)(3) and (c)(6) are two of the most common IRS tax-exempt statuses for nonprofits. To qualify for either exempt status, a nonprofit must meet specific tests outlined by the IRS (www.irs.gov/charities/article/0,,id=256970,00.html). One common requirement of a tax-exempt entity is that your net earnings may not benefit private shareholders or individuals. After they're organized, 501(c)(3) and (c)(6) organizations are both required to file annual IRS forms.

So which exempt classification is right for your planned organization? Here are some common differences:

- **501(c)(3):** This classification is for organizations operated exclusively for charitable, educational, religious, literary, or scientific purposes. They include membership associations if the purpose of the organization is to advance the profession with respect to educational activities. With 501(c)(3) organizations, lobbying and political activities are significantly restricted, and they'll lose tax-exempt status if the IRS determines that they've engaged in substantial lobbying activities.

  Advantages of the 501(c)(3) classification include enhanced fundraising options, such as eligibility to receive tax-deductible charitable contributions, gifts of property, and many grants, and eligibility to receive other state and local tax exemptions (for example, sales tax). One example of a nonprofit 501(c)(3) is the Urban Justice Center's Street Vendor Project.

- **501(c)(6):** Organizations with a 501(c)(6) classification are operated to promote a common business interest and to improve business conditions in the industry. They often include a membership organization or industry trade association, advancing a common business interest. A 501(c)(6) is allowed a wide-range of lobbying, yet it's required to disclose to membership the percentage of its annual lobbying dues. Dues or other payments to a 501(c)(6) are only deductible to the extent that they serve an ordinary and necessary business purpose of the payer. Examples of nonprofit 501(c)(6) include DC Mobile Food Vendors Association (DCMFVA) and SoCal Mobile Food Vendors' Association (SoCalMFVA).

As you can see, within the world of the 501(c), several similarities and distinct differences exist, and the (c)(3) and (c)(6) classifications represent only two of several types. When creating a new nonprofit organization for the mobile food vendors in your area, be sure to consult with both legal and tax professionals to help you make an informed decision. For additional help, you can contact the National Food Truck Association (www.nationalfoodtrucks.org).

Familiarizing Yourself with Local Laws

Laws will govern just about every aspect of your food truck business, from the types of food you can serve to the ability to stay in a metered parking space so you can sell your fare. To include all the laws that pertain to a food truck business would take several more chapters and go beyond the scope of this book, so I out-line just a few in this section. Make sure you know (or hire someone who knows) the laws that are most likely to affect your business, including the following:

>> **Business formation laws:** Here, you have laws for the specific business structure you've selected (I discuss different structures earlier in this chapter).

>> **Consumer protection laws:** These laws are against fraud or unfair business practices.

>> **Employment laws:** These laws regard hiring and firing employees, overtime pay, child labor, disability, workers' compensation, unemployment, employee rights, employee safety, and discrimination.

>> **Environmental laws:** These laws include recycling laws and laws for dispos-ing of the hazardous waste materials your truck or commercial kitchen may produce.

>> **Tax laws:** These laws pertain to filing tax returns and paying taxes, including sales tax, withholding taxes, corporate taxes, pass-through taxes, and both state and local taxes.

>> **Trademark and patent laws:** These laws and similar laws pertain to ownership or intellectual property rights.

>> **Zoning laws:** Typically, these laws include local ordinances that regulate parking, signage, and whether mobile vending is allowed in a specific area.

REMEMBER

Until now, you probably haven't worried too much about the legal issues associated with running a food truck, and you may still be on the fence about whether the additional costs of hiring a lawyer, accountant, and insurance provider are really worth it. But if you're seriously thinking about launching a food truck business, going it alone is a big mistake. These professionals are trained to interpret business-related laws, and those who specialize in the laws specific to the food service industry can be worth their weight in gold. I provide guidance on how to find and work with these professionals in the earlier section "Identifying the Help You Need."

Looking at Food Truck Licenses and Permits

When you open a food truck, you have to acquire many licenses and permits in order to operate your truck. What's the difference between a license and a permit, you ask?

>> A *license* is a legal document issued by a government agency that gives you the agency's permission to do something or use something. In some cases, licensing is granted after some kind of test to make sure the person receiving the license is capable of doing a specific activity; however, a business license doesn't usually require an examination of any kind.

>> A *permit* is a type of license granted by a government agency. Permits usually regulate safety and are typically granted following an inspection.

In the following sections, I explain some of the licenses and permits you may need and note some pointers for securing them.

Examining some of the paperwork you may need

The business licenses and permits you'll need for your food truck business differ for each city, county, state and country. Also, some areas may require you to register your business annually, collecting a fee each time. To find out what you need for the area your business will be located in, talk to your county or city clerk.

TIP

The laws and regulations of any area are subject to change, so you may want to join your local restaurant or food truck association to stay informed on the changes in laws and local government officials and how they'll affect your business. A simple Internet search can help you find these organizations, or you can speak with current food truck owners in your town to find out what organizations they belong to.

Here are some of the licenses and permits you may need for your food truck business:

>> **Business license:** Depending on the area you operate in, you may be charged a percentage of your gross sales or a simple yearly fee to operate your business.

>> **Vehicle license:** Because your business is on wheels, you'll have to make sure the truck itself and its drivers are properly licensed. Depending on the length and weight of the vehicle, certain states may require a commercial driver's license to operate your truck.

>> **Health department permit:** Just as any restaurant is required to be inspected by the health department, your mobile restaurant will also need the review and approval of your local health department to verify that the food you prepare is being maintained and created in a safe manner. Check out Chapters 13 and 21 for information on what the health department looks for and how to pass important inspections.

>> **Food handler's license or permit:** Having one of these licenses or permits is necessary to sell edible goods. Each county and state has its own set of rules and fees. Health inspectors will regularly inspect your truck to make sure you're running a clean mobile food business. Most states require you (and all your food handling staff) to take a one- to two-day course on food safety.

>> **Fire certificates:** The fire department will undoubtedly inspect your food truck if you're using cooking equipment on board. They'll educate you on the regulations you need to follow, and they'll do routine inspections on your food truck fire suppression system.

>> **Music license:** If you intend to play music in your truck (and play it loud enough for your customers to hear) and if your local laws allow, you may need a music license to play copyrighted music. The license is necessary even if you play music from personally owned CDs.

WARNING

Although this list isn't complete, it's a good sampling of the most common forms of approvals you'll need. Operating without a required license or permit can expose your business to fines and penalties. In some cases, those fines can be levied for each day you remain out of compliance, which adds up fast.

Going through the paperwork process

REMEMBER

Before you even think about obtaining licenses and permits, you need to apply for a Federal Employer Identification Number (EIN), which identifies you to the government as a business owner. You can get this number by visiting the IRS website (www.irs.gov) and answering a few questions about the type of legal structure you want your business (as I discuss in the earlier section "Surveying Different Structures for Your Food Truck Business"), how many people will be part of your business, where your food truck business will be located, and even why you're applying for the EIN; afterward, you'll be issued your EIN.

Unfortunately, you can't take care of all your licenses and permits in one stop because the requirements for mobile food vendors rest with more than one government agency. As a result, securing all the necessary paperwork can quickly become a tedious process. It requires multiple follow-up calls, so expect delays and be sure to allow plenty of time to get your licenses and permits and any inspections and approvals needed. Speak with other food truck owners in your area to find out how long this process took them and whether they can give you names of people to work with directly in the licensing department or tips they may have to help you speed up the process. Also be prepared for multiple inspections and having to do a little more than you originally planned for in order to meet local codes.

TIP

If you don't have time for this administrative paper chase or if you prefer the peace of mind of having a professional do it, you can always hire an attorney or permit expeditor with experience in the food service industry. Certain business licensing services are also available on the Internet through business services, such as LegalZoom (www.legalzoom.com) and BizFilings (www.bizfilings.com).

Buying the Insurance You Need

As with any business, the owners of mobile food trucks need to protect themselves and their business. While other food service businesses face potential insurance claims every day, food trucks face additional risks, for which they need different types of insurance. In the following sections, I talk about the basic insurance coverage you need as well as extra certificates.

Covering insurance basics

REMEMBER

Working with an insurance provider who understands the needs of the mobile food industry is important. Many insurance providers sell insurance for the traditional brick-and-mortar restaurants in your area and can tailor these insurance policies to your specific needs, so make sure to present all the aspects of your business to a prospective provider so he can find the best policy for you. Here are a few questions to ask when buying insurance:

>> Am I protected if I get into a car accident?

>> Does my insurance allow for a mobile business?

>> Do I have coverage for food poisoning claims?

>> What if the truck is stolen or vandalized?

>> Do the items I tow need special coverage?

Be sure to review your business in detail with your insurance provider to determine which (and how much) coverage is right for you. A typical insurance program for a mobile food vendor includes the following:

WARNING

>> **Commercial auto liability:** This insurance is designed for vehicles used during the course of business operation.

Be careful not to purchase only *personal* auto insurance that includes "business usage" because the terms of the commercial auto insurance and personal auto insurance policies differ. Generally, a commercial policy offers higher limits of insurance, allows for modified trucks, and permits different types of usage and travel radius. Also, a food truck is generally larger than a personal vehicle and has heavy modifications, so it needs extra coverage.

>> **General liability:** This insurance is a policy that offers several specific types of coverage served a la carte, where your start with several types of coverage and have the option to choose additional coverage if desired. Simply put, your commercial auto policy is only one piece of the insurance puzzle. What will protect you when you've parked the truck, opened your service window, or even set up tables? General liability often includes protection from claims that arise from bodily injury and property damage, as well as covering the food that you sell.

>> **Business personal property:** If you want insurance protection for equipment that isn't permanently mounted to your truck (such as a barbeque or smoker you tow behind your truck) and isn't covered under your commercial auto policy, you should consider this type of coverage.

Note: Although you may have coverage for liability risks while towing these items, typically no coverage exists for replacement if it's damaged.

>> **Workers' compensation:** This insurance takes care of medical bills for employees injured on the job.

>> **Unemployment insurance:** This insurance pays your out-of-work, former employees until they find another job.

>> **Umbrella liability:** Umbrella liability coverage (also known as *excess liability*) provides additional protection above and beyond your automotive, general liability, and workers' compensation policies. For example, if your general liability policy provides $1 million in coverage but a claim settlement calls for $1.5 million, your umbrella policy would cover the additional half-million dollars.

REMEMBER

When your insurance provider is putting together your automotive insurance quote, he'll require a list of your drivers so he can check each of their motor vehicle reports (MVRs) on his own. If you have an ineligible driver, most competitive insurance companies will pull their quote. You're then stuck with having to use an insurance company that charges you an arm and a leg to cover the poor driver. To avoid this situation, be sure you always check a person's MVR prior to hiring him or allowing him to drive your food truck. Require all potential drivers to go to the Department of Motor Vehicles or Secretary of State and get a copy of their MVR. Within the last 36 months, no prospective driver should have more than

>> One moving violation and two accidents

>> Two moving violations and one accident

>> Three moving violations and no accidents

None of your drivers should have any serious moving violations (such as driving under the influence, a suspended license, or an auto felony conviction).

Adding additional insured certificates

One insurance topic many new food truck owners are unfamiliar with is the need for additional insured certificates. An *additional insured* is a term for a person, firm, or other entity that's afforded the same protection under the insurance policy as the insured (food truck). Most property owners and event planners require this paperwork when they invite food trucks onto privately held property for a food truck event. In some cases, if you'll be attending an event that's held on city- or county-owned property, a government agency will also ask to be included as additional insured.

Essentially, the venue or event is protecting itself from any bodily injury or property damage your business may cause at its event. Some insurance carriers charge $25 to $100 per certificate, which can add up to a significant hidden cost if you attend multiple events throughout the year.

Not until I started organizing local food truck events did I realize the importance of these certificates. Unfortunately, the insurance providers that aren't familiar with these types of food truck operations often fail to mention the cost or even realize a truck may need additional insured certificates. To prevent your business from incurring these unexpected added costs to operation, hire an insurance provider that's familiar with this type of added coverage.

REMEMBER

When you're getting insurance quotes from potential insurance providers, have them do the following:

>> Place you with an insurance carrier that doesn't charge for these certificates

>> Offer you a blanket (unlimited) additional insured option (which could add about $500 to your annual premium)

Chapter 7

Parking and Presenting Your Food Truck

C hances are you've heard the phrase "location, location, location" in regards to setting up a business. Well, this phrase is just as important to operating a mobile food truck. The key to locating areas to park your truck is finding spots that are easy for your customers in your targeted market to reach. Maybe your community allows trucks to park on the streets, but what streets should you park on? Does your local community college or university need another food option for its students? Will it be better to operate solo, or should you team up with other food trucks to create a mobile food court? Use the suggestions in this chapter to discover the best locations in your community to operate from. (Of course, make sure you can legally park in the spots you've chosen.)

You also need to make sure your truck can attract the attention of hungry pass-ersby and those who may not be familiar with you. In this chapter, I cover the basics of developing a look and atmosphere that matches your truck's concept and that explains to those walking by why they should stop and place an order. After you've formulated a logo and design for your truck, you need to figure out a way and a medium for getting that design on the truck; I share the pros and cons to using a vehicle wrap or paint and either installing the design yourself or hiring a design company to do it for you.

TIP

Although the location you park your truck during the day is where you'll bring in your profits, you also need a location to park your truck overnight or during the time it's not on the road. Check with your local municipality to find out where commercial vehicles can park; in most cases, you'll be required to park your truck at your commercial kitchen. (See Chapter 9 for more info.)

TIP

Create partnerships with those who own trucks that complement yours. Working in teams can be very conducive to both businesses; for example, savory and sweet trucks parked in the same area work well together.

Discovering Where the Street Traffic Is

Finding good street locations for your food truck to park and operate in is vitally important to your chances for success. Starting up a food truck is nearly impossible without having a street location where customer traffic can get to you. (When I say *traffic,* I don't mean only automotive traffic but also pedestrian traffic.)

Carefully investigate both the foot traffic and the vehicle traffic surrounding your street location and make sure there's enough to build a good customer base. If you park on the street in locations where there isn't enough traffic to survive, you may doom yourself before you even begin.

You also want to find out who lives or works around your potential street locations and make sure they're the customers you want to attract (according to the guidelines in Chapter 3). If you offer a more upscale menu, for example, don't locate yourself in the chicken wings and beer neighborhood. You can usually get a feel for a location by the kinds of businesses already there, but do some research to back up your instincts. In the following sections, I describe different options for getting the info you need.

In addition to finding out who lives or works in the area you're planning to operate your truck in, you also want know when these people are actually in the area. While the lunch crowd may consist mainly of people working at the local businesses, the morning and evening crowds may be people who live in the area and are looking for meals before or after the times they work.

TIP

Try to get the Twitter handles of businesses in the area and give them a shout-out when you're going to be parked near them. Often, businesses will send out email announcements informing their employees of your location for you. (Check out Chapter 16 for more about using Twitter and other social media sites to market your business.)

Relying on others' research

If you're interested in research that's already been compiled, your first stop should be the office of your local development group or chamber of commerce; they can provide information on both vehicle and pedestrian traffic, as well as the demographic statistics of the people who live in the area. Commercial sources, such as Scan/US (www.scanus.com), can also help you determine the demographics on car traffic and pedestrian traffic.

WARNING

Having a busy location with no place to park is almost as bad as being in a dead zone. Unless you base all your business around foot traffic, which usually works only in downtown areas or business districts, your customers will need adequate parking. You aren't going to get walk-up customers if they have nowhere to park their cars. Drive around the areas you're researching and look for locations where customers can park and are able to walk to your operating location. If no parking options are close, you may want to adjust the exact spot you park your truck so it's closer to where potential customers can park.

TIP

If finding a good start-up location is a struggle, reach out to other food truck owners in your area. If they seem hesitant to give you information on their best spots, you can find out by merely checking their website or following them on Twitter; however, observe the food truck code and be careful not to infringe — no poaching.

Calculating foot traffic yourself

Understanding the level of foot traffic at specific locations around your area is very useful in determining where the potential for success is greatest and where you want to park your truck from day to day. If you're interested in researching this information on your own, follow these steps to calculate foot traffic in the areas where you're interested in operating:

1. **Determine when you plan to be open for business and calculate the foot traffic during these time periods at each location you want to investigate.**

   In all likelihood, every location's foot traffic will vary at different times, so make sure to count traffic over a slightly longer period than your target time (15 to 30 minutes before and after your planned operating hours).

TIP

   If you'll be able to stay in one location for multiple work shifts, it may be in your best interest to count traffic for the entire day to hone in on the best times to operate.

2. **Put together a gridded worksheet with each of your selected time periods listed down the left-hand side, and list different classes of pedestrians along the top, such as elderly, adults (with and without children), and bicyclists.**

   Use five-minute time increments to allow an accurate profile to be calculated at the end of the process.

3. **Find a safe location from which to observe pedestrians, and identify a visual reference point, such as a parking meter.**

4. **Put a tick in the appropriate pedestrian class box every time someone passes your reference point during a given time period.**

TIP

   Pay attention to small groups of three to eight people, which can make or break a stop. Food trucks are innately social, and people like to go to them with their friends.

5. **Repeat this counting until the entire window of time (for example, 11:45 a.m. to 1 p.m.) has been completed.**

6. **After you have your numbers, total the columns and rows for each time slot and class of pedestrian.**

   The column totals allow you to see whether one specific class has the potential to generate a particularly high demand over the entire time window. This data can be used for a variety of purposes, such as planning your menu for each time window.

   The row totals identify overall demand during each five-minute period and provide an accurate profile of the traffic totals. Understanding this data may even help to confirm whether each location you're considering fits the customer base you're striving to attract to your truck.

Figure 7-1 shows you an example of what your chart may look like for a time span from 11:45 p.m. to 1 p.m. (Your chart, of course, would cover a longer time span; Figure 7-1 is a condensed version.)

If you have multiple locations to check out, you can repeat this process for each spot and then compare the locations and consider the best times to operate in each place. Many trucks are in large enough cities to conduct lunch and dinner operations five days a week without repeating a single location each week, whereas others operate the same amount of time but park in only one or two locations each week.

TIP

If you find the perfect street spot to operate your truck, but the spot gets taken long before the time period you plan to operate, you can hold the parking spot with another car until your food truck arrives. This way you're guaranteed a spot for the day.

Pedestrian Classification					
Location:					
Time Period	**Adults without Children**	**Adults with Children**	**Elderly**	**Bicyclists**	**Total**
11:45-11:50 a.m.					
11:50-11:55 a.m.					
11:55 a.m.-12 p.m.					
12-12:05 p.m.					
12:05-12:10 p.m.					
12:10-12:15 p.m.					
12:15-12:20 p.m.					
12:20-12:25 p.m.					
12:25-12:30 p.m.					
12:30-12:35 p.m.					
12:35-12:40 p.m.					
12:40-12:45 p.m.					
12:45-12:50 p.m.					
12:50-12:55 p.m.					
12:55-1 p.m.					

FIGURE 7-1:
An example of a DIY chart for measuring foot traffic.

Exploring Other Excellent Parking Options

The fact that your business is mobile gives you a fantastic advantage over brick-and-mortar restaurants. If you find that the spots you initially work from don't provide enough traffic for you to succeed, you can merely move to another location and try again.

Parking on streets with the right amount of traffic (see the preceding section) isn't your only option. A huge number of different locations are available for you to work from, any of which may provide you with great foot traffic to your truck. You find out about them in the following sections.

Although you can and should attempt to operate your truck from many places, you shouldn't waste your time on some spots. Avoid areas that aren't well lit or are known as high-crime areas. You shouldn't risk the security of your staff and customers if you know an area has a risk of criminal or seedy activity. Ultimately, you need to know the target customers you want to attract to your truck and avoid areas and situations that aren't attractive to that market.

Food truck meet-ups/events

Food truck events are popping up across the country, many of which have been started by food truck owners themselves. These meet-ups or events typically involve multiple trucks offering various savory and dessert options to their visitors. Some cities, like Miami, Florida, and Orange County, California, have been able to schedule weekly events that attract thousands of foodies from those areas.

To find events in your area, speak with other truck owners, check your local newspaper, or find local or national food truck websites (such as www.mobile-cuisine.com) that publish lists of these events throughout the year. If existing food truck event series are running, find out who the organizer is and what the requirements are to enter. Some groups require you to pay a minimal entrance fee, but the amount of traffic that visits these events can far outweigh the cost of admittance.

Business parks and office complexes

If you're located in an area with industrial or business parks, contact some of the businesses in the park. The building manager or human resources group is your best bet for finding someone who can grant you permission to serve the businesses' employees. Most of these buildings house hundreds of workers who are tired of eating out of vending machines or out of their less-than-creative cafes. In some cases, these businesses will even help advertise your truck to your prospective customers. Breakfast and lunch hours are the primary times to operate in this type of location.

College campuses and local parks

With the current state of the economy, many state-run colleges have cut services on campus. In many cases, their food service is part of these cuts. Reach out to the college administration (start with the facilities management group) to find out whether you can help feed their students. A college campus can be a fantastic place for a truck that's just starting up to build loyal customers, because students fit right into the demographic of individuals looking for tasty, high-quality but inexpensive food.

TIP

College kids love food trucks, but they also love to charge their food purchases on credit or debit cards. Be sure to be well equipped to handle these transactions. For more on the subject of accepting credit cards, check out Chapter 12.

Local parks are another great spot to park your truck; just make sure that if the park visitors are mainly children, their parents commonly join them. Check with the city park district to find out whether mobile vending is authorized or whether vendors are required to pay a fee to sell their products from the parks.

Farmers' markets

Farmers' markets are a great option for food trucks because they typically cater to local farmers and food producers. Research all the farmers' markets in your area but realize that not all markets are alike. Some will be more appropriate for your food truck than others. Think about the distance to each market, the size of the market, the rules and regulations the market has, and the type of customer it attracts. You can get this info from the market manager or the market's website.

After you identify a market you're interested in joining, contact the market manager to inquire about applications and entry forms. The best time to apply is at the beginning of the market year (during the winter season, because many markets shut down in areas where the temperature drops near or below freezing). Expect the application process to take up to a few weeks, or even a few months. This timing depends on the number of applications they have to review, whether or not they have a board that reviews and votes on applicants, and/or the size of the market. Some require an interview, an application fee, and/or a one-time, weekly, monthly, or yearly fee to participate in the market.

Airport cell phone lots

Food trucks have invaded almost every metro region in America. Why should the airports (the first glimpse travelers get of the cities they're visiting) be left out? A few airports have recently brought food trucks to their cell phone parking lots and taxi staging areas. Los Angeles, Orlando, and Tampa International have the most robust programs.

All Dolled Up: Presenting Your Vehicle

If there's one sure way to kill your food truck before you even get a chance to open your service window, it's failing to decorate the exterior of your truck properly. Don't spend all your time and effort filling the inside of your truck with expensive kitchen equipment and then scrimp when it comes to your truck's appearance.

You only get one first impression! Although it may sound cliché, it's absolutely true. Someone driving or walking by your truck will, on average, have five seconds to decide whether she's comfortable ordering from your menu. It doesn't matter how good your food is; your customers' first impression is based on what they see, and they buy with their eyes.

In the following sections, I describe the items that should appear on your truck and in your logo. I also explain your options for truck decoration and help you decide who should have the honors of outfitting your truck.

Knowing what to include on the exterior

Depending on your daily driving routes, your food truck will be seen by thousands of people every day. So what should you include on its exterior? You can include your logo and images that display your food items in a colorful and appetizing light. Also include anything that you feel your customers need to know about how to find or follow you at a later date, such as your website URL, phone number, or the ways they can follow you on Facebook or Twitter.

REMEMBER

Limit the amount of text you have on your truck to your company and contact information. Most viewers will see it from a distance, so it must be large and clear enough to be easily read. Don't be tempted to cram too much information onto the truck; be concise and use images to attract the interest of potential customers.

REMEMBER

A lot of planning needs to be taken into account before you finalize your truck's appearance. Try to keep in mind what you want your customers to see and where you want that art or information to be. Putting your menu and/or contact information on the right side of the truck is very important because when you're parked street-side, customers will be walking up to (and therefore viewing) the passenger side to get to your service window. You can use the left side of your truck to add images of your food along with your logo and contact information.

TIP

When wrapping your truck, don't forget about the roof. This adds a little extra bang for your buck in urban communities, where there are tall office buildings. Placing your Twitter name or website address on your roof will give those working in office buildings a way to find out who you are and what they are missing out on.

Creating a memorable logo for your food truck

Establishing a logo for your food truck helps people remember your business and think of it when they're in the mood to order something from a food truck. For some people, designing a logo is an exciting task that allows them to tap into their creative side. For others, it can be a dreaded chore with too many options to choose from.

When creating a logo to use for your business, think about how you want it to be perceived, because every element in it matters. It's like developing the perfect recipe. Everything needs to be of high quality (the colors, fonts, background, image, and so forth) and in the right quantity. Make sure your logo is completely authentic and infused with your personality. It needs to also convey your concept, which I discuss in Chapter 2.

REMEMBER

So where do you begin? Whether you're designing your logo yourself or are hiring someone to help, having a clear idea of what you're looking for will help you get to the finish line in no time. Here are some tips:

>> **Keep it simple.** The simpler your logo, the easier it will be to recall. After all, being memorable is the primary purpose of your branding for a food truck business. So hone in on your brand's core message, pair it down to two or three key phrases, and then use these phrases as starting points for conceptualizing relevant shapes, colors, or actions. (For example, the color yellow can define cheer, happiness, joy, playful, sunshine, and warmth, or you can choose to use concentric circles to represent continuity and shelter.) If you get too fanciful and complicated, your logo's meaning may get lost and customers may not be able to identify it. You don't want people looking at your logo and asking whether it's supposed to be a hamburger or some sort of plant.

>> **Don't be too literal.** Subtlety is the key to an effective logo design. The fundamental goal of the design is to spark recognition by the viewer as quickly as possible, and that relies on simplicity. Don't use fancy fonts or complicated images. No one likes logos that take several minutes to understand their meaning.

>> **Stay away from trends.** Your logo can be with you for years, whereas what's cool today can be tired and dated tomorrow. Trends come and go, but a timeless logo needs little tweaking to adapt to new ages.

>> **Select size carefully.** Keep in mind that what matters is not how big your logo is, but how big its elements are in relation to each other. If your logo is poorly proportioned, important parts may become hard to recognize when it's shrunk down for smaller usage (such as on your website or business cards). Similarly, when you blow it up for the truck, other elements may dominate. Keep your logo design to a logical ratio.

>> **Stick with a limited color range.** Try to use a maximum of three or four colors. This tactic helps ensure that you're using each color for a specific reason.

>> **Make your logo easy to describe.** The golden rule of branding your food truck is that a logo must be describable. Like Nike's "swoosh" or McDonald's "golden arches," your logo needs a simplicity and uniqueness that can be conveyed by description. Clear colors and describable shapes make your logo more memorable for those seeing it, which, after all, is its primary purpose.

Now that you understand the basic principles of good logo design, you're on your way to designing the perfect logo for your food truck business. Let your creativity flow and start by brainstorming many different designs. Try out a few of the final contenders with friends and family to get their feedback.

TIP

If you have problems coming up with a logo design you're excited about, I recommend hiring a professional graphic design agency to assist you with this task. The main benefit of hiring an agency is that you get a team of designers who have industry experience and know what type of colors, fonts, and graphics work best for the mobile industry. You can find many graphic design firms by getting referrals from food truck owners who have already developed their graphics. Or another resource may be food truck builders in your area who typically use one or two different graphic design companies to help them design the graphics for their clients.

If budget is an issue and you want to see many design options, 99 Designs (www.99designs.com) is a great resource for crowdsourcing. After you post a description of what you are looking for, you will start receiving designs from around the world. They offer several investment levels the lowest being $299 up to $1,000. The more you offer, usually gets more experienced designers will submit ideas for your project. If you don't like any of them, you don't pay a dime.

Deciding how to decorate your truck

After you decide what info to include on your truck and design a logo, you need to decide how to apply all that good stuff to your truck. You have a couple of options for the exterior decoration of your truck. You can have your truck either wrapped in vinyl or painted:

>> **Wrapping your truck in vinyl:** The most common industry practice is wrapping the truck in vinyl because of the unique nature of this medium partnered with eye-catching designs. Marketing studies have supported that vehicle wraps are actually read and remembered better than any other form of advertising, except TV ads. Vehicle wraps look great for years, depending on weather exposure and how well you take care of the wrap. Although vinyl manufacturers guarantee the material for five to ten years, the actual life span of a vehicle wrap will be considerably less. In addition, wraps that stay on vehicles longer than three years tend to bond more strongly to the surface and make wrap removal more time consuming. A decent wrap will cost between $3,000 and $5,000.

If you operate in a city with buildings taller than three or four stories, consider wrapping the top of your truck. Think about what people on the upper floors looking outside their windows will see when you drive through or park in these areas. In most cases, they'll see a blank white truck top, with nothing differentiating you from the local delivery truck. But if your roof is branded and includes your contact information, they may just make the choice to come downstairs and place an order.

>> **Painting your truck:** Paint is another, although less common, option for adding graphics to your truck and is about half the price of most full vehicle wraps. The downside to paint is that unless you invest even more in a professional painter, you can't get the same quality and detail in smaller painted graphics. Your investment is about $1,000 to $3,000 for the paint option.

Don't attempt to paint your vehicle yourself unless you have experience in truck painting. Not only do you risk spending a lot of time and money to do the painting yourself, but you also risk the chance of doing a poor job and having to get the painting redone by a professional — and coughing up even more money.

If you choose to have the main body of your truck painted, you can still install a partial wrap that features your logo and contact information.

Figuring out who should wrap your truck

When your truck is finally ready to get dressed, you have two options at your disposal: (1) finding a company to help and (2) doing the decorating yourself.

Finding a quality graphics company to help

Don't overlook the importance of your vehicle's wrap installation. Why? Your food truck's wrap is one of the most effective methods you have to get your marketing message to your customers. Simply said, by installing a vehicle wrap, you transform your truck into a mobile billboard. You can target your favorite locations and take your message to your targeted audience by merely driving down the street or parking on it.

When searching for a company to perform this task, you need to select one that can meet your needs. Here are issues you should consider when searching for the right vehicle graphics company:

>> **Specialization:** Just as you wouldn't let a general practice doctor perform your brain surgery, you shouldn't trust a sign shop to handle the specialized creation and installation of your truck wrap. You need to hire a professional

and qualified company that specializes in designing and installing vehicle wraps. You can search your area for these professionals in the yellow pages or online. I also suggest speaking with food truck builders in your area to get referrals for the companies they use to wrap the trucks they produce. One such company that's started specializing in food truck wrapping is Custom Vehicle Wraps (www.customvehiclewraps.com).

>> **Design:** The most important aspect of your truck wrap installation is its overall design, including your logo; it portrays your brand in the eyes of your audience. The old adage "you get what you pay for" still holds when it comes to vehicle wraps. Avoid a company that offers to "throw in the design for free." Before contracting any company, ask to see a portfolio of other food truck designs the company has done. Also make sure the company you contract provides you with a custom design.

>> **Materials:** Using poor materials can cause you to waste a lot of money. Ensure that a company uses a good-quality material, including a film laminate on top of your graphic project, in order to protect your investment. Also look for companies that offer you a warranty on their work.

REMEMBER

>> **Legal knowledge:** Almost every state and local municipality has its own specific laws and regulations that govern the use of imagery in any form of advertisement. These laws also govern what you can display on your truck. You need to be sure that the company you select to wrap your truck has a full understanding of these laws. This knowledge will save you from problems getting approval to operate on the streets and prevent you from having to pay to have a graphic removed if it can't be approved.

Wrapping your truck yourself

If you have experience in applying vinyl graphics, you may choose to attempt wrapping your truck yourself. However, you shouldn't do a full vehicle wrap yourself unless you have years of experience and enough friends to help you install the wrap properly. If you do decide to wrap the truck yourself, read this section carefully and be sure your graphics are no larger than 4 or 5 feet across — if they're larger, hand over the reins to a professional. You don't want to spend money on printing out a graphic if there's a chance you may incorrectly install it and have to pay for a professional to do it in the long run.

To install a wrap on your food truck yourself, you'll need the following basic tools:

>> **A tape measure:** For accurately positioning your wrap.

>> **Masking tape:** For positioning the wrap before you install it.

>> **An air-release tool:** For removing air bubbles.

Inexperienced installers often use razor blades to pop bubbles. This practice is dangerous because it creates a slit in the film that leads to a stress point, which can cause the film to lose its strength or integrity.

>> **A squeegee:** For applying the wrap.

Some installers actually use two different squeegees: a standard hard squeegee for the general work and a felt squeegee for the detailed areas. Felt squeegees help you avoid scratching the vinyl in hard-to-wrap areas.

>> **A razor knife (with break-off blades):** For trimming away excess vinyl.

>> **A heat gun:** For heating the vinyl on more complicated applications.

Install your wrap in temperatures between 50 and 90 degrees Fahrenheit — 70 to 80 degrees is the optimum range. Whenever possible, apply wraps indoors, which helps control the temperature and reduces the amount of wind and dust you have to deal with.

When you're ready to install your food truck graphics, follow these steps to apply them like a pro:

1. **Clean and dry your truck thoroughly.**

   Preparing your vehicle for wrapping isn't just a matter of driving it through the car wash. All dirt and oil must be removed from the vehicle's surface to ensure a proper bond of the vinyl's adhesive. Any lingering dirt, even the minutest of dirt particles, will show through the graphic installation. Any oil residue can lead to poor adhesion and bubbling of the wrap material. Use warm soapy water to hand-wash your truck, and use a grease remover to get rid of those tough spots.

   A common mistake during the preparation process is failing to allow the vehicle to dry fully. It can take up to 24 hours for your vehicle to dry completely, especially in humid or cold areas.

2. **Touch up your truck's paint job.**

   Any paint imperfections and stone chips need to be touched up; otherwise, they'll show through the vinyl and may cause it to wear, tear, or prematurely peel.

3. **Remove any elements, such as mirrors or wiper blades, that will force you to make extra cuts or unnecessary marks in the vinyl.**

4. **Tape the design to the exterior to make sure everything is positioned correctly.**

5. Remove the backing of the film and apply the wrap.

You can use a heat gun to help remove bubbles and allow the vinyl to flex and bend over curved surfaces. All movements over the vinyl should be firm and in a sweeping motion to avoid the formation of bubbles in the first place. If bubbles do appear, remove the vinyl in that area and try again. Using a firm — but not sharp — plastic squeegee can help avoid bubbles.

After you've completely installed your graphics, caring for vinyl is similar to caring for paint work. Use a standard car soap to wash the vehicle and apply a wax polish (unless you have a matte finish). Avoid the use of caustic cleaners such as tar remover.

3

Preparing to Open Your Service Window

Chapter 8

Creating Your Food Truck Menu

A well-planned and developed menu is the keystone of any successful food truck operation. It tells the story of your business, assists you in promotion, establishes your budget, and keeps your brand fresh in each customer's mind. Your food truck menu should create an impression on your customers that stays with them long after they've ordered from it. In addition, it must convey your brand in a manner that makes diners excited to visit, want to come back, and want to recommend it to family and friends.

In this chapter, I go over what you need to know to plan your food truck's menu, from determining what you'll serve, to properly laying out the presentation of your menu, to determining when it's time to change it up.

What Do You Have Today? Making Major Menu Decisions

Creating a good menu is part art form and part science. Just like a great artist, you should create something truly inspiring and original when putting your menu together. The scientific part of the equation involves the construction of a menu that not only matches your concept but also takes into account the type of equipment available to create your delectable meals. Run-of-the-mill belongs with a corporate chain sports bar, not your food truck. In the following sections, I provide all the tools you need to create a menu that brings customers to your service window time after time.

Matching your menu to your concept

REMEMBER

In Chapter 2, I go into detail about how and why you must put together a sound concept for your food truck. Now it's time to take that information and develop a menu that matches it. In other words, you need to create a menu that matches the concept and the atmosphere you want your customers to experience. Without taking this step, you may start adding menu items that confuse your customers, so answer these questions:

>> **Will your truck sell ethnic cuisine?** If so, make sure all the items on your menu represent the culture or country you're showcasing. For example, if you plan on a Mediterranean concept, be prepared to serve Greek or Middle Eastern dishes. You can also fuse two cultures together as long as one of the cultures is the basis of your concept, such as fusing Mexican food and Korean food like Kogi BBQ (www.kogibbq.com) did with their famous Korean BBQ tacos.

>> **What menu items do you potentially have in common with competitors?** If you're in an area that already has food trucks with a similar concept you plan to use, look at their menus and create items that may be similar, but put your own twist on them. Changing ingredients and flavor profiles can create differences that get customers to come to you, even though the menu items may seem similar to other trucks. For example, your menu may include a hamburger with hand-cut French fries, while your main competitor offers a plain burger with boring old frozen fries. (Flip to Chapter 3 for more details on researching your competition.)

>> **What are your hours of operation?** If your truck is going to be serving a breakfast crowd, your customers will expect to see breakfast items. On the other hand, if you'll be serving a lunch or dinner crowd, you probably shouldn't include an omelet on your menu, unless your concept is breakfast for dinner.

Building your menu with a few handy hints

Creating your food truck menu can be overwhelming. What dishes should you offer and what should you skip? The ideal menu offers a balance of unique dishes and old favorites that match your concept (see the preceding section). Avoid a menu full of food fads, such as low- or no-carb offerings. Although you want your menu to be exciting and trendy, you need to include cuisine favorites as well.

Here are some additional pointers for putting together your menu:

» Make sure your menu items are easy to prepare. Unless you plan to compete with local fine-dining establishments (and really, what food truck can?), you need to be able to prepare your menu items quickly. Any menu item that takes abnormally long to cook or prepare can bog down the line at your service window during a rush. I'm not saying that you shouldn't offer great presentations, but just make sure they're simple.

» Use ingredients in more than one dish to keep food spoilage to a minimum and to stretch your budget. For example, if you offer various proteins for a sandwich or wrap, try to offer other items that can include those same proteins.

» Gather the core group of menu items you want to serve. Being realistic about how many items you'll be able to serve from the limited space in your truck will help you determine the number of menu items you start with. The basic premise of "quantity doesn't equate to quality" definitely applies to food trucks. Most food trucks across the country average between 6 and 12 menu items.

As you build your menu, keep the financials in the back of your mind. Each item on your menu should be affordable to customers but priced to keep your profits up. Expensive ingredients result in high-priced menus. This doesn't mean that you should use the cheapest food available, but you need to balance high and low food costs for a reasonable profit margin. In addition, balancing expensive items, which are prone to price fluctuations, with items that have stable costs can help maintain your desired menu prices. So go ahead and have some lamb and beef on your menu, but be sure to temper them with some less expensively priced chicken and/ or pasta dishes. (I talk about menu pricing in full detail later in this chapter.)

Linking your menu to your equipment

The size and types of equipment in your commercial and food truck kitchens will play major roles in determining the items you can include on your menu. The larger the kitchen and the wider the range of equipment, the more menu items you can offer. However, if you try to offer too large or complex a menu out of a tiny food truck kitchen (which can be done, though it isn't easy) you may run into serious problems during busy times. Having proper stations set up in your kitchen will also help you and your staff from cross-contaminating menu items. (I go over cross-contamination in detail in Chapter 13.)

For example: If you choose not to install a fryer due to space limitations, then you shouldn't add items like French fries, onion rings, and other fried foods to your menu, even if your customers continually ask for them. If you expect sandwiches or salads to play a prominent role on your menu, be sure you have enough room for a sandwich or salad station in one or both of your kitchens.

TIP

If you're planning to use a concept that will have you making styles of food that require specialty kitchen equipment, be sure your truck or commercial kitchen has the space or ability to have it installed. Here are some of the styles of cuisine (and typical related equipment) that may require more than a flat-top grill, convection oven, or deep-fat fryer in your equipment list (check out Chapter 9 for full details about kitchen equipment).

>> **For Chinese/Thai food:**

- Bamboo steamer

- Rice cooker

- Wok

>> **For Greek/Middle Eastern food:**

- Gyro machine

- Juice machine

>> **For Hispanic food:**

- Cheese melter

- Chip warmer

- Salamander broiler

>> **For Indian food:**

- Rice cooker

- Tandoori oven

>> **For Italian food:**

- Meat slicer

- Pasta rollers

- Pasta cookers

- Pizza oven
- Pizza prep table
- Sandwich grill/press

REMEMBER

You can find most of the preceding list of equipment online or at a local kitchen equipment supplier. If the equipment will be located on your truck, you'll have to come up with the means to mount it to the truck for safety. In addition, if you're retrofitting a truck that already has a generator installed in it, be sure it'll be able to supply ample power for your additional equipment.

Validating Your Menu with Taste Tests Before You Go Prime Time

So you've put together the menu of your dreams. Great — now what? Taste-test all your menu items before making a final decision to serve them from your truck. Modify or discard any food that doesn't meet your quality standards. This testing is an important technique to control the quality of the food you may ultimately serve to the public.

TIP

Hosting a taste-testing party or running a short term pop-up restaurant are ways you can get feedback from friends, family, staff, and even local foodies. Offer samples of menu items to the party participants and record their responses and body language when sampling. Getting these reactions can be an invaluable source of feedback before you open your food truck, before you try a new recipe of an existing menu item, or before you start offering a new menu item.

When preparing to taste-test a menu item, review the recipe, noting ingredients and preparation procedures. Set up criteria for these tests based on the following:

>> Appearance

>> Taste

>> Temperature

>> Texture

Now answer the following questions about each item:

>> How does the item look?

>> How does the item taste?

>> Is the item at the proper temperature?

>> Is the texture of the item correct (moist, firm, crunchy, and so on)?

>> Is the item acceptable to serve?

If you determine that a menu item isn't acceptable to serve, decide whether you can modify it to meet quality standards or whether you should simply discard it. Determine how you can change the recipe or preparation procedures to result in a product that makes the cut.

REMEMBER

Practice the following food safety and sanitation measures when conducting taste tests:

>> Take a small sample from the pan with the serving spoon.

>> Place the sample on a separate plate.

>> Return the serving spoon to the pan. (Don't use the utensil you serve with as a tasting utensil.)

>> Don't taste the food sample over the pan.

TRAINING EMPLOYEES ON TASTE

You can organize taste-testing meetings as part of your staff training so your employees can accurately describe menu items to inquisitive customers. You can take this training procedure a step further by administering blind taste tests to your employees. Seat them at a table and blindfold them, and then serve small samples of various menu items, one at a time. Have them smell, taste, and try to guess what each sample is. Doing these taste testings helps the staff recognize food items by taste and smell and distinguish differences in items with similarities.

These taste tests also allow you to watch and learn while your employees partake in what they serve your customers. If the team says, "This is terrible," that item may have little chance of success. If they say, "This is fantastic," their enthusiasm can become the foundation for a great promotion by the staff. If they fall in love with a particular item, they'll become ambassadors for the product, and their recommendation to customers becomes a personal testimonial rather than a script.

Pricing Principles: Figuring Out How Much to Charge

After you've finished drawing up your food truck menu, you may find yourself wondering, "Well, what now?" Pricing your menu can be an intimidating task if you've never done it before. How much will you have to charge to make a profit? What prices will customers think are too high? What happens if you price yourself out of the local food truck market?

A variety of aspects affect a food truck's menu pricing. Be sure to understand the following factors and how they affect your truck before you begin pricing:

>> **Direct costs:** These costs are associated with the food itself. They involve the cost of the food, how you portion the servings, and how much food is spilled, overcooked, thrown away, or otherwise wasted during the preparation process. (See Chapter 10 for more about calculating food costs.)

>> **Indirect costs:** Indirect costs don't include the actual ingredients that make up a dish but instead cover the aspects of your food truck that add perceived value or quality. These aspects provide significant basis for charging higher prices. The labor to prepare a menu item is an indirect cost. Menu items that require time, effort, artistry, or talent to prepare merit a higher menu price than something that requires simply heating and plating.

>> **Changing food costs:** Many raw commodity food items, or basic ingredients with minimal quality variance, may fluctuate as often as daily. For example, flooding in California could wipe out a lettuce crop, causing the supply to drop and demand to increase. You may want to set your menu prices slightly higher for items that tend to swing in price, especially for when food costs increase unexpectedly. This way, you'll avoid losing money even when paying slightly more for those products.

>> **Competition:** Always keep an eye on your competition. You or a staff member may consider even checking out a rival food truck to see what you can improve about your own operation.

Although you can't control every cost factor, you can take some simple steps to help keep your menu in the appropriate price range. Knowing how to calculate menu prices is important, so get out your calculator, brush up on your algebra, and price that menu with the help of the following sections.

Determining your food truck menu's price points

Your prices are specific, but your *price point* is the range of prices your menu items fall into. Food trucks are a category of food service operators where a meal falls into roughly the same range of prices. *Price point* is actually a marketing term, because we all have expectations of what price we're willing to pay for various qualities of products or dining experiences.

Most customers may be willing to pay a dollar for a double cheeseburger at a fast-food joint, but when they get in line at a food truck, they may pay $10 for a specialty double cheeseburger. The *price point* describes the point where cost and quality scales intersect for customers. Some people may recognize the value of your $10 burger but can't afford it, and some would never pay $10 for a cheeseburger, regardless of whether they can afford it. It's a way of determining how to set the price of an item, and more importantly, how to develop products for price/quality points where a product doesn't exit or where you have more customer demand. You may want to develop a $7 cheeseburger that's still a premium product but is more affordable to the person who can't afford the $10 burger and doesn't seem outrageous to the person who won't buy the $10 burger.

REMEMBER

Customers will pay more for quality food, but exactly how much more is something only they can answer.

What does your local market consider a fair price for the food you're preparing and serving from your food truck? You can't just throw prices onto your menu without considering what your community is already paying for similar products from competing food trucks. You must consider what other food truck businesses are charging for the same type of food you're offering. If you're going to charge more than your competitor for the same dish, you have to be able to justify your price with added value.

TIP

Added value can mean larger portions or more exotic ingredients. Whatever your prices, they must offer value to your customers. If your customers don't think your food is worth what you're charging, you won't have enough business to make money, no matter what your pricing method is. Consumer research points to a number of elements that can add value to a particular menu item or to your entire menu. These elements include

>> Premium ingredients

>> Appropriate portion sizes or a variety of sizes

>> Perceived freshness

>> Included extras at no charge

>> Uniqueness

>> Select use of *natural* and *organic* labels

Checking out menu pricing methods

Setting prices for the products you sell from your food truck is one of the most crucial components to running it, because the prices you set directly affect your ability to sell, cover costs, and generate your desired level of profit. Restaurant food cooked on the premises is normally priced on a per item basis. Typically, prices of menu items vary according to food costs (the actual amount it costs you to make dishes) and sometimes according to demand. For example, if your truck is famous for serving a unique dish, you may be able to use a higher markup to your costs of preparing it.

REMEMBER

Most food service establishments target food-cost percentages between 20 and 40 percent. In other words, if a menu item's total food costs are $2, its sale price should be between $5 (40 percent) and $10 (20 percent). You can adjust the actual percentage you use as you deem necessary. For items that require more time and labor to prepare, you may have to increase the percentage to keep your pricing competitive.

New restaurant and food truck owners alike typically use one of the following methods to determine menu pricing (I discuss each method in detail in the following sections):

>> Food-cost percentage pricing

>> Factor pricing

REMEMBER

These methods are merely guidelines for your use and aren't absolute rules. If your market will bear menu item pricing that exceeds what you come up with by using these methods, *do it!*

Food-cost percentage pricing

The *food-cost percentage pricing* method is the most widely used method for menu pricing. To determine prices with this method, you need to know the target food-cost percentage and the actual food cost for the item, which you plug into this formula:

Food cost ÷ target food-cost percentage = menu price

For example, suppose you have a cheeseburger on your menu with a food cost of $1.50 (meaning that the ingredients used to make one cheeseburger costs you $1.50), and your target food-cost percentage is 35 percent. The calculation to price this item is as follows:

$$\$1.50 \div 0.35 = \$4.30$$

TECHNICAL STUFF

To get an idea of how various cost percentage affects your prices, take a look at these numbers:

Percentage	Food Cost	Menu Price (min)
20	$1.50	$7.50
25	$1.50	$6.00
30	$1.50	$5.00
35	$1.50	$4.30
40	$1.50	$3.75

REMEMBER

Food cost is only one part of the equation here. This formula doesn't take labor or other operational costs into consideration. So the lower you can get your food costs, the better off you'll be and the more you'll have left over for labor and overhead.(Check out Chapter 10 for the full scoop on managing food costs.)

Factor pricing

The *factor pricing* method uses a factor, such as 30 percent, that represents food-cost percentage. To determine prices with this method, you multiply the food cost by your pricing factor. To calculate the pricing factor and the menu price, you need the target food-cost percentage and the actual food cost for the item, which you plug into this formula:

100 ÷ target food-cost percentage = pricing factor

Food cost × pricing factor = menu price

For example, suppose your target food-cost percentage is 30 percent. Divide 30 into 100, and you get 3.33 as your pricing factor. If the food cost is $1.50 and the factor is 3.33, you end up with the following:

$$\$1.50 \times 3.33 = \$5.00$$

WARNING

This method doesn't take into consideration that some foods have a higher cost than others. Factoring has the potential to overprice high-cost food items and underprice low-cost items.

Applying psychology to your pricing

Pricing psychology is one of the most fascinating areas of menu development. Psychologically speaking, a huge difference exists between $9.99 and $10. Pricing theory says that menu items ending in an odd number (fractional pricing) convey a greater bang for your buck than when rounded up to the next whole dollar. Customers believe that when people price their product fractionally, they've priced it as low as possible, hence the odd number. Customers will completely ignore the last digits, which sets a lower pricing in their head. Research also shows that prices ending in 98 or 99 convey much more savings than all other prices, including 49, 50 or 75.

With that said, many food truck owners feel that adding change to a price creates more problems than the possible increase of sales is worth. Due to the fact that many food truck customers make their purchases with cash, food truck owners find it much easier to simply price menus with whole dollars to prevent the need to spend additional time making change for their customers. If you choose to use this method and find your food cost for an item is at a 50 cent mark or higher, round up to the next highest dollar; round down anything below the 50 cent mark.

Another example of pricing psychology is the elimination of the dollar sign next to prices on your menu board. By pricing a menu item at 6 rather than $6, you soften the price in such a way that it can cause your customers to disassociate the number they're viewing with the actual dollars in their wallet. A number without a $ is much less intimidating. (See the next section for more about designing your menu board.)

Designing Your Menu Board

After you've written a list of fantastic menu items and priced them properly, you need to create the perfect menu design. This task may sound easy enough, but an effective menu design is more than just scribbling your menu items on a menu board or printing a list of items on white paper. Colors, fonts, layout, descriptions, and engineering are all integral parts of creating an effective menu design in any format, as you find out in the following sections.

REMEMBER

Your menu's job is to sell those meals you want to sell. To be the most effective, your menu must communicate the proper messages and lead your guests to those high-profit items. Proper menu design and engineering will have a profound impact on your sales, profits, and customer satisfaction.

Honing your menu board's colors, fonts, layout, and descriptions

Your menu color scheme and font should reflect your truck's concept (see Chapter 2 for tips on developing a concept). For example, if you're opening a Mexican-themed truck, using vibrant colors, such as red, turquoise, purple, and green, may be good choices for your menu and menu board. These same colors would look out of place on the menu of a crêpe or cupcake truck, though; those types of trucks may benefit from softer, pastel colors.

The same can be said for the fonts you use on the menu. If you're hand-printing your menu on a dry-erase or chalk board, you have a little more flexibility with the font or style you use, but if you're planning to use any printed menu materials, be sure to keep fonts within your truck's theme. You can use fancy fonts, such as Script or Broadway, for section headers to match your concept, but I recommend using amore readable font, such as Arial or Times New Roman, for your menu item listings and their descriptions. You don't want to confuse or hinder someone from reading your menu because the font is difficult to read.

WARNING

Don't select a letter font that's too small or difficult to read. Your menu needs to be readable for customers without confusing them.

The layout of your menu is also an important consideration. Menus from most restaurants are typically arranged sequentially from sides to entrees then to desserts and beverages. If your menu board has enough room, you should copy this style; any printed menus (and even your website menu page; see Chapter 15) should definitely use this stylized format. Having these separate sections clearly identified with bold headings or borders helps customers easily navigate through your menu. And highlighting items with a star or other symbol draws customers to popular or special dishes.

TIP

Depending on the amount of space you have on your menu board, consider adding pictures of your food. (I cover photography in Chapter 15.) Be sure to avoid adding too many pictures or busy backgrounds, though, because they can make the menu hard to read.

Your menu descriptions should appear below each item's name and make a customer's mouth water. Don't be afraid to explain what's in a dish and to use ethnic names to add a bit of authenticity to the item description. Incorporating geography or local history into a menu item description is also a fun way to make your menu unique. As an example, a Maine lobster roll sounds appealing even if you're ordering it from somewhere other than the East Coast.

Although customer culinary intelligence has improved over the years with the popularity of television programs that cater to foodies, don't assume that everyone who walks up to your service window is familiar with all the culinary jargon that you and your staff use. Using technical terms can confuse and even annoy some customers. Recently popular terms such as *al dente* or *mole*, however, add a touch of spice to your menu without overdoing it.

Beware the following when it comes to menu descriptions:

>> **Avoid making descriptions too long.** A sentence or two is fine, because you want to intrigue customers. If they have more questions about the menu item, your staff can give further information about a dish or recommend what other customer favorites are. (Besides, long descriptions clutter any design!)

>> **Be sure you and your staff can educate customers if they ask what particular terms mean.** Advise your staff not to appear condescending when answering a food jargon question, no matter how simple it may seem to them. This type of attitude can be off-putting and keep a customer from returning or spreading the good word about your truck.

Considering additional menu presentations

Although most food trucks rely on a main menu board to advertise their fare, you may want to consider other avenues, such as print materials. Supplementing your food truck's menu in additional take-away menu formats can help customers who may be interested in visiting again or even hiring you to cater a future event.

>> Printing one-page menus allows your followers to remind themselves of your menu the next time they plan to hunt down a food truck for a quick and delicious meal. These menus should mimic the colors, fonts, layout, and descriptions of your menu board (as I discuss in the preceding section) to tie into the overall concept of your truck. Be sure you update this menu as often as you update your main menu board. Nothing turns a customer away faster than finding out the menu that got them back to your service window doesn't match the menu you're selling that day.

>> If your business model includes catering (see Chapter 18), be sure you have printed materials to provide customers who want you to cater their next birthday, party, or even wedding. Include your prices and menu options but maintain the format you develop for your main menus.

ENGINEERING YOUR MENU

Engineering isn't a term frequently used in the context of the food industry. Simply put, *engineering* is about applying technical, scientific, or mathematical knowledge to get a desired outcome. *Menu* engineering is about taking a more structured approach to building a menu.

The two key measurements required for menu engineering are the contribution and popularity of each menu item:

- *Contribution* is the amount of money you make from a menu item. You calculate contribution by subtracting the entire recipe cost from the sale price.

- *Popularity* is the number of a menu item sold during a given period as compared to other items. The sales numbers can be based on actual results from a point of sale system or estimated or forecast sales.

You can use contribution and popularity to classify menu items into the following groups:

- Stars — High contribution and high popularity

- Plow Horse — Low contribution and high popularity

- Puzzles — High contribution and low popularity

- Dogs — Low contribution and low popularity

These classifications provide a structured approach for planning your menu layout. You can use menu engineering to help steer your customers toward the items classified as *stars* and *puzzles,* which are those that make you the most profit.

Most people don't read a menu from page to page like they read a book. Instead, they quickly scan menus, almost randomly, to find information and items that appeal to their tastes. The beauty in a food truck menu board is that you have a limited number of menu items and you usually list them in a vertical stack. If you want to sell more *stars* or *puzzles,* you need to place those items where the eye naturally looks first. Customers typically purchase the first two items and the last item listed in each category. By placing your most profitable items in these positions, you can usually count on selling more of them. You can also highlight a particular item or set of items on your menu by placing boxes around them.

Hiring a Consultant (If You Need One) to Help with Your Menu

Every food truck owner has his own challenges; this aspect is just part of life in the business world. If you don't have a strong culinary background and need assistance in putting your menu together, hiring a local chef or a consultant with the expertise, answers, and solutions you need may be a great option.

WARNING

You need to do some soul searching before you hire a consultant. Are you willing to listen to what she has to say? Are you willing to change your menu or menu items? If not, hiring an outsider will be a waste of your time and money.

TIP

If you perform an Internet search on "food truck consultant" or "restaurant consultant," you'll see no shortage of firms and individuals who proclaim to be professional thought leaders in the food industry. However, in discussions with food truck owners who've had successful consulting experiences, most tell me that they found their best consultant candidates by getting referrals from other food truck vendors.

When you find consulting candidates you're interested in hiring, make sure you take the time to interview each one.

>> Speak with candidates in depth on the services they provide and how they can assist you.

>> Get their personal background as well as the background of any additional staff members they may employ to work on your account.

>> If you already have a concept in mind, ask them to prepare a dish that they feel would be able to work into a future menu; if you don't have a planned concept yet, ask them to prepare something they feel would work well as a menu item from a food truck.

Taste the item they make and have them discuss the ingredients, the preparation requirements, and how much they would charge for that particular item. If they can't give you a competent response to any of these questions, they likely won't be able to provide you with the full service consulting you need.

>> Finally, ask them for a list of references you can contact to find out how they performed as a consultant. An important question to ask a candidate's references is whether they'd hire the consultant again. If they hesitate or don't give a heartfelt response, it may be time to move onto the next candidate.

After you've hired a consultant to assist you in developing your menu, have her help create the menu and recipes before you hire your staff. The project should include tasting and modifying recipes and creating a recipe book with pictures, product specification, and detailed preparation steps. If you want to get even more detailed, you can have the consultant create a training video that shows the preparation of each item. Doing so is a great way to document all the recipes and cooking steps so all you have to do is hire a chef to execute these items. This step eliminates being at the mercy of an employee who keeps all the recipes in his head.

REMEMBER

You have the overall responsibility for the success of your business, so stay on top of every aspect of developing your menu. Using a consultant requires *your* money and *your* time, so make sure the consultant understands that you don't want any surprises in regard to her designs and fees. Menu consultants have different ways of billing for their services, so ask for a fixed fee for the scope of services to be performed. Ultimately, you'll have to determine whether the total cost is reasonable in proportion to the benefits you'll receive.

Deciding When to Change Your Menu

One of the toughest things for an established food truck owner to do is to change his menu. A common fear is that removing the wrong item off the menu will result in the truck's business slowly vanishing or that raising prices will chase off current customers.

In most cases, these fears never become reality. After a menu change, owners are often relieved that they made the change and are thankful for the smiles of customers. Although most price changes go unnoticed, the longer you wait to change your prices, the higher you'll have to increase the price and the more likely they'll be noticed.

TIP

Instead of waiting a year and raising a price by $1, you should raise prices incrementally every three or four months. Frequent changes result in higher cash flow throughout the year. I also suggest making changes to your menu items at least three or four times a year. Doing so gives you the opportunity to keep the menu new and exciting and allows you to make the smaller price increases.

Chapter 9

Finding a Commercial Kitchen for Your Food Truck

One of the first things you need to do when planning for your future food truck business is to find a commercial kitchen for your truck to call home. In Chapter 6, I point out that local zoning ordinances in the majority of cities and towns throughout the United States limit the places that food trucks can operate and park. Most municipalities require mobile food units to be parked at a state-licensed commercial kitchen. But your commercial kitchen is much more than a place to park your truck — you'll also dump your gray water, receive food deliveries, prepare your products, and store your food there when it's not on the truck being sold.

In cities where cooking isn't allowed onboard the truck, the cooking and packaging of the food you sell must also take place in a commercial kitchen. Due to the size limitations of your truck's kitchen, you'll want to prep all your food in your commercial kitchen anyway, unless you tow around a full-sized catering trailer. Most food truck kitchens are able to store enough food for only one work shift at a time. The tools you need to prepare your food alone are likely to take up far too much room to be stored on your truck. So there's just no way around finding a commercial kitchen for your food truck.

In this chapter, I describe the issues to take into account when choosing the proper commercial kitchen for your mobile food business. I also provide some outside-the-box kitchen options for you to consider.

Getting to Know Commercial Kitchens

Finding a commercial kitchen that works for you is an integral part of bringing your gourmet mobile food business to life. The location, cost, type, and size of your commercial kitchen determine many aspects of your business, including the types of dishes you can make, the capacity of events you can handle, and where your service and events can be located. When looking for a commercial kitchen, you can direct your search by the type of food you want to make and the scale of your food truck operation.

TIP

To maximize the usefulness of a kitchen, you must first consider your equipment requirements. You can't know what equipment you'll need until you develop your menu items, so if you haven't already done so, head over to Chapter 8 where you find out how to create your menu. You can then use your menu as a guide for making a list of the equipment your kitchen must have.

In the following sections, I describe different commercial kitchen choices, explain how to find kitchens in your area, and outline some guidelines for you to use as you evaluate kitchens.

Exploring commercial kitchen options

For most new food truck owners, a *shared-use commercial kitchen* is the most viable option. A shared-use kitchen (also referred to as a *kitchen incubator* or a *cooperative kitchen*) provides a fully equipped, commercially licensed facility that's available for rent by the hour and leased out to multiple food trucks or chefs.

Because you share this kind of space with other businesses and the rent you pay is usually based on a time-per-use basis, you're able to save money instead of racking up overhead costs by building or owning a commercial kitchen of your own. The problem that some food truck owners run into is finding that they need to use the facility at the same time other local food trucks are attempting to use the kitchen. This scenario can cause backups if more than one business needs to use the same equipment.

Although a shared-use kitchen is a great resource for food truck owners, a number of other options — such as restaurants, schools, social clubs, and churches — can be used as your commercial kitchen. I cover these options later in this chapter.

Finding commercial kitchens

After you have an idea about the kind of kitchen you want, you can start shopping around to find the best pricing and amenities for your commercial kitchen. Start your search by using your local white pages or speaking with other food truck owners to find out which commercial kitchen they use. They may — or may not — suggest using their current kitchen, but talking with active operators is a good way to assess the going rates in your area. Your local health department can also provide you with a list of registered commercial kitchens in your area. Some municipalities even provide these lists on their websites.

TIP

Due to the growth of the mobile food industry, you may find a lack of commercial kitchens in your area that suit your needs. If this is the case for you, the following websites may help you locate a kitchen that may be a bit farther away but still feasible. These websites can locate commercial kitchens throughout the country, and they provide maps along with links and contact information for each kitchen in their registries.

>> Commercial Kitchen for Rent: www.commercialkitchenforrent.com

>> Culinary Incubator: www.culinaryincubator.com

Evaluating commercial kitchens

Before you sign a contract with a commercial kitchen, spend time in the prospective facility with a culinary consultant or your staff. Having multiple sets of hands and eyes on the equipment and layout is helpful in determining the pros and cons of each kitchen you investigate. Foremost, make sure the kitchen has the equipment you need and plenty of space for your staff to work. The following sections give you the information you need to evaluate any commercial kitchen's equipment and layout.

REMEMBER

No matter what kind of kitchen you find in your area, make sure it's been approved or certified by your local health and building departments. In almost all municipalities in the country, if your kitchen doesn't have proper certification, your truck can't be approved for permits. To verify that a kitchen has been certified, ask to see its license. Kitchens are required to place their license in open view.

Taking inventory

Although the equipment in commercial kitchens may vary somewhat, most kitchens are equipped with the following standard items:

>> **For prep work:**

- Can openers
- Cutting boards
- Dough rollers
- Food blenders
- Food processors
- Knife sharpeners, steels, stones, and gloves
- Mandolins
- Meat grinders
- Meat saws
- Mixers (countertop and handheld)
- Scales
- Slicers and vegetable cutters
- Thermometers
- Timers

>> **For cooking:**

- Broilers, salamanders, and cheese melters
- Charbroilers
- Commercial ovens
- Crêpe makers
- Flash-bake ovens
- Griddle-tops, hot plates, and sandwich grills
- Infrared cooktops
- Microwaves
- Panini grills
- Pasta cookers
- Pizza and deck ovens

- Ranges
- Rice cookers
- Rotisseries
- Steamers
- Toasters

» **For frying:**

- Fry baskets
- Fryer station
- Oil filtration and shortening disposal units

» **For holding/warming:**

- Countertop food warmer
- Hold oven
- Holding cabinet

» **For refrigeration:**

- Ice machines
- Walk-in refrigerator and freezer

Be sure to verify that the following supplies, which may or may not be provided, are available if you know you'll need them:

» Frypans and saucepans

» Knives

» Ladles, whisks, tongs, spatulas, and utensils

» Oven mitts and handle holders

» Pastry bags

» Pie, cake, and baking pans

» Pots

TIP

If you find a commercial kitchen that suits almost all your needs but is missing a single piece of equipment you need to prepare your food, speak with the owners of the facility. Most kitchens allow you to bring in additional pieces of equipment if needed. Just make sure the kitchen provides adequate and secure storage for any equipment you supply so you can leave it there. You don't want to lug large or otherwise cumbersome items in and out of the kitchen every day.

Checking out the kitchen layout

When conducting a search for a commercial kitchen, keep in mind that a well-designed kitchen will increase your profits by reducing the amount of kitchen labor required to prepare your food. If your staff knows where everything is located and doesn't have to run back and forth between stations, prep and cooking times in the kitchen will be more efficient.

Commercial kitchens lay out their equipment in many different ways. There's no set rule on the configuration style that will work best for your business, but knowing about the following two basic methods of equipment grouping can help you make an educated decision:

>> **Assembly-line:** The assembly-line design is ideal for a food business that produces large quantities of the same type of food, such as tamales, pizzas, or sandwiches. In an assembly-line configuration, the kitchen is laid out according to the order of use, and the pieces of equipment are generally set up in a line. Figure 9-1 shows an example of an assembly-line kitchen design.

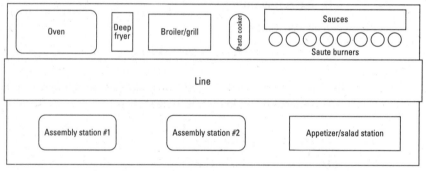

FIGURE 9-1:
A sample
assembly-line
kitchen layout.

© John Wiley & Sons, Inc.

>> **Zone-style:** In a zone-style layout, the kitchen is divided into different blocks. Generally, you have a block for food preparation, a block for cooking, a block for refrigeration, and a block for sanitation and cleaning. The zone-style configuration works well for food trucks that have many types of food on the menu. This layout allows you to prepare in one area while already-prepared food is cooked in another area. (See Figure 9-2 for an example of a zone-style kitchen design.)

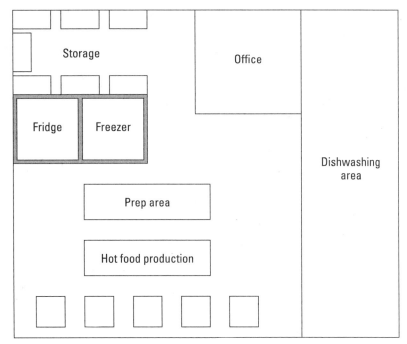

FIGURE 9-2:
A sample zone-style kitchen layout.

Both assembly-line and zone-style kitchen configurations can be (and, if possible, should be) ergonomic. An ergonomic configuration represents the ideal kitchen in many ways. Ergonomic spaces tend to be well thought out and designed for maximum labor efficiency. This layout means your kitchen staff spends more time producing your products and less time walking back and forth to prepare the food and clean. Ergonomics operates on the theory that the fewer steps and moves your employees need to make to complete a task, the better. Ergonomics can also help reduce injuries and fatigue.

TIP

Don't worry if you can't find your dream kitchen; finding the perfect kitchen layout can be difficult. You may have to go with a suitable kitchen that can fit you in during the hours you need.

Determining the size of commercial kitchen you need

Commercial kitchens' sizes range greatly, and the needs of each food truck owner differ just as much. The average commercial kitchen is roughly 2,000 square feet. The general rule in kitchen design is that for every person you serve, you need 15 square feet of kitchen space, but I've seen kitchens much smaller serve many more.

When you're investigating commercial kitchens for your use, instead of going into a kitchen with a specific size in mind, look at a kitchen to see whether it will meet your specific needs. A commercial kitchen should do the following:

- >> Provide storage space for raw materials
- >> Provide space for food being prepared
- >> Provide adequate storage for your equipment, cookware, and cutlery
- >> Provide enough space for safe movement of staff
- >> Provide an area for checking in stock

Figuring proximity to your territory

Just as important as the locations you choose to operate your truck from, the location of your commercial kitchen plays a similarly significant role. You don't want to spend a lot of time driving back and forth between your stops and your commercial kitchen between shifts. If at all possible, try to keep your kitchen within 15 to 20 minutes from the majority of your stops. The more time you spend on the road traveling, the less time you'll be able to spend selling your products or doing tasks in your kitchen or office.

CONSIDERING "GREEN" KITCHENS

Most commercial kitchens use excessive amounts of water and energy, and many followers of the food truck industry are becoming increasingly aware of a kitchen's impact on the environment. Since its inception, the mobile food industry has been an active participant in the movement to improve environmental sustainability. Therefore, finding earth-friendly commercial kitchens can be a responsible and smart business strategy as a food truck owner.

The amount of energy and water used, along with the waste produced in the creation of food, makes the food service industry one of the least sustainable. A food truck's commercial kitchen pollutes the air, water, and soil simply by being used. Finding a kitchen that's gone green helps you reduce your impact on the environment.

Although you may not receive the direct cost savings involved in a green commercial kitchen, you may receive the indirect benefits. By finding a commercial kitchen that has a green rating, your rents may be smaller than those being offered by other kitchens. If you do find a commercial kitchen that hasn't achieved a green rating, you may try to talk the owner into striving for a green rating by pointing out some of the benefits he would receive with the rating, including the following:

- **Lower energy bills:** An upgrade to energy-efficient equipment can almost halve energy usage, and local governments and utility companies around the country offer substantial rebates for consumers purchasing Energy Star–qualified equipment.

- **Lower water bills:** Taking steps to conserve water can save the kitchen owner a large amount of money on utility bills.

- **Reduced air pollution:** Using green cleaning supplies and lowering energy consumption can greatly reduce the amount of harmful emissions indirectly caused at your commercial kitchen.

- **Reduced landfill usage:** The consistent creation of waste produced at commercial kitchens not only takes up space in landfills but also contaminates air, water, and soil.

- **Less water usage:** Fresh water supply is being rapidly depleted, causing some states to declare water shortages. Using a kitchen with water-saving equipment and policies can greatly reduce your water usage.

If you're looking for a green commercial kitchen, ask the kitchen owner to provide you with proof of its green certification. There are organizations that provide guidelines and certifications to each kitchen. The following provide the standards for those looking to make the necessary changes to go green:

- Energy Star: www.energystar.gov

- Green Restaurant Association: www.dinegreen.com

- Green Seal: www.greenseal.org

- U.S. Green Building Council (USGBC) and its LEED Green Building Rating System: www.usgbc.org/LEED

Exploring Other Kitchen Options

Depending on your area, you may find that either all the shared-use commercial kitchens are full (or not taking on any additional renters) or that the available selections don't meet your requirements. Don't fret; a number of other valid solutions exist, which I explore in the following sections.

Commercial kitchens are designated by the state and local health departments and can take form in a number of different venues, from a local restaurant to the church around the corner, from the VFW Hall to your local high school. Because these organizations provide food to the general public, their kitchens must go through the same permitting and inspection processes as the shared-use kitchens do.

Renting from a restaurant

Renting a restaurant kitchen during a time when the restaurant is closed is a solid option for a food truck owner. This arrangement is likely to cost less than using a traditional commercial kitchen because the restaurant owner isn't relying on your usage fees (kitchen rental isn't his core business). The space would otherwise go unused during the restaurant's off-business hours, so the money it collects from you for using the kitchen is gravy. Furthermore, you know exactly when you can (and can't) use a specific restaurant's kitchen, and this knowledge helps you avoid the scheduling issues that can occur with a shared-use kitchen.

Knowing what a restaurant pays in rent each month can be helpful in your negotiations. For example, if a restaurant pays $3,000 per month in rent and you offer to rent the kitchen in off-hours for half of that, the owner will likely take you up on your offer.

Checking out churches and synagogues

Many churches and synagogues have underutilized kitchens that they're often willing to rent out to local entrepreneurs. If you plan on serving kosher menu items, visit the synagogues in your area as well as the Jewish community center and other local Jewish organizations to see whether a kitchen is available for your use.

If you're a member of a church, speak with your priest, minister, bishop, preacher, or rabbi and volunteer to assume responsibility of overseeing the utilities, pest control, and/or other various kitchen inspections. Providing this type of service to your church can be rewarding, and it allows you to barter your personal time for the use of this licensed kitchen.

Some churches can't receive rent per se for the use of their facilities, so you have to find another way to donate to the church. One idea is to volunteer to cater church events. The resources of a professional chef and gourmet food for church events may be a match made in heaven for both you and the church.

You don't need to be a member of a specific church or religious group to find out whether it's willing to allow you to use its kitchen.

Considering social clubs

The local Moose Lodge, VFW, Elks Lodge, or a similar organization may have a health-inspected and certified commercial kitchen that you can rent for your food truck business. As with churches (see the preceding section), you may be able to use these kitchens rent-free if you agree to cater events for the organization as a means of payment or donation.

Scoping out schools

My final suggestion for locating a licensed commercial kitchen is to reach out to educational facilities. The lunch lady isn't allowed to serve students out of her home kitchen, so schools are required to prepare their meals in their own commercial kitchen, meaning it likely has the licensing you need for your food truck business.

Depending on the size of the student population, a school's kitchen may be the perfect place for you to prepare your mobile cuisine. Call local culinary schools, high schools, and universities to find out whether they have a licensed commercial kitchen. Speak with the kitchen manager and ask about times when the kitchen may be empty and available for your use.

TIP

If you grew up in the area, first check with the schools you attended. Being able to play the "I'm an alumnus" card is a great way to start the conversation.

Chapter 10

Purchasing and Managing Supplies

t's no secret that when it comes to business, especially the mobile food industry, you have to spend money to make money. After all, you have to pay your employees, buy your food, and ensure that your truck provides the proper atmosphere you're trying to present with your concept (among other things). But just because you have to spend some money doesn't mean that you have to break the bank to have the food truck you want. As a food truck owner, you can save money in a lot of ways and not compromise your menu, but the biggest way you can save money is in the way you purchase and manage your food.

In order to produce your menu items for your customers, you have to purchase high-quality raw materials — your truck's food, beverages, paper goods, equipment, and so on. To get all the materials you need, you typically have to purchase food and supplies from one or more suppliers every week. Paying the lowest price for the highest-quality products ultimately makes you more money.

In this chapter, I cover how to make a list of the supplies you need and choose suppliers, as well as how to maintain an efficient inventory system of the food you don't immediately use so you can minimize your bottom line and maximize your profits.

REMEMBER

Because you'll purchase equipment for your business infrequently after you start up, most of this chapter focuses on food and beverages (see Chapter 9 for info on purchasing kitchen equipment). However, you can use the principles in this chapter to purchase anything for your food truck.

Assembling Your Supply List

REMEMBER

Before you can begin purchasing your food and beverage supplies, you have to put together a list of the items you need. Just as you'd set up a grocery list for your personal use at home, generating a supply list for your food truck should be based on the needs of your menu. Look at your menu (see Chapter 8 for help with creating one), and put together a comprehensive list of all the ingredients you need to prepare these items for your customers. Follow these guidelines for setting up your own list:

>> Add all the ingredients necessary to make your menu items, and be as specific as you can. If you need shredded Cheddar Jack cheese for your tacos, for example, be sure to specify that rather than listing just "cheese."

>> Group all like items into categories. Most of the suppliers you deal with group their products with common classifications, like baked goods, dairy products, and meat/poultry. Following this tip makes it easier to purchase like items from the same suppliers, which helps you save money on your food purchases.

>> You may not be able to complete the list yourself before you find suppliers, but your list needs to be as complete as you can make it (item name, category, and *projected weekly volume* — in other words, how much of a given item you expect to use in a week) before you can begin the process of finding suppliers. When you start speaking with suppliers, they'll help you determine what type of unit sizes you can get for each specific item (such as cases, tubs of particular weights, and the like).

>> When you're drawing up your supply list, consider all the factors involved in preparing your menu items. You may choose not to spend a lot of time prepping all the food on your menu. If so, you may be willing to spend some extra money purchasing pre-made items, such as sauce bases, pre-cut meats, or prepackaged baked goods. If your concept requires that your food be "from scratch," then by all means, include all the items you need to create it.

Table 10-1 is one example of how to organize supplies (this list is partial).

TIP

You can get a quick estimate for your projected weekly volume of each of these items by breaking down each menu item into ingredients and amounts needed for each serving. Multiply these totals with your projected weekly sales count for each menu item (which I discuss in Chapter 8) to get your projected weekly volume.

TABLE 10-1 **A Partial Sample List of Supplies**

Item	Category	Projected Weekly Volume
Bread, French roll, 1.5 oz.	Baked goods	360
Bread, sticks, 2 oz.	Baked goods	750
Bread, 3-ft. loaf, Italian	Baked goods	100
Pizza dough balls, 20 oz.	Baked goods	240
Butter, unsweetened, 1 lb.	Dairy	3
Butter, whipped, 5-lb. tub	Dairy	3
Cheese, Cheddar Jack, shredded	Dairy	6
Cheese, mozzarella, fresh	Dairy	5
Cheese, Parmesan, shredded	Dairy	6
Cheese, provolone, longhorn	Dairy	6

Working with the Best Suppliers for Your Food Truck

After you've determined what supplies you need, the next step is finding someone who will be able to provide them for you at the times you need them. In the planning stages of opening your food truck, locating suppliers whom you can build a strong, long-term relationship with is important. They're going to be your source for the food you serve, so you want to be able to trust that your deliveries will be made on time and with the quality you expect. Therefore, you must take the proper steps to find someone you can count on.

In the following sections, I explain how to find, interview, and choose suppliers; I also note how to negotiate terms and establish beneficial long-term relationships with them.

Finding potential suppliers

The ultimate goal in selecting a food supplier is to find one who will offer you high-quality food with good pricing. You'll have the opportunity to work with numerous food suppliers, and in some cases, you may choose to have multiple suppliers for your products, such as meat and produce; however, you may be able to find a supplier who can provide you with the bulk of your food supplies from under one roof.

Large national suppliers, such as Sysco (`www.sysco.com`) or US Foods (`www.usfoods.com`), can provide highly discounted rates for their products because of the high volume of food they distribute. You may find that their minimum orders are too high for a single food truck, but if you're friends with other food trucks in your area, you can group together to place orders large enough to meet their minimums.

TIP

Although you likely won't be able to purchase all your products from a single supplier, keeping track of a lot of invoices wastes time and energy. Try to meet your needs with the fewest possible suppliers.

To prevent spending a lot of time trying to locate specific suppliers, you can use a number of quick and easy ways, such as the ones I discuss in the following list, to locate the exact suppliers you need for opening and maintaining a successful mobile food business.

>> **Speak with fellow food truck and restaurant owners in your area.** These professionals have been in the business long enough to have found the most proficient suppliers in your area and can make recommendations that are based on the experiences they've had and learned from.

>> **Search online for local food and restaurant suppliers.** Almost every type of product you require can be found on the Internet. You can take advantage of online business directories that list suppliers and even search for suppliers based on the type of supplies you're looking for. If you want to search specifically for a supplier in your area, many of these sites have an option for you to enter your zip code. Another benefit for using online business directories is that they often provide information about suppliers who offer very competitive prices on their products.

TIP

Check out the following sites to help find the suppliers (and supplies) you need:

- Food Business Review: `www.food-business-review.com/suppliers`

- Foodservice.com: `www.foodservice.com/foodshow/restaurant-distributors.cfm`

>> **Attend restaurant industry trade shows.** At these trade shows, you can obtain information about various restaurant suppliers' products and services. You have access to supplier literature and may even be able to talk to restaurant supplier representatives. You can find a list of these trade shows at your local chamber of commerce or from the National Restaurant Association (`www.restaurant.org`), which sponsors many of these shows across the country.

No matter which avenue you use to find a supplier, you must take the time to speak with the ones you're interested in using. After you've created your supply list, write the name of at least two suppliers next to each item to create a comprehensive list of suppliers you'll interview (see the next section).

Interviewing and choosing potential suppliers

When it's time to meet your supplier candidates, be sure to meet them at their facility or warehouse (if they're local). Doing so allows you to see how they store and handle their merchandise before delivering it to their clients. You don't want a supplier with a shabby operation providing you with food that will be attached to your brand. Look for cleanliness and organization; a dirty or unorganized facility tells you that they don't take their business seriously, so why would that change in how they feel about yours?

Here are some questions to ask a supplier during an interview:

>> How long has your company been in business?

>> What are your payment terms and return policy?

>> Do you have online shopping available?

>> Do you have a minimum order; if so, what is it?

>> What is your delivery schedule for this area?

>> Do you place food items in coolers or walk-in freezers?

>> What discounts do you have (volume, early payment, cash, and so on)?

After you've interviewed each supplier candidate, you must select one for each of the items you need to purchase for your menu. (Note that one supplier may be able to supply multiple items from your list.) Take the following into consideration as you select your supplier(s):

>> How the candidate answered your questions

>> Whether he has competitive pricing

>> His ability to meet the standards you're looking for in your food and service

>> Whether he's received good referrals from food truck or restaurant owners in your area

Negotiating with your selected suppliers

When you find a supplier who appears to fit your needs, you have to negotiate terms to your business relationship with him. Be sure to settle all your business terms before locking into a food supplier. Some of these terms may include the following:

>> **Product prices:** Negotiating product prices is part of your discussion with any supplier. The first and most obvious way to get a better price is to ask for it, yet few people do. Also, never accept a supplier's first offer. If you do, you may find that extra charges begin to appear because the salesperson thinks you'll just accept them. Start low and trade every concession for something specific that you value: "I'll do this if you do that."

Another avenue to follow during your negotiations is to seek other benefits than just product prices. Before narrowing the discussion down to price, find out what else the supplier may be able to do for you, such as give you extended payment terms or offer you lower delivery charges if you agree to let him deliver when it suits him.

TIP

Although salespeople may not be able to give you additional discounts, their marketing department may be able to contribute in other ways, by providing your truck with a free branded refrigerator if you sell its brand of soda, for example. Suppliers often have a separate marketing budget and are eager to find good ways to spend it.

>> **Item quantity:** For the products you purchase, you want to be assured that the standards in item quantity are maintained. Provide the supplier a copy of your supply list (discussed earlier in this chapter) and have him help you determine the average unit amount you need to order each week to meet your projected weekly volume. For example, your supplier can help you figure out whether you need to order a 50-pound sack of flour every other week to meet your baking needs.

>> **Payment terms:** The industry standard is to pay suppliers within 30 days or less from the time you receive your supplies, but some suppliers may offer you more flexibility, so be sure you know these terms before you sign any type of agreement.

TIP

>> **Delivery schedule:** Most suppliers across the country work with other companies in addition to yours, so you may need to negotiate a delivery schedule that works for both parties. Don't schedule your weekly deliveries when your truck will be on the road. Most food truck owners choose either early morning or weekend deliveries.

Establishing good supplier relationships

Orders get placed, trucks deliver products, and invoices get paid. Unfortunately, this type of business strategy does nothing to establish a strong association with your suppliers. A good relationship is based on the promise of long-term collaboration. Supplier reps need long-term partnerships to succeed.

Cultivating a healthy relationship with your suppliers can be very helpful as your business grows and market trends fluctuate. Leveraging your supplier relationships can produce both immediate and long-term results for your business because your suppliers often have access to research on industry news and trends as well as consumer behaviors that you can tap into to better forecast your business trends. This research can be critical in terms of answering questions or resolving problems you run into with the products you receive. For example: If the fish you use for your bestselling menu item has increased to $10 per pound or the Wagyu beef always has veins down the middle, having a good rapport with your supplier can help you find out the real reason behind these issues and help you make revised ordering decisions to improve your food prices and quality.

TIP

The best way to build a rapport with your suppliers is to become one of their valued customers by doing the following:

>> **Paying on time:** You can negotiate for favorable payment terms before you place an order, but after you place your order, be sure to pay for it on time.

>> **Personalizing the relationship:** Visit your suppliers' offices and invite them to visit your truck while you're at a spot close to them.

>> **Sharing information:** Keep your suppliers aware of what's going on in your business. Tell them about changes in key personnel, new products you're considering, or special promotions you're planning.

Developing good relationships with suppliers isn't a complicated process. Be communicative, treat them fairly, be demanding (coupled with loyalty), and pay them on time. It's just that easy.

TIP

You have to be able to contact your supplier representative at all times during business operations, so be sure to have his office, cell, and home phone numbers at your fingertips. If a problem arises or you need to make changes quickly, you need to be able to reach your supplier rep promptly. Also, getting to know your primary food reps and their bosses can emphasize their obligation to assist in making things right. Working with your suppliers is the ability to work together for mutual benefit in a variety of circumstances.

Building an Efficient Inventory System

Your *inventory* is the food and other supplies that you've purchased and placed in storage. Whether the value of the food is $500 or $10,000, until you sell it to a customer, it isn't doing anything for your business, other than taking up space, tying up money, and in some cases, spoiling. Inventory is nothing more than a cost until it's sold. Also, the larger your inventory, the less money you have available for other aspects for your business.

Because most of your inventory is highly perishable, if you fail to use an item within its limited shelf life, off to the garbage it goes, along with some of your hard-earned profits. In an ideal world, you should maintain a level of inventory large enough to allow you to serve your customers without running out of an item. Not only that, but you should also run out of a particular item *only* at the same time as the next delivery truck pulls up to the back door of your commercial kitchen.

Being able to maintain a proper level of inventory is a key step in running a successful food truck business. Without an efficient inventory management system in place, keeping the proper amount of inventory on hand can result in potential losses showing up in a variety of forms. Spoilage, theft, over-portioning, waste, cooking errors, and unrecorded sales are just a few of the ways you can lose money. With food cost being such a large portion of your total business, wasting just a small portion of your total food cost can represent a lot of money lost.

In the following sections, I explain how to figure out the right inventory level, and I show you how to calculate and keep an eye on your food costs. I also describe how to prevent theft and reduce waste so your costs stay low.

Determining your proper inventory level

REMEMBER

An easy way to determine whether you're carrying an appropriate amount of inventory is to calculate your *number of days of inventory.* This number tells you how many days your existing inventory will last, based on how much food you're using in an average day, which translates to your average daily food cost. Calculating your number of days of inventory is a two-step process. (*Note:* To do the following calculations, check your financial statements for the number of days in the period, food cost for the period, and ending food inventory; also see Chapter 4.)

1. **Calculate your average daily food cost, using this equation: Average daily food cost = food cost ÷ number of days in period.**

   So if your food cost for the period (say, 30 days) is $15,000, you're average daily food cost is $15,000 ÷ 30 days = $500.

2. **Calculate your number of days of inventory with this formula: Number of days of inventory = ending food inventory ÷ average daily food cost.**

    For example, take the ending food inventory (on your balance sheet), say, $5,000, and divide by the average daily food cost you just calculated, so $5,000 ÷ $500 = 10 days' worth of food on hand, or days of inventory.

REMEMBER

This calculation tells you that at the end of a 30-day period, you had about ten days' worth of food on hand. For most food trucks, this amount is far too excessive an inventory. Most food truck owners optimize food inventory at three to five days of food on hand. Ideally, they have less than a week of produce and fresh products and more than a week in the freezer and dry storage areas; however, the average of all their food products on hand is about five to six days. So the entire inventory turns over every week or so.

In the preceding example, having ten days' worth of inventory probably indicates that you have too much food on the shelves. If operationally feasible, lowering inventory levels to three to five days of sales will cause your food costs to drop almost immediately.

Many variables come into play when planning for a food truck event. Some variables to consider when planning how much food to bring include event size, total number food vendors, pricing by other vendors, type of event, event fees, and weather.

TIP

Don't reduce your inventory levels to the point that you're constantly running out of products. Instead, reduce or eliminate the amount of "excess" inventory that you don't need and won't use.

Calculating and monitoring weekly food costs

To make sure you're keeping up on your food costs, you need to calculate them every week. Although many restaurants determine their costs only monthly, a problem arises with this strategy: If your monthly profit and loss (P&L) statement shows that your food costs have increased, it may be too late to correct the problem because you're probably four to six weeks beyond the point that the problem surfaced. By reviewing your costs weekly, you're able to find the problem and eliminate it as soon as possible.

An easy way to monitor your food costs every week doesn't need to take much time, either. Take a look at Figure 10-1, which is a simple form you can put together in a spreadsheet to record and keep track of daily purchases. To use this log, list each of your food invoices in the left-hand column and add their totals into the appropriate subsection on the right.

DAILY INVOICE LOG: FOOD & BEVERAGES								
Week Starting/Ending Dates		7/1	to	7/7				
					Food Purchases			
Supplier		**Date**	**Invoice Amount**	**Cheese**	**Meat**	**Produce**	**Grocery**	**Beverages**
Total Food Purchases								
Beginning Inventory								
Ending Inventory								
Actual Food Cost								

FIGURE 10-1:
Keep track of your daily food purchases with an invoice log.

© John Wiley & Sons, Inc.

At the end of the week, you simply total the food column to get your total food purchases for the week. You can then use a form similar to Figure 10-2 to list your daily sales figures, food purchases, and the beginning and ending inventory for the week. First, place your daily sales numbers in the top row of the worksheet; add them up and put the sum in the *Total* column on the right side. Then, take your total food purchases total from Figure 10-1 and place it in the *Purchases* column in the *Food* row in the *Cost of Sales* section. Add your inventory figures to the *Beginning Inventory* and *Ending Inventory* spaces. Add your beginning inventory to your purchases; subtract your ending inventory from this number. Now, divide this total by your weekly sales and you're left with a percentage that represents your cost of goods.

WEEKLY FOOD COST WORKSHEET												
Week Ending Date 7/7												
	Monday	**Tuesday**	**Wednesday**	**Thursday**	**Friday**	**Saturday**	**Sunday**	**Beginning Inventory**	**Ending Inventory**	**Total**	**%**
Sales											
Food	$0	$1,200	$1,200	$1,440	$1,750	$1,820	$0			$7,410	100%
Cost of Sales								**Purchases**			
Food								$2,103	$579	$459	$2,223	30%
Gross Margin										$5,187	70%

FIGURE 10-2:
Monitor your weekly food cost with a simple worksheet.

© John Wiley & Sons, Inc.

Prepare this report every Monday morning so you can see your food cost from the previous week. If something is out of line, such as a huge spike in your beef cost from the previous week, you'll know about it right away and will be able to act on it for the current week.

Preventing theft

Employee theft contributes about $52 billion a year in lost profits, and approximately 95 percent of all businesses experience employee theft. Finding the root causes behind the theft and improving prevention measures is a much more involved process. A good prevention program is never 100 percent effective; however, that doesn't diminish the importance of taking steps to prevent theft in your food truck business.

Common types of theft include the following:

>> **Under-ringing sales:** An employee sells something for $15 but rings up only $5; the employee puts the $15 in the register and at the end of the shift, pockets the extra $10. Because the cash in the drawer matches the transactions listed on the register tape, the theft goes unseen.

>> **Tearing up order tickets:** An employee serves a customer and the customer pays the check, but instead of putting the money and ticket in the register, the employee tears up the order ticket and pockets the cash. You have no record of that specific order or the money from the transaction.

>> **Stealing food or taking supplies:** An employee eats food without paying for it (and without permission, such as a free meal plan during his shift) and/or steals office supplies, such as paper or postage, for his personal use. Although these thefts may seem small when you look at them individually, they're as bad as taking cash right out of your register and can really affect your bottom line if they happen on a regular basis.

REMEMBER

So what can you do to curb these issues? The following tips can help:

>> Require a receipt for every transaction. Ask customers to request a receipt with their orders by posting signs at the service window.

>> Require that the cash register drawer be closed after each transaction. Never leave a register unlocked when unattended. And never leave the register key with a register.

>> Get your employees involved, and ask your staff for suggestions on how to eliminate theft.

>> Conduct employee background checks during the hiring process (see Chapter 11). When employees aren't screened properly, you spend more time and money training new employees to replace any dishonest ones.

>> Keep low amounts of cash in the cash register drawer; doing so can also help deter would-be robbers. When they see small amounts of cash in the register, they're less likely to take the risk of getting caught.

TIP

Pull all large bills ($20 and larger) out of the cash drawer regularly and place them in a secure location, such as a money belt.

>> Conduct physical inventory checks often and at irregular intervals. Also make routine spot checks to make sure your inventory matches your records. Define individual employee responsibilities for inventory control, which helps establish accountability on their part.

WARNING

Despite your best efforts, a dishonest employee can find a way to steal from your business. If you happen to suspect theft taking place, call your local police department. Don't attempt to play detective to try to solve the crime yourself, and don't ever jump to unsubstantiated conclusions. A false accusation can result in embarrassment and possibly an expensive civil case against you.

Reducing waste

REMEMBER

Food waste and spoilage has a huge effect on your food truck business's gross profit. You purchase food with the intent to sell it, but because you must throw some spoiled items away, the result is wasted sales. Reducing food spoilage is something that your food truck business should be doing from its inception, but reducing waste can be one of the most difficult tasks because you have to take so many steps. If you can isolate those steps and take them one by one, your profits can increase while your spoilage decreases. These steps include purchasing, receiving, storage, and usage procedures.

1. **Make sure you or your staff is ordering the proper amount of ingredients.** Before ordering, check the inventory to make sure you don't order something that's already in stock.

2. **Make sure you inspect all your produce deliveries.** Sometimes a supplier can short you or add more product than you ordered. Also, make sure the perishable products you've ordered arrive in peak condition. Check each product for temperature and quality. If one of the items doesn't meet your quality standards, refuse to accept it. If this happens repeatedly, you may want to look for a new food supplier.

3. **Use products that are at the end of their life cycle first.** If you can create specials to use these items, your spoilage should see immediate improvement and profit.

4. **Review your storage methods.** Correct storage methods can increase a product's shelf life. Mark your incoming products with a black marker or grease pencil. Write the day they were received so the older products can be used first.

   Keep certain fruits and vegetables separate to prevent food spoilage. Some fruits, such as apples, peaches, and bananas, release ethylene gas as they age.

Other fruits and vegetables, such as carrots, berries, and leafy greens, absorb the ethylene. Ethylene causes fruits to ripen, but it can also lead to spoilage if too much is present.

Store dry goods, such as rice, grains, and pastas, in plastic or glass containers with an air-tight seal to reduce food spoilage.

5. **Order supplies to bring your inventory to a two-order period par level.** That is: If you order an item daily, such as produce, order enough to have a two-day supply, including the inventory you have on hand. If you order dry stores weekly, subtract the inventory you have on hand from what you expect to use over the next two weeks and order the difference.

6. **Track your waste.** Posting a waste sheet allows staff to record what is thrown away. Dates, product, volume, the reason for the waste, and employee initials should be included. This information helps track reoccurring incidents that might suggest over-ordering of a product. It can also help track if there is a particular employee that might be part of the waste problem.

Chapter 11

Hiring and Training Your Food Truck Team

Outside of your concept (see Chapter 2) and menu (see Chapter 8), your employees will become the lifeblood of your food truck. Sure, they'll be your biggest expense and the cause of many headaches, but they'll also assist in the process of making you money. Your business will be unable to function properly if you don't have the right quality or number of employees to assist you in its daily operations. Your success, in part, depends on how effectively you manage your business, but your staff plays just as critical a role because without them you won't have a business to manage.

The food service industry is one of the most frustrating places to hire and manage a good staff. Turnover is high and the workforce is much younger than average; at the same time, good service is paramount to your success. Although the mobile food industry is relatively new and finding qualified and competent employees can be difficult, you must strive to hire, train, motivate, and retain the best people for your truck staff; I provide helpful guidelines for doing so in this chapter.

REMEMBER

Behind every successful food truck is a loyal and dedicated staff. That kind of staff doesn't just materialize on its own; it must be built from the ground up.

Finding and Hiring the Staff You Need

Whether you're opening your first food truck or simply hiring due to employee turnover, as the owner, your job is to consistently understand what your business staffing needs are. In the following sections, I show you how to identify the positions you need to fill, along with how to find the perfect candidates to fill these roles. I also look at a range of topics, from posting a job advertisement in your local newspaper to reviewing resumés and selecting which candidates to bring in for interviews. Finally, I clue you in on what documentation you need to get your new employees ready to start working.

Identifying your dream team

Unlike restaurants, food trucks are often operated by a small staff composed of individuals working a variety of roles. The size of your truck will help you determine the number of staff members that can efficiently and comfortably work inside of it (you can check out different sizes and types of vehicles in Chapter 2). In some cases, food truck owners have two or three sets of employees: those who work on the truck and others who work at the commercial kitchen or in the office. You base the number of employees you hire on the amount of people your truck can handle (most food trucks can hold two to six workers) as well as how many workers you need in the commercial kitchen to prepare the food before it makes its way onto the truck.

TIP

The fewer people you need to hire, the better. Always know exactly how many *[insert what you sell here]* it'll take to pay an employee for the day.

REMEMBER

Even if you plan to handle many of the operational duties inside your truck, you'll need to fill several positions to ensure smooth operation of your food truck so it can be successful in this fast-paced industry. These positions fall into two categories:

>> **Front of house:** In the food service industry, the term *front of house* (FoH) refers to the customer service that involves interacting with, serving, and cashing out your customers from the moment they approach your service window until they leave. Your FoH employees are the public face of your food truck because they're the representatives your customers interact with in most cases.

>> **Back of house:** The *back of house* (BoH) staff performs all the other operational tasks of your food truck, such as cooking, cleaning, and even the bookkeeping (check out Chapter 6 for information on finding a great accountant). Because most trucks can house only between two and six employees comfortably, many of the BoH staff are responsible for multiple tasks.

I describe the positions within these two categories in the following sections.

Service window attendants

Service window attendants, who are in the front of house, take customers' orders, serve food and beverages, prepare itemized checks, and accept payments. They must be professional, polite, and reliable. These staff members need to be familiar with the menu, including how food items are prepared, what they taste like, and whether special orders are permitted. Service window attendants should also know the daily specials, if you have any, so they can inform the customers.

REMEMBER

Because your food truck will likely be a high-paced environment, be sure to hire someone for the service window attendant position who can keep up with the pace while staying polite and friendly — and with a smile.

Managers

The manager position runs the show in the back of house. Ultimately, the manager's responsibilities include all the functions in your food truck business, from overseeing the commercial kitchen and truck operation to filling in for last-minute absences of regular employees. Unless you plan to hand over these responsibilities to someone else because you're unable to cover all the shifts the truck operates or because you own more than one food truck, you (the owner) will act as the manager of your food truck.

The manager opens and closes the truck, purchases food and beverages, opens the register, tracks inventory, trains and manages employees, works with suppliers, and manages your truck's marketing. Depending on the size of your organization, a manager takes on all the administrative and managerial duties of the kitchen while maintaining a dual role as a chef or cook.

The chef and cooks

The chef (part of the back of house) is responsible for all that goes on in your kitchens (both the truck's kitchen and the commercial kitchen). The chef should be involved in the hiring and training process of cooks and other BoH staff, if possible. The chef is responsible for the daily menu as well as buying supplies and equipment. One of the main differences between a chef and a cook is a culinary certification. Most food truck operations have one chef on the truck, and the remainder of the kitchen staff are cooks.

Cooks (also part of the back of house) are one of the most integral parts of a food truck dining experience, because, no matter how well your service is, your customers judge by the taste of their meal. A cook's responsibility may encompass more than just cooking; a cook may also be responsible for supervising and training other kitchen staff members.

REMEMBER

The most important factor to consider when hiring a chef or cook is his experience. The best-case scenario is to hire someone who has experience as well as an eagerness and strong knowledge of the food style your truck serves. If a cook or chef is professionally trained, be sure he can handle the speed of a busy kitchen because food truck kitchens can run a lot faster than some styles of restaurants. Having a food safety certification, such as a ServSafe Certification (`www.servsafe.com`), is also a plus and is normally required training for all food truck employees (see Chapter 13 for introduction to food safety). Although chefs and cooks don't need to be as personable as your service window staff, they should be able work as part of the team.

Kitchen workers

Kitchen workers in the back of house weigh and measure ingredients and stir and strain soups and sauces. They also clean, peel, and slice vegetables and fruits and make salads. They may cut and grind meats, poultry, and seafood in preparation for cooking. You may also require them to move the prepped food from the commercial kitchen to the truck, unload the truck at the end of each day, and wash the truck at the end of the day when you bring it back to the commercial kitchen for the night. Determining how many separate kitchen workers you need depends on the amount of work you need done to prepare the food before it gets onto the truck. Although many truck owners have separate staff to take care of these tasks, it's not uncommon for the kitchen workers to work as cooks on the truck as well.

The driver

Depending on the size of your food truck and the vehicle driving requirements in your area, you may have to hire a driver for your truck who has a commercial driver's license. Verify these requirements before you purchase a truck so you know ahead of time whether you'll have to hire a driver separately or whether you'll need to require a staff member to also hold a commercial driver's license.

TIP

To prevent the need to hire a separate driver for your truck, look into the process of attaining a license in your region and, if at all possible, get licensed yourself.

Sourcing your staff

After determining what types of positions you need to fill, the biggest problem you'll face is finding good candidates to hire. The first thing you should do is determine how you define a great candidate. If you skip this step, you won't be able to explain what you want in job descriptions and postings, and you won't know what to look for when you're sifting through resumés. When you begin the process of staffing your food truck, you'll be looking for individuals with either a specific skill set, such as having experience working in a fast-paced kitchen, or certain personality traits, such as being friendly and outgoing with the ability to provide great customer service, or better yet, a good mix of the two.

You can find the right people to staff your food truck in several ways, including the following:

>> **Word of mouth:** If you have family, friends, or former co-workers who know talented people or have contacts in the mobile food or restaurant industry, seek them out. These people are often able to offer trustworthy recommendations of experienced individuals who are looking for work. You may even ask your most reliable employees (if you already have some) to recommend their friends or people they know who would be a good fit for your business.

>> **Online postings:** The Internet is a gigantic information hub. You can post job openings on a variety of websites, and conversely, people looking for jobs can now browse and apply to jobs entirely via the Internet. Some of these job posting sites include Monster (www.monster.com), craigslist (www.craigslist.com), Indeed (www.indeed.com), and LinkedIn (www.linkedin.com).

>> **Local newspaper and trade magazine advertisements:** Although newspaper and magazine subscriptions have dwindled over the years, these ads can still be a good way to find candidates for your food truck enterprise. Before you spend any money on posting a local newspaper ad, do some research into the subscriber demographics and make sure they cater to the types of individuals you're looking to hire. Some food industry trade magazines you may want to check out include National Restaurant News (www.nrn.com), Mobile Cuisine (www.mobile-cuisine.com), and QSR Magazine (www.qsrmagazine.com).

>> **Local schools:** Reaching out to local high schools, colleges, or culinary schools can be a great way to find full- and part-time staff. Talk to the school administrator to find out whether the school has an intern program where these students can receive credit for working at a job in their projected career path. In some cases, you can hire these individuals without having to pay them because they're receiving school credits for doing this work; however, students will normally be able to work for you in this type of program for only one semester.

Although rookies and interns are good candidates to hire, be sure you have some veteran kitchen talent who can handle the heavy lifting.

TIP

Online and print ads are currently the most popular way of finding food truck staff members for one simple reason: Hiring is a numbers game. The more people you're able to reach, the more people will respond, and you're bound to find a few diamonds in the rough.

Some people in the food truck industry will tell you that a good way to find the most qualified candidates is to poach them from your competition; I won't advise that, though. The truth is that if you attempt to lure employees away from other truck owners, you're more likely to have the same thing done to you, and at the same time, you create a level of animosity between you and those truck owners.

Writing an effective job description

Creating effective job descriptions isn't rocket science, but unless you have experience writing them, it can certainly seem like it. To develop an ad that attracts the best candidates, you need to provide enough information to draw their interest. Including the following items in your job ad can help you do just that.

Job title

This specification may be one of the most important aspects of your ad. Why? The job title is one of the first things a job seeker sees when searching through the want ads. So what will differentiate your ad from the other culinary jobs in your market? The answer is easy: a creative job title. For example, instead of listing the title as "cook" or "line cook," try spicing it up a little with something like "creative, customer-oriented line cook."

Company info

Provide some insight into your company by including the following information in your ad:

>> Brief description of the business

>> Cuisine your food truck provides

>> What type of training employees can expect

>> Why someone would want to work for you

>> Work environment (casual, formal, team-focused, flexible hours, and so on)

Even if your truck is widely known in your area, be sure to include this information in your job ad; it can help "sell" your company to prospective candidates.

Job description

Candidates want to know what they'll actually be doing in this position. Provide a comprehensive description of the position, including

» Detailed overview of the responsibilities for the position

» Reason for position opening (growth, expansion, new position, and so forth)

Requirements or qualifications

Outline the skills required for the position. Differentiate between the actual skills required and those skills that'd be helpful to have to do the job. Some of these requirements and qualifications may include

» The desired or minimum number of years of experience for the particular job position

» Specific culinary work experience

» Education or certifications needed

» Miscellaneous (organizational skills, leadership skills, communications skills, willingness to work long hours, and so on)

How to apply for the position

A job posting isn't complete without a call to action. Include one or more of the following ways to receive resumés and/or applications and references:

» Email

» Mail

» Website (be sure to specify how to find the employment section within your website)

Also provide specific instructions to what format the resumé should be submitted. For example, you may request that resumés be submitted in MS Word as an attachment to an email or cover letter.

Interviewing candidates and choosing staff to hire

After you have a good selection of candidates, it's time to begin the interview process, which I describe in the following sections. I always advise that you don't hire an applicant without first scheduling an interview, no matter how promising his resumé is. The interview process is important, because it gives you the opportunity to thoroughly examine all the job applicants who want to work for you.

Starting off on the right foot

When you call applicants to invite them to a face-to-face interview, make sure you're prepared with the appropriate materials that will help you make the best choice for your team. At the interview, you should have the applicant's resumé and/or employment application, a written job description, an interview evaluation form (or a notebook that includes questions you plan to ask and space for you to note the candidate's answers), and any other materials you may need to reference during your meeting.

At the beginning of the interview, ask questions to help the candidate feel at ease, such as where he lives, what activities he enjoys, and what his plans are for the upcoming holidays. Avoid asking yes or no questions because people tend to give only one word answers. Instead, ask questions that will encourage the applicant to talk about himself.

Getting to the heart of matters

To transition into more of the important factors you're looking for, have the candidate discuss his current place of employment and what type of work he does there. Then have him tell you what three things in a workplace are the most important to him. This type of question helps you determine whether your business fits what he's looking for.

Moving on, start asking questions that help you understand what type of accomplishments the candidate has in his past jobs. Here are a few examples:

>> What are the three most important results you've achieved at your current job or at your last two places of employment?

>> Give me an example of a major customer-related/food-related/staff problem you had to solve. What was the issue and how did you resolve it? Whom did you ask to help? What was the result and outcome? What was its significance? What were your three biggest obstacles?

>> What is your current salary? What range are you looking for?

Beware of these red flags from candidates, which can predict negative situations you want to avoid bringing into your business:

>> They can't give reasons for leaving their last job.

>> They don't want their references checked.

>> They've had many jobs in the last year or more.

Wrapping things up

Just as you ease into the questions at the beginning of the interview, you want to ease out of the tough questions with ones that a candidate should be able to answer without too much trouble. These questions give you an idea about whether the candidate is actually interested in working for you, and if you choose to hire him, how quickly he can start. You can close the interview with the following questions:

>> Based on what I shared with you, do you feel you can do the job?

>> What is your interest, on a scale of 1 to 10, in this position?

>> What time frame are you looking to start a new job? How soon can you give notice if I make you an offer?

>> Where else are you interviewing? Do you have any offers? How do you feel about them?

Some legal consequences exist for asking certain questions during the interview process. These taboo topics you *may not* ask about include the following:

>> Birthplace

>> Date of birth, or age

>> Marital status or children

>> Race or skin color

>> Religious practices

Visit the U.S. Equal Employment Opportunity Commission website at www.eeoc.gov for details.

If you're still considering a candidate for the position by the end of the interview, give him the opportunity to ask you questions about wages, policies, training, and scheduling. Be sure you have your employee handbook nearby in case you need to reference it (I discuss this handbook later in this chapter).

Making decisions after the interview

TIP

I recommend at least two rounds of interviews for positions in the kitchen. The first interview should be a sit-down, formal interview for screening individuals and for figuring out how they may fit into your business (see the preceding sections); the second round should take place in the kitchen and include a cooking test, which can test their knife skills as well as their ability to prepare one of the items off your menu. If you're hiring for a head chef position, you can have the candidate prepare a plate of something he thinks could be used as a menu item. This type of interview structure gives you an idea of an individual's personality and cooking skills.

After a candidate makes it past your first two rounds of interviews, use the reference list he provided on his application. Calling past employers, supervisors, instructors, or co-workers can provide a candid look into the candidate's prior employment or activities. These names and numbers are there for a reason, and you're obliged to research your potential hires as fully as possible.

REMEMBER

When determining which types of employees you need to build your team, hire a good balance of people — different maturity or age levels, talents, personalities, and experience levels. However, be sure to hire people who fit your concept, values, and culture. Don't hire someone who won't work well with his co-workers. Your staff should feel comfortable and confident working alongside one another, so do as much pre-screening as possible to be sure you build the best team you can.

Providing must-have forms for new hires

After you've selected and hired the best candidates for your staff, you need to put together a couple of government forms as well as some internal documents for the new hires to complete. You'll also want to give them a personal copy of your employee handbook, which includes all your policies and procedures (see the next section for building this handbook), and you may want to have them sign a document that confirms they received, read, understood, and agree with all the attached policies.

TIP

I recommend keeping these forms on hand for new employees you hire after you open your truck. Having these forms available and ready as you need them will help make the hiring process go quicker and smoother.

>> **I-9 (required):** Every employee must complete this form in order to work in the United States. You, as a business owner, must hold onto these documents for three years after hiring an employee or one year after the end of his employment with you.

>> **W-4 (required):** This IRS document allows your employees to claim the amount of tax to withhold from their paycheck. The fewer dependents an employee claims, the greater the amount of tax that will be deducted from each of his checks.

>> **Attendance calendar (optional):** This form allows you to track an employee's sick days, vacation days, and other days off.

>> **Emergency contact card (optional):** This form comes in handy should you have to take an employee to the hospital and need to contact his family or friends to let them know of the situation. Typically, an employee lists his spouse, parent/guardian, or close friend as an emergency contact.

REMEMBER

Maintain a file for each of your employees that includes these forms in addition to their job application and/or resumé. Doing so is a good business practice, and having these documents together and readily available is important in case your business is ever audited.

Using E-Verify for Employment Eligibility Verification

Any employer in the United States found guilty of hiring employees who are not authorized to work in the country may be subject to civil fines or criminal penalties. What could this mean for you? Penalties start at $3,200 per worker for a first offence up to a maximum of $16,000 per worker for a third offence. The good news is that food truck vendors are not expected to be experts on immigration or the documents that establish employment eligibility authorization.

By participating in E-Verify, you can ensure that your food truck is compliant with immigration laws. E-Verify (www.uscis.gov/e-verify) compares information from the Form I-9 to data from the Department of Homeland Security and Social Security Administration. It is a voluntary, free, fast service. An E-Verify case must be created for each hire no later than the third business day that employee starts work. By participating in E-Verify, legally, it is presumed that the employer has complied with I-9 requirements.

Don't risk your truck's future by not using these simple employment eligibility verification tools. Not only do you risk fines or jail time, you but risk your other employee's job security.

Setting Up and Using Policies to Live By

An employee handbook is an essential tool for your business. It brings a level of professionalism to your hiring process and provides a blueprint for each employee's obligations.

You may think that putting together an employee handbook is a waste of your time because you're already busy with all the other details required to get your truck on the road. However, if you take the time to construct this document, you'll find it provides several advantages. Here are a few reasons an employee handbook is necessary:

>> **It answers frequently asked questions.** Putting together (and updating) an employee handbook helps you out because the handbook can include answers to questions that all new employees seem to ask. Employees can then refer to the handbook later for questions that may arise after they've worked with you for a while.

>> **It gives employees the security of knowing that everyone is being treated the same way.** If you have a handbook with policies and procedures in place, you don't have to worry that you're giving one employee some benefit that you didn't give others (as long as you stick to those policies!).

>> **It allows you to establish procedures early on.** Creating a handbook helps you figure out how you'll handle common kitchen or truck procedures. Having a process in place for when certain situations arise is a great way to keep stress levels low.

>> **It helps you deal with problem employees.** Even if you have only one employee, having clear processes for evaluating, disciplining, and terminating employees helps you work out any problems. Following written policies in these situations helps minimize legal issues.

In the following sections, I describe the policies you should include in your employee handbook and explain how to take disciplinary actions when needed.

Require all new employees to read the handbook and sign a form to acknowledge that they've read and understood it; keep a record of their signatures. You should also review the handbook with employees every year or whenever you make changes to it.

Knowing what to include in your employee handbook

Start compiling your handbook with a basic outline, and jot down some notes. The following list contains some of the standard items included in many employee handbooks:

>> Welcome letter

>> History of the company

- >> Organizational chart of the company
- >> Statement of Equal Opportunity Employment
- >> Proof of right to work (I-9 form)
- >> Training
- >> Termination, suspension, and discipline
- >> Attendance policy
- >> Work schedules
- >> Breaks and lunches
- >> Payday procedures
- >> Overtime
- >> Vacations
- >> Holidays
- >> Sick leave
- >> Jury duty
- >> Family leave
- >> Injury or accidents
- >> Driver authorization
- >> Smoking
- >> Drug and alcohol policy
- >> Firearms or weapons
- >> Theft
- >> Tardiness
- >> Sexual or other harassment
- >> Insurance
- >> Uniforms and grooming standards

REMEMBER

Make sure you're complying with both state and federal laws. Review labor laws in your state and check out the United States Department of Labor website (www.dol.gov). Include a disclaimer that the handbook isn't a contract. An attorney doesn't need to write the handbook, but if you do have an attorney, have her review the policies to be sure you're on firm legal ground. Keep it simple and straightforward, though; don't let your attorney turn anything into legalese that your employees can't understand. A lack of understanding can be the cause of a future lawsuit.

TIP

You can find many samples of policies on the Internet, or you can get your attorney to help you create some. (Figures 11-1 and 11-2 show policy samples. Figure 11-1 is an attendance policy, and Figure 11-2 is a drug and alcohol policy.) Also, you can ask local food truck or restaurant owners if they'll share their handbooks with you, but don't just take a handbook and put your name on it. Change it to make it your own.

Attendance Policy

Being on time and ready for work is part of good attendance. If you are late or plan on being absent, you place an extra burden on fellow employees. If unusual circumstances cause you to be late or absent, you must call your supervisor at least two hours in advance so that someone can be located to cover your shift until you arrive. If your supervisor isn't available, you should leave the following information with another manager:

- Name
- Reason for absence or lateness
- When you expect to be in
- Phone number where you can be reached

Leaving a message does not relieve you of the responsibility of speaking with your supervisor personally. You must continue to call until you make contact with your supervisor. Do not rely on friends, relatives, or fellow employees to report your absence or lateness.

Absences of more than one day must be reported daily, and a doctor's certificate of illness may be requested for any absence due to illness. Consecutive absences will require a doctor's note. Absences of more than four days due to illness or disability will require an approved medical leave of absence.

Failure to follow the proper call-in procedure may result in disciplinary action.

FIGURE 11-1:
A sample
attendance
policy.

Taking disciplinary measures

People are human. Mistakes happen. No matter how skilled or well-intentioned they are, your staff is bound to slip up from time to time and violate policies in your employee handbook. In those instances, you need to consider taking disciplinary measures.

FIGURE 11-2: A sample drug and alcohol policy.	**Drug and Alcohol Policy** The illegal use, consumption, possession, distribution, or dispensation of drugs or drug paraphernalia and the unauthorized use, possession, or being under the influence of alcohol, controlled substances, or inhalants on company premises, in company vehicles, or during work hours are prohibited.

Feeling uncomfortable with disciplinary situations is normal, and most people aren't trained to deal with unacceptable employee behavior. Most people try to avoid conflict; however, an employee's actions aren't going to get better unless he's aware of a need to improve. The situations won't disappear if you ignore them, even if a problem employee leaves. You may face feelings of distrust, frustration, and a lack of commitment from other employees if you don't take a stand and properly discipline problem employees. Just as children test their parents, every one of your staff members is watching you to determine what your boundaries are. If you ignore unacceptable employee behavior, you're indicating to your staff that that behavior is okay, which can lead to more problems down the road.

REMEMBER

Inconsistent disciplinary practices can lead to problems. Charges of favoritism or discrimination, for example, can come from inconsistent discipline. Make sure the actions you take are predictable based on your policies set forth in your employee handbook (see the preceding section).

In the following sections, I help you decide whether discipline is required and walk you through the steps of a disciplinary discussion with an employee.

Figuring out whether discipline is needed

Before taking any actions against a staff member, ask yourself the following questions:

>> **Am I providing a good example?** Discipline isn't effective if you appear to be a hypocrite (for example, trying to discipline an employee on attendance issues when you regularly arrive late). Good leaders lead by example.

>> **Do I know all the facts?** Take the time to investigate when the situation warrants it.

>> **What is the employee's performance record?** If you have an employee with a consistent record of outstanding performance, consider whether the fault outweighs his past performance.

>> **What level of severity does this warrant?** Traditionally, the disciplinary process begins with a verbal warning as part of a progressive discipline system. If the behavior continues, a written warning should follow. If these warnings don't correct the situation, another written warning or suspension to provide time to investigate the circumstances is usually appropriate. Finally, if the behavior continues, you may decide to terminate the staff member. (See the next section for details on holding a discussion with an employee in need of disciplinary action.)

REMEMBER

These actions can warrant immediate dismissal:

- Possession of or use of drugs or alcohol on company property

- Sexual harassment

- Threatening employees or customers with violence

- Theft

- Sleeping on the job

- Insubordination

Holding a disciplinary discussion

If you've determined that discipline is required, make sure you're prepared for a discussion with the employee. You should have written documentation that includes date and place of infraction, factual details, specific rules that have been violated, steps to be taken, and a disciplinary form requiring signatures from you and the employee.

TIP

If an employee refuses to sign a disciplinary form (indicating he has read and understood the document), note this non-action on the signature line.

As I note in the previous section, disciplinary action usually starts with a verbal warning. When giving a verbal warning, be sure to put it in writing, even if just as a personal note. Administer the verbal warning in a private environment — not in front of customers or other employees — and do so *after* you've documented the warning in the employee's file. Doing so keeps you from forgetting to document it later. Also, having that written documentation is important in the case of a terminated employee who brings a legal suit against you — the more documentation you have, the better.

Here are a few steps that can help make your disciplinary discussions with employees more effective:

1. **Describe the issue or offense.**

   Refer the employee to the appropriate policy that he failed to uphold so he understands why his actions are being disciplined.

2. **Ask for the employee's reasons behind the offense (and listen to his response).**

   Knowing why the employee did what he's being accused of is important. In some cases, extenuating circumstances may have triggered the offense, and you may want to take those into consideration as you determine what actions to take.

3. **Describe the action you're taking and explain why.**

   Let the employee know what you plan to do and give him the specific reason behind your decision. Doing so helps the employee understand why he's being disciplined in the way you chose.

4. **Indicate follow-up action and set a follow-up date.**

   Don't let a lot of time pass before you follow up with the employee; usually, just a few days will suffice.

5. **End the discussion on a positive note, indicating confidence in the ability of the person to change his faulty behavior.**

   Don't let this discipline become an issue between yourself and the employee. After you've disciplined the employee, make an effort to move on and leave the issue in the past.

Note: If the offense warrants terminating the employee, you may skip the last two steps because they're no longer applicable.

REMEMBER

Discussions revolving around disciplinary actions are difficult and unpleasant. However, putting off these discussions can undermine your entire business, including your staff. Try to have these discussions before the end of the shift the offense took place or at the beginning of the next shift the employee is scheduled for.

Training Your Staff

Of course, you need to train staff members when they first join your team, however, ongoing training for all staff is also essential, not only because everyone on the staff can stand to learn more, but also because creating a culture of steady learning helps you improve retention rates and make your employees more effective at what they do.

The primary goals of an effective training program are to define the major functions of the job each staff member holds and to make sure they're able to perform their individual tasks and responsibilities. For the entry-level employee, training includes various aspects and tips specific to the job and the mobile food industry.

For your more experienced employees, ongoing training helps them polish their skills and reiterate the knowledge they already have. The length of training each individual needs depends on the amount of experience he or she has in the food service industry.

You should begin training on an employee's first day on the job, starting with appearance, hygiene standards, and aspects of the dress code, such as what type of shoe to wear to prevent slip-and-fall injuries. Other areas of training include learning the menu, cooking or food preparation, service standards, cleaning, safety (see Chapter 13 for details on safety practices), and how to deal with irate customers (check out Chapter 17 for information on this topic).

REMEMBER

A properly trained staff keeps your food truck running efficiently and increases customer satisfaction. Customers are more apt to patronize your business when the staff is well trained in hospitality and service.

WARNING

Failing to properly train employees can result in serious consequences. For example, if employees aren't trained properly on the correct temperatures to serve some foods, such as meats, customers can get sick with a food-borne illness, which can lead to health department infractions and eventually the closure of your business. Cross-training individuals in all areas of your food truck operation and food safety is a must for any food truck operation.

Avoid falling into the trap of thinking, "I just can't afford to train my employees right now." Training your employees doesn't have to suck up a lot of your budget. You can implement an effective training program for very little cost, as long as you're willing to put in the time. One way to save time and money on employee training is to have your experienced staff members train those who aren't as well educated on a particular subject. For example, if you have a few employees who want to learn more about working the grill or want to improve their butchery, you can have the grill masters or expert butchers on your staff teach their co-workers.

TIP

The food service industry has always had relatively high turnover work rates, making employee training a constant task for management. Here are some simple guidelines to help you maximize employee retention and reduce turnover:

>> **Have patience.** Remember that Rome wasn't built in a day. As such, training a cook or service staff member takes time.

>> **Avoid criticism.** Nobody likes to hear he's been doing a job the wrong way, so be positive and encouraging instead. In most cases, if an employee hasn't learned a task properly, the trainer has missed something in the lesson. Try to use the approach of offering a "better way" to complete a task. For example, instead of yelling or making a scene if a new cook put together a food order improperly, pull him aside and show him how you've found an easy way to remember the process.

>> **Put yourself in the trainee's place.** Even though some tasks may now seem easy to you, they may have taken you days or even weeks to learn. So give your new staff member ample time to learn new tasks.

>> **Set realistic objectives.** You have to set goals that the new staff member can achieve. Let him experience success in each step along his training path. For example, set a goal for a new cook to master the cooking and presentation of your menu items within a certain amount of time after walking him through all the steps. Give a more experienced cook less time.

>> **Use your best resource for training — your employees.** One of the best resources you have at your disposal to accomplish the training of new employees is your existing team. Have the new person shadow one of your top performing staff members for a few days. Not only will this help him figure out the details of his new job, but it will also give him your best example of a good employee.

>> **Create clear expectations.** Nothing is more confusing to a new employee than contradictory or constantly changing expectations. This trap is easy to fall into, because everybody in your company will have expectations for the new guy. Make clear to the new employee and to the rest of your staff what your expectations are for them so you avoid crossed signals.

>> **Set a positive example.** Ultimately, your employees look to you for cues on how they're performing. The best way to improve new employee and overall staff retention is to set a positive example for all employees to follow. Create a positive work environment that values constructive criticism and mutual support.

Making Staff Schedules

REMEMBER

Without proper time management and employee scheduling, running your food truck business can quickly get out of hand. Your employees are an important component to your business that can turn your business into a profitable venture if you plan their shifts properly. Organizing and communicating your employees' work schedules makes things easier for you as a manager and keeps employees happy by giving them advanced notice as to when and how often they're assigned work. Here are some guidelines:

>> **Make a list of all your current employees.** Before you can create a fully functional schedule, you must know every member of your team.

>> **Create a list of available work hours you need filled.** On days when you're catering events, you may have more hours available than days where the truck is making only regular stops. Depending on the tasks you need

completed each day, your employee shift schedules can be as short as two hours and as long as eight hours or more.

» **Separate your employees into two groups: full time and part time.** If an employee works only part time, he likely won't work as many days as your full-time employees and will typically work shorter shifts. This shorter schedule allows you to schedule part-time employees to help prep the food before it's loaded onto your truck or to meet the truck after hours to clean it for the next day.

» **If you have a large enough group of employees, create a form so each employee can choose his preferred work schedule**. Knowing your employees' preferences helps you place them in an available work shift that's convenient for everyone.

» **Set up defined ground rules for the employee schedule.** For longer work shifts, create specified times for short breaks, lunch breaks, or dinner breaks. If a scheduled shift is extremely short (less than four hours), make sure the employee understands and agrees to no breaks or unscheduled breaks. You'll also need to restrict the number of work hours for an individual employee to allow him to maintain his current work status.

» **Post the work schedule at least one week in advance.** Doing so gives your employees an opportunity to review the schedule and allows them to notify you ahead of time if any changes need to be made before the week arrives. To give your employees confidence in giving you advanced notice of scheduling issues, assure them that if a conflict occurs, you're willing to work with them.

» **If you can, try to keep the same schedule each week so your employees can get into as much of a routine as possible.** Because of the nature of the mobile food industry, you won't always be able to maintain the exact schedule from week to week, but giving your employees some order is better than none at all.

» **Make schedule changes as far in advance as you can.** The more notice your employees have, the better your whole team will function.

You can save yourself some time by setting up your employee work schedule in a spreadsheet (like the one in Figure 11-3) or other computer program. You can then use that same program to keep track of expected work hours and planned time off for yourself and your employees.

Lunch		
1. John	Prep	8–10 a.m.
2. Erica	Prep	8–10 a.m.
3. Hannah	Truck	10 a.m.–2 p.m.
4.	Truck	10 a.m.–2 p.m.
5.	Truck	10 a.m.–2 p.m.
6. Rick	Truck/Drive	10 a.m.–2 p.m.
Dinner		
1. John	Prep	2–4 p.m.
2. Hannah	Truck	4–8 p.m.
3. Ally	Truck	4–8 p.m.
4.	Truck	4–8 p.m.
5. Rick	Truck/Drive	4–8 p.m.
On Call		
1. Tessa		
2.		

FIGURE 11-3: A sample staff schedule.

© John Wiley & Sons, Inc.

Motivating and Retaining Your Staff

The mobile food industry is much like any other sector of the food service industry, where employee turnover is common. You must be prepared to hire great people who you'll someday lose to another job, higher education, or relocation. However, your staff is one of your greatest assets, and keeping them motivated and retained in a competitive job market is crucial to the ongoing health and success of your business. High staff turnover not only results in a significant cost to your business but also can have a negative ongoing effect by fostering an unstable, and inconsistent work culture. When it comes to keeping your staff motivated and retained, you have several techniques at your disposal, as you find out in the following sections.

Offering competitive wages

Studies show that nearly one-third of all employees who choose to leave their workplace leave for a better-paying position elsewhere. You can help avoid this turnover by offering competitive wages and rewarding employees with a raise when you notice consistently high performance. Even a small increase can keep your best employees from jumping ship.

If you're going to hire and retain qualified staff members for your food truck, paying them with a salary or hourly wage that matches or exceeds what's offered throughout the food service industry is vital. Although paying peanuts may save a few dollars in the short term, you can seriously damage your business if you can't retain your staff members because you're paying under the current industry standard.

Before setting up a pay package for any role on your staff, research the average rate of pay offered by the competition for a similar position. You can do this research by consulting job websites, such as Monster (www.monster.com), LinkedIn (www.linkedin.com), or Simply Hired (www.simplyhired.com), or reviewing data on the Bureau of Labor Statistics website at www.bls.gov, where you can find detailed information for the typical salary rage for jobs held in the food service industry.

If you can't attract the right applicants to fill your job vacancies, chances are you may have to increase the amount of money you're offering, even if you feel the pay is competitive. The more demand that exists for an individual's labor, the more he can expect to be paid.

Providing basic employee benefits

Offering basic employee benefits provides many paybacks to you and your employees — number one is staff retention. An attractive employee benefit package helps recruit good employees and retain them as well.

If you decide to offer benefits to your employees, you have different choices based on your and your staff's personal situations:

>> **Insurance:** Perhaps the most sought-after benefit but also the most expensive is health insurance. Two common types of insurance are

- **Fee-for-service plans:** These plans reimburse members (employees and dependents), regardless of what doctor or hospital they go to.

- **Managed care programs (including HMOs):** These programs focus on preventive health and are generally less expensive for both employee and employer, but your employees are limited to which practitioners and facilities they can visit to receive maximum benefits.

  In addition to health insurance, you may provide dental insurance and vision care.

>> **Retirement plans:** Most of today's plans include 401(k)s. Employees have their own accounts and can take the money from these funds with them

when they switch companies. They can also contribute as much as 15 percent of each paycheck into this fund.

Offering a retirement plan for a small food truck business may not be realistic when you first start up. Over time, you'll need to determine whether you can afford these types of benefits and whether your staff members typically stay with you long enough to contribute.

You can find more information on employee benefits by visiting the websites for the Employee Benefit Research Institute (www.ebri.org) or the U.S. Small Business Administration (www.sba.gov).

Considering creative benefits

Although offering basic benefits, like insurance and retirement plans, isn't easy or cost-effective for all small businesses, creative benefit packages can give your employees similar value at a fraction of the cost. A little creativity in demonstrating to your staff that you care about their well-being can go a long way.

Creative benefits should complement the salary instead of substituting for good pay, and ideally, some benefits should be personalized to individual staff members to ensure that they're beneficial and meaningful. Here are some examples of perks you can offer your whole staff:

>> **Direct deposit:** Provide your staff with the option of having their checks directly deposited into their bank account. Direct deposit saves time and clears the funds faster.

>> **Free or discounted meals:** A common food service industry benefit to staff members is being able to buy discounted meals or receive free meals when they're working, or even buy a discounted meal when they're not working.

>> **Education plan:** Today's workforce requires lifelong learning to keep pace with the changing demands of employment. You may not be able to pay the tuition costs of an MBA program, but offering some community college or culinary course reimbursement can be affordable — and beneficial to your business.

Some other simple yet creative benefits and perks to consider include the following:

>> Additional days off for staff birthdays

>> Complimentary gym membership or movie or sporting event tickets

>> Work-life balance benefits, such as flexible working hours, working from home for your office staff, study leave, or child care assistance

>> Yearly off-site team-building experiences

>> High-quality, personalized holiday and birthday gifts

>> Magazine subscriptions

Conducting performance reviews

Setting clear, measurable performance objectives for your staff and reviewing them at regular intervals is a crucial factor in promoting and retaining a high-quality staff. These performance objectives provide your employees with focus and motivation as well as a sense of accomplishment and morale when objectives are met or exceeded. They also enable you to measure the performance of your staff and identify any particular strengths that can be leveraged or weaknesses that may need to be addressed.

An effective performance and review system includes

>> Setting clear objectives for each staff member, such as improving the time it takes to prepare certain menu items or improving on customer service techniques

>> Providing necessary resources for growth (tools and training)

>> Scheduling regular appraisals (every 6 or 12 months)

>> Rewarding staff members who meet or exceed their performance objectives with tickets to a concert of a band they enjoy or to a game of the sports team they follow

>> Addressing weaknesses or under-performance with training

>> Setting new objectives to keep staff challenged and motivated

Boosting morale in other important ways

An employee has numerous reasons to leave a job, such as inadequate pay and a lack of benefits (I discuss salaries and benefits earlier in this chapter). However, high stress levels can amplify those reasons. Here's what you can do to ease tensions and boost morale:

>> **Encourage open communication.** Part of your job is to ensure that your employees can work together as a team, even when they may not like one

another. A food truck doesn't allow a lot of room for staff members to separate themselves if issues occur. If a situation arises, speak to the whole team in private about cooperation and its importance in running the business. If need be, take further action, such as mediating a private conversation with just the involved parties.

As the top level of management, be sure to promote healthy communication between yourself and the staff as well as between staff members. Hold staff meetings frequently. Greet and talk with each of your employees daily. Let your staff members know what the future has to bring the business. This type of open dialogue will show and make them feel that they're a part of your business and its successes.

» **Offer opportunities for advancement.** Whenever possible, consider each employee for potential advancement within the company. For example, take note of an employee's performance and interests, and offer training programs for the kitchen workers who work in the commercial kitchen and want to move up to line cooks in the truck. These types of advancements can boost morale as well as interest in making your business succeed.

» **Reward employees of the month.** One motivational technique that has shown success over the years is an employee-of-the-month program. This award, based solely on job performance, highlights an individual who's shown outstanding drive, performance, and effort in a given month.

You can post the person's picture in a prominent area in the truck or at your commercial kitchen and give a few perks for that month, such as a designated parking spot close to the entrance of your commercial kitchen. This type of reward won't cost any money to implement, but the results can be huge. It gives the employee public and in-house recognition.

IN THIS CHAPTER

Determining where to establish your office

Gathering necessary office gear

Talking about payment options

Chapter 12

Setting Up Your Office and Managing Money Matters

Although your truck and commercial kitchen are where your business will make its money, your office will be the place from which you'll distribute the money you make to pay for your business as a whole. The office is the brain of the business because it's where information for the entire organization is collected, processed, and stored.

You need to regard your business office as being as important as your truck and your commercial kitchen to help maximize your mobile food business's productivity and protect your valuable data. In this chapter, I discuss choosing an office location, getting the office gear you need, and dealing with payment issues.

REMEMBER

You may notice that one area that isn't covered in this chapter is payroll. There's a good reason for that: It's a heavy topic that can have an entire book written about it. Payroll is an issue that's consistently researched by new food truck owners; if you have any questions about it, speak with your accountant, who can help you set up your payroll system and merchant bank accounts as well as pay your taxes (flip to Chapter 6 for details on how to find an accountant if you don't have one already).

Deciding Where to Set Up Your Office

Early on your path into the mobile food industry you have to choose whether to set up your business office in your home or to rent or lease commercial office space for this function. This decision can significantly impact your business financially, so I give you the pros and cons of both choices in the following sections to help you make the right one for your food truck business. I also help you figure out what to look for in a commercial office if you decide to go that route.

Home offices versus commercial offices

Although the reasons for wanting to work at home are obvious, doing so isn't the best option for everyone. On the other hand, renting or leasing commercial office space can drain your wallet and hurt your business before you even get started. I cover the advantages of home offices and commercial offices in the following sections.

REMEMBER

Both working from home and renting or leasing office space can be great options for food truck owners. The key is to figure out which one is best for *your* needs. Ultimately, your business will suffer the consequences if you make the wrong choice, so be sure to choose wisely. Don't rush this choice, and don't let anyone else influence your decision.

The pros of a home office for your food truck

Obviously, having a home office is your most affordable option. Not having to drive to the office in the morning before you make your way to your commercial kitchen is also very convenient. Another pro to having your office at home is that your family will probably enjoy having easy access to you when you're not prepping food or driving around town selling it.

Based on these factors alone, a home office may sound great; however, you should only choose to do your office work from home if you meet these criteria:

>> You have a separate space available for your office that's not a part of your normal living area. This separate space is important because you need to be able to balance your work and your personal life, and having them flow between each other without any separation can negatively affect both areas.

>> Your home has all the necessary resources and room for the equipment your office needs (I describe this equipment later in this chapter).

>> Your office work requires a minimal amount of staff interaction outside of your truck.

>> You primarily communicate with suppliers by phone or email, not in person.

>> You have the legal right to operate this portion of your business from your residence.

TIP

Working from home can be much simpler than renting or leasing a separate office, but it may put you in violation of zoning and other laws that regulate residential and business spaces in your area. Familiarize yourself with the legal and tax laws that affect home-based businesses, such as the home-office tax deduction, and be sure to check out your city's and county's zoning regulations relating to home businesses.

>> You have a reliable meeting spot where you can hold face-to-face meetings outside of the home when necessary.

>> You're self-motivated and highly disciplined when it comes to work.

REMEMBER

You must be honest with yourself on this point. If you're the type of person who can be lured away from your business tasks to do odd jobs around the house, a home office isn't for you.

The pros of a commercial office

Operating your office from a space outside of the home has some clear benefits. A "real" office can give your food truck business a more professional appearance in the eyes of the public. It also gives potential suppliers and staff the ability to meet you in your office and feel comfortable doing business with you there.

REMEMBER

As tempting as it is to place your business name above a storefront marquee or office space placard, only consider this option if

>> Your business has the need for several full-time employees to maintain the office functions. For example, if you want your accountant and/or office staff in one place, handling the business tasks that aren't handled in the truck or kitchen, you may benefit from having a "real" office.

>> You can afford the rent or lease payment and sustain it even at times when sales are slow.

>> You're easily distracted and wouldn't function well in a home-based working environment.

What to look for in a commercial office

Suppose you decide to lease a commercial office instead of working from home; the search for a space is now on! You have many things to look for when you're searching for the best commercial office space to lease. You want a space that expresses who you are as a business and has all the necessary amenities without breaking your budget. The following sections list items to think about when selecting a solution to your office needs.

Location, appearance, and size

Location is one of the most important factors to consider when you're choosing your commercial office. You want to choose an area that's close to your home as well as your commercial kitchen. Appearance is also crucial; it should be well maintained and look good on the inside and out. Your office says a lot about you to your employees and suppliers, so make sure you choose a space that looks professional. You want the space to be clean and inviting; if you share a building with other businesses, make sure they have professional-looking offices, too.

The size of your office should reflect your needs. If you'll be working there alone, you'll be able to rent a smaller space. On the other hand, if you have a number of permanent employees who will work out of the office, you may find you need a larger space with multiple offices and maybe a conference room.

Potential problems

WARNING

You want to look out for possible problems you may run into when it comes to choosing your office. Be aware of the following before you sign on the dotted line:

>> Make sure parking isn't going to be an issue. You should be certain that you'll have enough parking spaces for yourself, any employees who will work there, and anyone else who may visit.

>> Read your lease completely before you sign it and find out whether there are penalties for leaving early. For example, you may find another space that better meets your office needs, or you may find that the location just isn't working for you; in these situations, you'll want to know whether you have the option to break your lease and whether there are penalties for doing so, such as losing your security deposit.

>> Find out what costs the landlord is responsible for. Who maintains the grounds surrounding the building, and who's responsible for each individual utility bill or the air conditioner if it stops working? Will the office come furnished or will you need to bring in your own furniture? Determine which of these issues concern you and find out the answers before you sign the lease.

Price

You want to get the best value for your money, but this doesn't necessarily mean choosing the lowest-cost office space. You should price a few different office spaces and decide which one suits your needs based on the criteria in the preceding sections. For example, you may find a low-cost option that's close to your home and your commercial kitchen, but if it's too big and has limited parking, you may want to pay a little extra for something smaller with better parking options, even if it's a few miles farther.

TIP

Real estate brokers and agents are great sources of information on local leasing rates. They can generally give you an average figure for the cost of commercial space per square foot per year in your preferred locations.

Creating Lines of Communication with the Right Office Equipment

Your food truck acts as your storefront to sell your fare from, but operating a business entails much more than just your sales. You need to manage your staff members' schedules, their pay, your supplies, and your inventory. You can't efficiently complete these tasks while sitting in your truck. In the following sections, I discuss the main equipment you need for your office to operate as your business's communication hub. (Flip to Chapter 10 for an introduction to purchasing and managing supplies; check out Chapter 11 for the scoop on creating staff schedules.)

TIP

The following sections cover the tech gear you need to run your office, but don't forget the old-fashioned stuff! You can outfit your office with the following:

>> Calculator

>> Desk and chair

>> Employment forms

>> Envelopes

>> File folders

>> Filing cabinets

>> Paper

>> Postage machine with scale

>> Safe

Relying on your computer

REMEMBER

The computer system you select for your food truck business will become the data center for many of your business's administrative and management duties. You must purchase a computer system that meets your needs. When considering this choice, you need to determine how the computer system will be used within your business. Some of the questions you should ask yourself include the following:

>> **Will the computer be used in multiple locations?** If so, consider using a laptop, which can travel with you between your home, your office, your commercial kitchen, and even your truck. Make sure this computer can be connected to the Internet via Wi-Fi connection because you'll need to be connected wherever you end up working.

>> **Will multiple staff members need to use computers at the same time?** If you're hiring multiple staff members to operate your behind-the-scenes operations (see Chapter 11 for details on hiring), consider installing a computer network. By networking multiple computers, you're connecting each of these computers to a main computer that holds the software that will be used. This configuration allows multiple users to work within the same software package at the same time.

>> **What software will you need to run to maximize the efficiency of your business?** Some of the basic software your business needs includes the following:

  • A word-processing program for your business correspondence, such as Microsoft Word

- A spreadsheet application like Microsoft Excel to help you track your inventory

- A basic accounting program like Quicken or QuickBooks to allow you to keep track of your bank accounts, write checks, and manage your receivables, even if you don't do your own payroll

>> **What additional hardware do you need?** A printer is a valuable asset that allows you to print all your reports and correspondence. An external hard drive acts as an electronic file backup for all your electronic data.

Many things can damage your computer, and if you don't back up your data, you risk the chance of losing all the work you've already stored.

>> **How will you protect your computer and the data it holds from loss or damage?** Consider purchasing both security hardware and software to protect your system. All your computers should be connected to an uninterruptable power supply to prevent damage from occurring during power outages or power surges. Your computers should also have security software to prevent your system from being hacked or viruses from being inadvertently downloaded, which can cause numerous problems and keep your computers from running smoothly.

TIP

Unless you're familiar with setting up an office computer system, selecting the proper hardware (the computer equipment itself) to meet your demands can be a difficult task. If you feel you're in over your head in this area, I certainly suggest reaching out to other food truck owners to find out how they've solved their computer needs. If this path doesn't solve the problem, reach out to a computer professional. Many electronics stores have staff members who can advise you in choosing the right system. In some cases, they'll come to your home or office to install the system after you've purchased it.

Using the phone

Outside of the Internet, your telephone is your primary connection with the outside world. Many individuals choose to use a cellphone, but when it comes to your office phone, I suggest looking at a land line due to the number of options phone companies can provide you. In addition to choosing which phone company will provide your local and long-distance phone service (both of which are necessities), you may be offered call waiting, call forwarding, three-way calling, caller ID, and an incoming toll-free number. Base your choice on the services that will help you be the most productive:

>> **Call waiting:** While some people feel that the customer who's already on the phone comes first and the customer who's just calling in should leave a message to be called back, others want the option to place a caller on hold

while they take another call. The cost for this feature is nominal, so the choice is ultimately up to you, but even if you do choose this option, you can always send an incoming call to voice mail.

>> **Call forwarding:** If you have a separate business line that isn't mobile, this feature allows you to route all calls from one phone (such as the office phone) to another one you know you'll have access to, including a cellphone.

>> **Three-way calling:** If you spend a lot of time on the phone with multiple vendors, this option can come in handy. Being able to provide a conference call can be a lot easier than relaying information between multiple people on separate calls.

>> **Caller ID:** I suggest you choose Caller ID when setting up your phone plan. An invaluable resource, it allows you to ignore personal calls and solicitations so you can reduce distractions and increase your productivity.

>> **An incoming toll-free number:** Because the majority of your food truck customer base will be relatively local, the cost of a toll-free number (those starting with the prefixes 800, 866, 877, and 888) may not be justified. On the other hand, if you plan to open up your business to delivering your products to national customers, you may want to consider this option.

REMEMBER

If you're operating your office out of your home, be sure to add an additional line to your residential phone plan to allow you to have a dedicated business line. Using your home phone is less professional and may cause potential clients to question the legitimacy of your business. One of the common pitfalls of using a home phone for business is having to share voice mail that uses a message from both family and the business, which may confuse your suppliers or customers.

TIP

If you have a high-speed cable connection, a voice-over-Internet protocol (VoIP) line can cut your phone costs significantly and may come with added benefits, such as the ability to receive voice-mail messages through email. On the downside, a VoIP line may not work during a power outage, may require rewiring a high-speed Internet connection and phone lines to the room you plan to work out of, and may require a little too much tech savvy. VoIP services are offered by phone companies, such as AT&T and Verizon, and other companies that specialize in VoIP services, such as Vonage.

Tracking sales (and so much more) with a point-of-sale system

A point-of-sale (POS) system is a computerized system that allows you to electronically track your sales, cash flow, and food inventory and can help simplify your bookkeeping process. (This system is a separate set of electronic hardware from the computer system I discuss earlier in this chapter.) A POS system can be a valuable addition to your food truck business because many of these systems process debit and credit cards. (I cover credit cards and whether accepting them is right for your business later in this chapter.)

One benefit of using a POS system is that it can track everything from food usage to your most popular menu items. Because the POS system acts as a time clock, it can also work with your payroll system, saving you a lot of time and money in bookkeeping. Along with facilitating the daily operations of running your food truck, POS systems can organize your profit and loss statement and can track your sales tax from each city you operate in. With this information, you'll be able to track the performance of your business operations, which I cover in Chapter 14.

WARNING

The biggest drawback to a POS system is that it's a computer. If the system crashes and you haven't backed up your data, you risk losing all of it, and this information is something the IRS may want to examine if you're audited. Also, a POS system doesn't have the same life span as the old cash register. You'll eventually need to replace parts and update its software.

Due to the size of the food industry, there are numerous distributers of POS systems; a few reputable ones include Hewlett Packard and Dell. Be sure to study the differences between the models and options. Not all systems are created equal. Some food truck sales groups, such as Mobi Munch (www.mobimunch.com), provide a POS system along with technical support to assist you if any problems surface when you purchase a vehicle from them. You can also speak with fellow food truck owners in your area to get recommendations on systems they've had success with.

TIP

If your food truck business will start off as a small operation, you may not need a POS system when you open, especially if you aren't going to take credit cards.

Investigating Payment Issues

These days, a great food truck isn't just about great food. Having a well-known, all-star chef can bring in a lot of business, but she's only an all-star if she works on a food truck that keeps the line at its service window full. Good food is good food, but if it's difficult for your customers to pay for their food, chances are they won't return.

In the following sections, I explore the different ways you can accept payment (cash-only or also credit cards) for your fare and help you determine which options are best for your business and your customers. I also help you figure out your food truck's refund policy for when a customer is unhappy with the product you served.

Deciding whether to go cash-only

Even though some countries like the United States have been plasticized by banks and credit-card companies, some vendors in the mobile food industry still feel that cash is king. So should you follow their lead and consider going cash-only? Here are some advantages:

>> One of the biggest reasons the food truck owners I've spoken with have resisted accepting credit cards is that the so-called "swipe" fees can average 2 to 4 percent per transaction for credit cards and 1 to 2 percent for debit cards. Those fees can definitely take a hit to your bottom line, especially given that food truck customers generally have smaller tabs unless they visit your truck as a large group.

>> A benefit of operating as a cash-only business is that when you ring up the tab and are paid, the money is all yours. When you get paid in cash, you get to keep it; you don't have to share it with your bank or credit-card companies, and you avoid credit-card chargebacks.

WARNING

Going cash-only has its downsides, though:

>> Many vendors have expressed that despite the high swipe fees, they're getting to the point where they can no longer afford not to accept plastic. You need to cater to the needs of your customers if you want to run a successful business. Sometimes customers don't have cash and an ATM isn't in the immediate area in which you've parked your truck. When you refuse to take a credit card from a customer and the customer has no other means to pay, it can leave him feeling embarrassed and rejected. The likelihood of that customer returning in the future diminishes drastically.

>> Running a cash-only operation means that you end up with a lot of cash on the truck. This situation can make you more susceptible to theft by employees or robberies than a business owner who accepts credit. No one is going to stick a gun in your face for a stack of credit-card slips, but if word gets out that your truck has a lot of cash on hand, that's another story.

TECHNICAL STUFF

Statistics show that customers spend more when plastic is involved. Customers spend up to 50 percent more with a card rather than cash because they aren't limited by what they have in their wallet. Customers also tend to feel the pain of paying when counting up those dollar bills.

When choosing whether to accept credit, you need to ask yourself whether you'd rather have 100 percent of nothing or 97 percent of $20 because you accept credit cards. Having a variety of ways for customers to pay maximizes your cash flow, and in the end, isn't that what will keep your business growing?

WARNING

Don't take advantage of accepting cash to avoid paying your taxes. Maintain strict receipts on all your cash transactions. Keep these receipts and either input them into your accounting software yourself or turn them over to your bookkeeper to take care of this task. The fact that you're getting paid in cash doesn't relieve you of the responsibility of paying taxes on that income.

Processing credit-card payments

The basics of credit-card processing are easy to grasp. Your first step is to select the right credit-card-processing company. You have no shortage of options here, so take your time to investigate what each one offers you. Then compare prices in order to find the best plan for your mobile food business. After making your selection, you set up a merchant account with your company of choice, and you receive and set up the equipment needed to process credit-card payments.

The actual act of processing a credit-card payment is easy to comprehend as well. When a customer makes a purchase with his credit card, his credit-card company must approve the transaction. Thereafter, the money is electronically moved into your merchant account by your processing company. The service or swipe fees are deducted and the balance is available to you. By logging into your account, you're then able to transfer or withdraw these funds. It's that simple.

As the mobile food industry continues to grow, so does the technology that allows mobile vendors to accept credit- or debit-card payments from their customers. While you have a number of credit-card-processing companies to choose from, in the following sections I profile two (Square and Intuit GoPayment) that are among the most popular in the food truck industry. Each offers slight variations in the plans it offers.

WARNING

Both of these systems are easy to use and relatively inexpensive, but to determine whether you're willing to use one of them (or any other credit-card-processing system), you must determine how much of each of your transactions you're willing to share to use their service.

Square

Square is the creation of Jack Dorsey (co-founder of Twitter). The card reader is plugged directly into your smartphone's audio jack, and software has been developed for both iPhone and Android products. It also runs on the iPad, which allows you to use its larger screen for payment processing.

With Square, both service setup and the card reader are free, and no contracts or monthly minimums are required. The service costs are on a per-transaction basis (2.75 percent and 3.5 percent plus $0.15 per keyed-in transaction).

After you've been approved to accept payments, Square sends the card reader in the mail (if you want a spare, you can purchase another card reader from almost any electronics store). You need to download the free Square iPhone, iPad, or Android application. From within these apps, you can specify whether you want to include a field for tips (by percent or dollar amount). The Square platform also offers a web-based business dashboard so you can view your transaction history in real-time or download it to your desktop.

After a card is swiped, you can either print out a receipt (the receipt printer isn't part of the free service) for the customer or send one directly to an email account that the customer provides.

For more information about Square, visit www.squareup.com.

Intuit GoPayment

Intuit GoPayment is the creation of Mophie and Intuit. Their platform comes as an all-in-one package, which is essentially an iPhone case with a card reader built into the bottom. These readers can be purchased at Apple Stores and online. Although the software for this system is available for a large selection of phones, this hardware is only compatible with iPhone 3G and 3GS.

The service is $19.95 per month, but you're also charged 1.6 percent and $0.25 per swiped transaction and 3.2 percent and $0.25 per keyed transaction. There are no setup or cancellation fees, or monthly minimums.

After your account is activated, you can use the free iPhone app to manage your account and view all transactions through the Intuit Merchant Service Center.

For more information, visit www.gopayment.com.

Exploring mobile payment options

Paying with your smartphone is all the rage. Near Field Communication (NFC) payments are very popular in mobile payment option that you as a vendor should consider. NFC allows consumers to swipe their mobile device in order to make a payment. Apple Pay and Android Pay make use of this technology, and it seems to be secure so far.

If your customers demand this convenience, you have several options when choosing a payment system, but you need to consider these factors:

>> **Cost:** The cost of using a mobile credit card reader varies, but vendors are typically charged a fee per swipe that ranges from 1.5% to 3%. Some of these

mobile payment options also charge a yearly or monthly fee. It's a good idea to find out if the mobile reader and the app you're interested in are free, and if you need to sign a contract. In terms of online payment services, there are typically no set-up fees or monthly fees associated with using a basic PayPal account.

>> **Flexibility:** Not all of your mobile payment options are compatible with all types of phones. Some apps only work with Android or Apple phones, while others have the ability to accept flip phones and other mobile devices. You should also find out if the mobile reader is versatile enough to accept all major credit cards.

>> **Ease of use:** The size of the device can be a factor when deciding on which of your mobile payment options to choose. Is it too big or too little? How does it connect with your existing system. You'll also want to determine if the money is deposited directly into your food truck bank account following the transaction.

Before you decide which mobile payment options to offer your customers, do your homework. Consider your age of your customers and their comfort using new technology. Conducting a thorough examination of the payment terms, program features, and benefits of each mobile payment system will ensure you get the best match for your food truck's payment-acceptance needs.

Handling returns and refunds

A very important aspect of starting and operating a food truck is quality customer service, because, without it, your business won't survive. One aspect of customer service that many food truck owners overlook is providing their customers with an easy refund or return policy. So be sure to keep customer service in mind while writing this policy.

I recommend that you have an easy-to-understand refund policy designed something like this: 100 percent satisfaction or 100 percent money back. If you're great at what you do, why not promise 100 percent satisfaction? Vow to take care of every customer complaint to the customer's complete satisfaction, including a full refund if that's what it takes.

Other refund options include offering customers a replacement meal or coupons that give free meals for their use in the future. Ask customers directly what they need to be satisfied and consider using their suggestion. If they choose a refund for their meal, only refund in the same form of currency used for the purchase. For example, if the customer purchased the item with a credit card, issue a credit to that same card.

REMEMBER

Make it a policy for you or your truck manager to pull unhappy customers aside to address issues when the customers are still at the truck. This task should always be performed by a manager, because an entry-level service window attendant may not be able to adequately address and solve the problem. Your managers should be capable of defusing any immediate trouble and assuring the customers that their issue will be resolved. Take a look at Chapter 17 for more information on how to deal with dissatisfied customers.

TIP

Place your food truck's return policy in plain view. Doing so makes it easier for the customer to understand upfront what type of refunds your business allows, and in some states, posting your refund/return policy is required by law.

4

Keeping Your Food Truck Running Smoothly

IN THIS PART . . .

Preparing yourself for common business-related problems

Avoiding food-borne illnesses and injuries in your truck

Keeping your food truck out of a mechanic's workshop

Looking at your business and properly evaluating its performance

Chapter 13

Running a Safe, Clean Food Truck and Keeping It on the Road

The exponential rate of expansion of the mobile food industry makes it one of the fastest-growing business sectors in the United States. The food service industry as a whole employed approximately 13 million workers in the United States in 2015, according to the National Restaurant Association, and with the current growth of food trucks, that number will only continue to increase. It probably comes as no surprise that this industry also comprises one of the largest groups of workers injured on the job in the U.S. Injuries and illnesses are costly and damaging, both for the employee and for the individual food business owner. Job injuries and illnesses contribute to absenteeism, light duty assignments or other work restrictions, high turnover, and higher workers' compensation costs.

Common injuries in food trucks include burns, lacerations, and sprains and strains. Many of these injuries are the result of slipping, tripping, falling, lifting, and/or repetitive motions — and these are just what can happen inside your kitchen. Your business is mobile; thus, a whole new area of driving-safety concerns needs to be addressed, too.

Food trucks must follow basic principles to ensure the health and safety of their employees and customers. Some of these rules are well known; others aren't as well known but are still critical to ensuring a safe eating and working environment. This chapter covers the topics of food and occupational safety as well as some truck maintenance suggestions that help you keep your food truck on the streets.

Making Sure Your Food Is Safe

When people walk up to your service window, they're making an unspoken agreement with you that they'll pay for the food they order and the service that comes with it. What they don't want to pay for are any problems, including health risks caused by putting something into their body that isn't healthy or safe. Your portion of this agreement is that you and your staff will keep your products safe for your customers to eat. However, even the best-intentioned food truck can run into problems now and then. Keeping yourself educated on the factors involved in safe food handling allows you to protect your customers as well as help educate your employees on the risks involved in serving your gourmet cuisine to the public.

Food-borne illnesses are caused by eating food contaminated with bacteria, parasites, or viruses. These illnesses can cause symptoms that range from an upset stomach to more serious symptoms, such as diarrhea, fever, vomiting, abdominal cramps, and dehydration. Although most food-borne infections aren't diagnosed or reported, the Centers for Disease Control and Prevention estimates that every year approximately 76 million people in the United States become ill from disease-causing substances in food. Of these people, about 5,000 die.

In the following sections, I provide guidelines on preparing, cooking, and storing food safely; fighting cross-contamination; and creating hand-washing procedures.

REMEMBER

Each state and local municipality has its own specific rules and regulations that govern mobile food vendors. Contact your local health department to find out which food safety laws have been adopted in the areas you'll be operating in.

KNOWING WHERE BACTERIA LURK

Harmful bacteria are the most common cause of food-borne illnesses. Some bacteria may be present on or in foods at the time you purchase them. Knowledge of what foods are carriers of particular bacteria can help you protect your customers from them. Some bacteria cause more serious illness than others, but only a few are responsible for the majority of the reported cases.

- **Campylobacter jejuni** is found in raw milk, untreated water, and the intestinal tracts of animals and birds.

- **Clostridium botulinum** is widely distributed in nature: in soil and water, on plants, and in the intestinal tracts of animals and fish.

- **Clostridium perfringens** can be found in soil, dust, sewage, and the intestinal tracts of animals and humans.

- **Escherichia coli O157:H7 (E. coli)** is found in raw milk, unchlorinated water, and the intestinal tracts of some mammals.

- **Listeria monocytogenes** can be found in milk, soil, leaf vegetables, processed foods, and the intestinal tracts of humans and animals.

- **Salmonella** is the most common bacteria found as a cause of food-borne illnesses and can be found in the intestinal tract and feces of animals; *Salmonella enteritidis* is found in raw eggs.

- **Shigella** is found in the human intestinal tract.

- **Streptococcus A** is found in the noses, throats, sputum, blood, and stools of humans.

Prepping, cooking, and storing food correctly

When food is cooked and left out for more than two hours at room temperature, bacteria, parasites, and viruses can multiply quickly. Most of these contaminants grow undetected because they don't produce a bad odor or change the color or texture of the food. Freezing food slows or stops the contaminants' growth but doesn't destroy them. The microbes can become reactivated when the food is thawed. Refrigeration also can slow the growth of some bacteria, parasites, and viruses, but in the end, thorough cooking is needed to destroy them.

REMEMBER

Most cases of food-borne illnesses can be prevented through proper cooking or processing of food, which kills bacteria, parasites, and viruses. In addition, because these contaminants multiply rapidly between 40 and 140 degrees Fahrenheit, food must be kept out of this temperature range. Follow these tips to prevent harmful contaminants from growing in food:

>> **Handle food with clean hands.** Always wash your hands for at least 20 seconds with warm, soapy water before and after handling raw meat, poultry, fish, shellfish, produce, or eggs. (I cover hand-washing procedures later in this chapter.)

>> **Wear gloves.** Make sure you wear gloves when preparing fresh fruits and vegetables served raw; cold meats, bread, toast, rolls and baked goods; garnishes such as lettuce, parsley, lemon wedges, potato chips or pickles on plates; or any food that will not be thoroughly cooked or reheated after it is prepared.

>> **Never defrost food on the kitchen counter.** Use the refrigerator, cold running water, or the microwave oven.

>> **Never let food marinate at room temperature.** Refrigerate it.

>> **Wash all unpackaged fruits and vegetables under running water just before eating, cutting, or cooking.** Scrub firm produce, such as melons and cucumbers, with a clean produce brush. Dry all produce with a paper towel to further reduce any possible bacteria.

>> **Prevent cross-contamination.** Bacteria, parasites, and viruses can spread from one food product to another throughout the kitchen and can get onto cutting boards, knives, sponges, and countertops. Keep raw meat, poultry, seafood, and their juices away from all ready-to-eat foods. (See the next section for a more in-depth look at the prevention of cross-contamination.)

>> **Wash utensils and surfaces before and after use with hot, soapy water.** Better still, sanitize them with diluted bleach — 1 teaspoon of bleach to 1 quart of hot water.

>> **Cook food to the appropriate internal temperature:**

- 145 degrees Fahrenheit for steaks and chops of beef, veal, and lamb

- 160 degrees Fahrenheit for pork, ground veal, and ground beef

- 165 degrees Fahrenheit for ground poultry

- 180 degrees Fahrenheit for whole poultry

Use a meat thermometer to be sure. Foods are properly cooked only when they're heated long enough and at a high enough temperature to kill the harmful bacteria, parasites, and viruses that cause illnesses.

- >> **Keep cold food cold and hot food hot.** Maintain hot cooked food at 140 degrees Fahrenheit or higher; maintain cold food at 40 degrees Fahrenheit or lower.

- >> **Refrigerate or freeze foods promptly and properly.** If prepared food, perishables, produce, or leftovers stand at room temperature for more than two hours, they may not be safe to eat. Set your refrigerator at 40 degrees Fahrenheit or lower, and your freezer at 0 degrees Fahrenheit.

   Don't over pack the refrigerator. Cool air must circulate to keep food safe.

- >> **Reheat cooked food to at least 165 degrees Fahrenheit.** Reheating food helps kill off any bacteria or other contaminants that may have grown after the food's temperature dropped out of its original safety range.

- >> **Wash sponges and dish towels weekly in hot water in a washing machine.**

TIP

Following the best practice guidelines of food safety handling is critical to your business. Although you may be tempted to reuse certain prepared foods, if you have a case of food-borne illness on your truck, it can affect not only your business but also the local industry as a whole. Customers will make no distinction between one truck and another.

Combating cross-contamination

Cross-contamination is the transfer of harmful bacteria, parasites, or viruses to food from other foods, cutting boards, utensils, and so on that aren't handled properly. Improper handling of raw meat, poultry, and seafood can create an inviting environment for cross-contamination. As a result, harmful contaminants can spread to your food and throughout your food truck.

REMEMBER

When handling food, follow these simple but important guidelines to prevent cross-contamination and reduce the risk of food-borne illness:

- >> Always wash your hands with warm water and soap for at least 20 seconds before and after handling food (see the following section for tips).

- >> Start with a clean slate before you prep and cook. Wash cutting boards, dishes, countertops, and utensils with hot water and soap.

- >> Use one cutting board for fresh produce and a separate one for raw meat, poultry, and seafood.

- >> Replace cutting boards when they become excessively worn or develop hard-to-clean grooves.

>> Never place cooked food back on a plate that previously held raw meat, poultry, seafood, or eggs.

>> Separate raw meat, poultry, and seafood from other foods in your grocery shopping cart and shopping bags, and in your refrigerator.

>> To prevent juices from raw meat, poultry, or seafood from dripping onto other foods in the refrigerator, place these raw foods in sealed containers or plastic bags on the bottom shelf of the fridge.

>> To aid in the prevention of cross-contamination, raw meats should be stored from above to below in this order: fish above raw meat such as pork or beef; then ground meats; then poultry on the bottom. Due to the cooking temperatures of each product, bacteria will be destroyed when cooked. For example, if juices from beef drip into chicken below it, that bacteria is destroyed at a lower temperature than the minimum cooking temperature of chicken.

>> Don't use sauce that was used to marinate raw meat, poultry, or seafood on cooked food unless you boil it first.

Implementing proper hand-washing procedures

Harmful bacteria or pathogens are found on almost everything we touch. People can carry them in or on their bodies, and pick them up when handling raw food or touching objects that have been previously contaminated. After your hands are con-taminated, these harmful organisms can very easily spread to the food you serve and cause illness to yourself or, even worse, your customers. Hand-washing is an important task for all food service employees to ensure you're serving safe food.

REMEMBER

Effective hand-washing helps prevent the spread of harmful bacteria, parasites, and viruses. Be sure you train each of your employees to follow these simple steps (see Figure 13-1):

1. **Wet your hands with warm water.**

2. **Apply soap to your hands and lather vigorously for at least 20 seconds.**

   Pay particular attention to fingernails, fingertips, and in between fingers.

3. **Rinse your hands with warm water.**

   Water is necessary! Although some hand-care products claim to be effective without washing or rinsing with warm water, hand-washing without water doesn't effectively remove soil, grease, and bacteria/viruses.

4. **Dry your hands with disposable towels or a blow-dryer.**

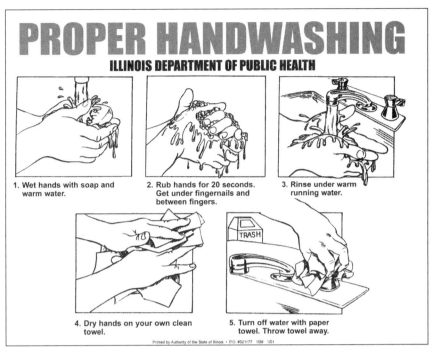

FIGURE 13-1:
You and your
staff should use a
proper hand-
washing
procedure.

Courtesy of the Illinois Department of Public Health

REMEMBER

All food service personnel must wash their hands at the following times:

>> Before starting work

>> After using the restroom

>> Before and after handling ice

>> Prior to and after using single-use gloves

>> While preparing food, as often as necessary to remove excess soil

>> When switching between tasks, such as preparing food and serving food

>> After handling nonfood items such as garbage bags or cleaning chemicals

>> After touching exposed parts of the body or clothes, other than clean hands

>> Between handling money and handling food, if not working solely at the register

REMEMBER

Hand-washing regulations vary from state to state. Contact your local health department or consult your state's food code for more information.

Keeping Your Food Truck Clean

As rewarding as it can be for you to prepare a gourmet meal for your customers, the mess created during the process can cast quite a cloud over an otherwise wonderful experience. Neglecting to clean your food truck's kitchen on a regular basis can cause especially detrimental consequences to you and your customers.

Because the truck kitchen is where much of your food preparation is performed, failing to clean your truck can result in your customers contracting food poisoning. An unclean truck is also an open invitation to insects or rodents to visit your truck. Maintaining a hygienic kitchen environment is absolutely essential. In the following sections, I list the gear you need, the tasks you need to perform on a regular basis, and the items that health inspectors check.

The cleaning supplies you need

Plenty of kitchen cleaning supplies not only significantly reduce your cleaning time but also reduce the amount of effort you need to put into the process, saving you the stress and strain of tough cleaning jobs. You can select supplies based on the types of appliances and surfaces you have in your food truck. (If you want to use green versions of these cleaning products, many brands are available.) Following are some of the most common cleaning supplies you'll need for cleaning and sanitizing your food truck:

>> All-purpose cleaner for the walls and floor

>> Broom

>> Degreaser

>> Glass cleaner

>> Mop

>> Oven cleaner

>> Soap

>> Sponges

>> Sanitizer

>> Stainless steel polish

>> Towels (paper and cloth)

Make sure you think through all the items you'll need to continually clean to help you determine what you need to purchase.

Due to the danger that the chemicals in many cleaning supplies contain, I recommend you store as many of them as possible at your commercial kitchen (see Chapter 9) or where you'll be detailing the vehicle every night. The small space inside your truck can become a hazardous area if these chemicals spill and begin filling the kitchen with their harmful emissions.

Keep your staff well trained in the safe handling of all these cleaners as well as the proper first aid to treat anyone who may wrongfully ingest one of these products (I discuss first aid in detail later in this chapter). Make sure each of your employees knows to keep these chemicals away from the food that's stored on the food truck.

Truck cleanliness 101

You're responsible for making sure your food truck employees are doing their job, which includes cleaning the truck during and at the end of a shift. Your main goal should be to ensure that the truck is safe and completely clean for its next use. The next time you and your staff members enter the truck, you should feel like you're stepping into a brand-new, untouched kitchen.

Here, I provide you with lists of tasks to help you maintain the type of cleanliness you should strive for daily. I also provide lists of tasks you should plan to do weekly, monthly, and biannually or annually.

Throughout every cooking shift, be sure to do the following truck kitchen cleaning tasks:

>> Brush the grill between cooking red meat, poultry, and fish.

>> Wipe down the cooking line and prep areas.

>> Switch cutting boards.

>> Empty the trash (use public trash receptacles to do this; don't use privately owned dumpsters).

After each shift, perform the following truck kitchen cleaning tasks:

>> Clean the fryers.

>> Clean the microwave (inside and outside).

>> Brush the grill.

>> Wash and sanitize all surfaces (cutting boards, the service window ledge, cooking line, and prep tables).

>> Empty and clean the steam table.

>> Cover all bins in the cooler with plastic wrap.

>> Wash the floor mats.

>> Sweep and mop the truck floor.

Take care of the following truck kitchen cleaning tasks at the end of each work day:

>> Change any foil linings on the grill, range, and flattops you use.

>> Wash the can opener.

>> Wash hood filters by hand or run them through a dishwasher.

Your weekly truck kitchen cleaning list should consist of the following:

>> Empty coolers and wash and sanitize them.

>> Remove lime on sinks and faucets.

>> Clean the coffee machine.

>> Clean the ovens. Be sure to follow the manufacturer's instructions.

>> Sharpen knives (okay, this isn't cleaning per se, but it needs to be done).

>> Oil cast-iron cookware.

TIP

To make things easy on you and your staff, schedule the weekly tasks on a single day each week (like every Sunday) to create a regular schedule for your team to follow.

Plan to do the following tasks on a monthly basis:

>> Wash behind the hot line (oven, stove, and fryers) to cut down on grease buildup, which is a major fire hazard.

>> Clean freezers.

>> Empty and sanitize the ice machine.

>> Calibrate ovens.

>> Calibrate thermometers.

>> Wash walls and ceilings.

>> Wipe down the dry storage area.

>> Restock your first-aid kit (I describe this kit later in this chapter).

>> Update your material safety data sheets, which outline how to safely use any chemicals in your kitchen.

Schedule your monthly tasks on a single day each month (like the first day of each month) to create a regular schedule for you to follow.

Last but not least, your biannual and yearly truck cleaning/safety list should consist of the following:

>> Clean the exhaust hoods twice a year.

Some professional companies specialize in hood cleaning. I highly recommend you use one instead of doing this job yourself because it can be very messy and time consuming. Simply search for them online or in your local yellow pages.

>> Check fire extinguishers (this task may need to be done twice a year, depending on where you live).

>> Check the fire suppression system.

>> Clean the pilot lights on gas kitchen equipment.

>> Have a professional pest control company inspect your vehicle for signs of pests, and have them removed.

To keep track of your annual inspections, conduct them when you bring your truck out of winter storage. If you live in an area in which you operate year-round, schedule these personal inspections the month before your annual health department inspection.

Thinking like a health inspector

The goal of health inspectors isn't to shut down your food truck or commercial kitchen. Their role is to enforce local food codes as well as to educate food service staff on proper food handling practices. When an inspector visits your food truck (typically once or twice a year, but make sure you contact your local health department to verify its requirements), he looks at certain areas to assist in protecting the general public. You need to understand what a health inspector is looking for in order to educate your employees as well as help you keep an eye on these items yourself. I tell you what you need to know in the following sections.

Check out Chapter 21, where I provide you with additional tips to help you pass your health inspections.

Critical inspection items

REMEMBER

At the top of an inspector's checklist are the critical items that relate directly to food-borne illness. These items are denoted in red on inspection sheets in many municipalities. Any violation of a critical item requires immediate attention and correction or a follow-up inspection will be scheduled to verify that the violation has been corrected. The following are typical critical items:

>> Observing proper hand-washing (I discuss hand-washing earlier in this chapter)

>> Confirming that your truck has the ability to provide proper amounts and temperatures of hot/warm

>> Making sure food is coming from an approved source (such as a retail grocery store that's properly licensed for food processing)

>> Ensuring that foods are kept at safe temperatures (see the earlier section "Prepping, cooking, and storing food correctly")

>> Verifying that no cross-contamination has occurred between raw and cooked products (see the earlier section "Combating cross-contamination")

Noncritical inspection items

REMEMBER

Although noncritical items aren't directly related to food-borne illnesses, they can still become serious problems if they're not corrected. Noncritical items like the following are usually listed in blue text on inspection sheets:

>> Labeled food storage containers

>> Current operator permit

>> Properly calibrated thermometers

>> Properly cleaned floors, walls, and ceilings

Potentially hazardous foods

Health inspectors must pay attention to potentially hazardous foods due to the heightened risks they present in spreading food-borne illnesses. These foods require precise time and temperature oversight for the prevention of bacterial growth and food-related illnesses. The health inspector will spend a lot of her time checking the food holding and storage temperatures of all your meat, poultry, and seafood products to ensure that they're kept at safe temperatures. (See the earlier section "Prepping, cooking, and storing food correctly" for more details.)

Food safety knowledge

Food truck owners are required to have a firm grasp of their local health codes as a prerequisite to operating a commercial food establishment. Your staff must have up-to-date training on food safety practices, and employees must be able to demonstrate a strong knowledge of safe food handling and preparation. In many cases, inspectors will quiz you and your employees on this knowledge.

Here are a few questions you or your staff may be asked:

>> Do you prepare any food in advance of service? How are these foods cooked, cooled, and reheated?

>> Do you have temperature records? Who records them? Where are the thermometers? How do you calibrate them?

>> What potentially hazardous raw foods do you prepare and serve (eggs, meat, poultry, seafood, and so on)?

>> Do you prepare foods from scratch? What is your food labeling process?

>> Where are your salad ingredients washed, and what is the process?

>> What is your procedure for limiting bare-hand contact with ready-to-eat foods?

>> What is your hand-washing and glove-use policy?

>> Do you have a written policy for an employee reporting illness or injury?

>> Who does your pest control?

>> What is your process to train new employees? Are your managers certified in food safety?

Check with your state Occupational Safety and Health Administration (OSHA) office to determine the required frequency of this training.

TIP

Employee health

When your employees are sick, you must make sure they don't handle and prepare food. To protect your customers, send sick employees home or give them a duty that doesn't involve handling food or utensils. Person-to-person contact is a leading cause of food-borne illness, and sick employees can easily transfer their germs to your customers, no matter how cautious the sick staff members are.

If one of your customers gets ill and the cause is rooted in your food, the health department has the authority to check your staff's medical records and take samples of the food they've prepared. The purpose of this action is to locate the exact cause of the illness in hopes of preventing further contamination. In some

WARNING

instances, food establishments have been shut down until all their employees are no longer sick and the establishment has been sterilized. To avoid this type of closure, and the consequent hit to your food truck's name, send your employees home if they show signs of a serious illness. Keep track of the time you send employees home and how long they stay out of work in their employee record. Doing so allows an inspector to quickly find out the specifics of the illness.

Protecting Your Food Truck Customers and Staff Members

The following sections provide tips and suggestions on the most common safety issues you'll run into as a food truck owner. The procedures, training, and drills you provide can help employees develop the knowledge and skills necessary to understand and prevent workplace hazards. Through teamwork, you and your employees can work together to prevent workplace accidents and injuries, and take appropriate action in the event of an emergency.

TIP

If you have questions with regard to the health and safety of your customers and employees, you can contact your local health department or the U.S. Department of Labor: Occupational Safety and Health Administration (OSHA) at 1-800-321-OSHA or www.osha.gov.

Avoiding injuries

Even though the space your kitchen takes up is minimal compared to many restaurants, the same types of injuries take place. Knowing how to avoid these injuries can help you prevent some of them from happening. Be sure to train your staff to observe the safety rules I discuss in the following sections to prevent them from becoming victims of injury.

Burns

Work-related burns are a leading cause of occupational injury in the United States. How can you avoid burn injuries in your food truck? Take the following precautions:

>> Avoid overcrowding on range tops.

>> Set pot handles away from burners, and never allow handles to stick out over the edge of the range.

- >> Adjust burner flames to cover only the bottom of a pan.
- >> Avoid loose clothing when working around ranges or ovens.
- >> Avoid porous fabrics, such as canvas, on your footwear because they don't protect feet from spills and burns.
- >> Check hot foods on the stove carefully by uncovering steaming food containers away from your face.
- >> Don't leave hot oil or grease unattended.
- >> Use hot pads when removing items from the microwave or oven, and lift lids cautiously to allow steam to escape.

TIP

Take extra–special care if you have a fryer on your food truck; fryer mishaps often result in burns. Here are some guidelines for fryer safety:

- >> Use grease-containing units that dump automatically.
- >> Use fryers that lower food automatically into the hot oil.
- >> Use splash guards on fryers.
- >> Use potholders, gloves, or mitts.
- >> Shake off excess ice crystals before placing a fryer basket in hot oil.
- >> Fill fryer baskets only halfway.
- >> Raise and lower fryer baskets gently.
- >> Don't stand too close to or lean over hot oil.
- >> Keep liquids and beverages away from fryers.
- >> Follow the fryer manufacturer's directions when adding new fat or oil and/or when disposing of oil.

Cuts, lacerations, and puncture wounds

Cuts, lacerations, and puncture wounds are some of the most common injuries reported in the food service industry. These injuries can be caused from handling knives or other cutting equipment. You can reduce their likelihood by implementing some simple strategies:

- >> Provide knives that are the right size and type for each job.
- >> Provide proper storage for knives (counter racks, wall racks, or storage blocks).

>> Keep knives sharp (dull knives are unsafe).

>> Keep handles in good repair; tighten or replace loose handles.

>> Never leave knives soaking in water.

>> Stop cutting and place the knife you're using in a flat, safe place if you're interrupted.

>> Pass a knife to colleagues by laying it on a counter, or pass it with the blade pointed down.

>> Never try to catch a falling knife.

>> Keep fingers tucked on the hand that's holding the food when you're cutting.

>> Never rush your staff; allow enough time to work safely.

>> Use a damp, sanitized towel under cutting boards to prevent them from sliding while in use.

Sprains and strains

Sprains and strains of muscles and tendons are common among food service workers. Improper lifting and repetitive motions are often associated with sprains, strains, and tear injuries in food trucks. With proper training and open communication between employees and managers, many of these injuries can be prevented. Use these tips to avoid sprains and strains while lifting loads:

>> Get help when the load is heavy, awkward, or unstable.

>> Hold the load close to your body.

>> Avoid twisting your body while lifting a heavy object.

Slips, trips, and falls

Slips and falls can occur on wet or contaminated surfaces. Common sources of slippery floors in food trucks include overspray from sinks, leaking equipment or pipes, food debris, and spills. You can prevent slip, trip, and fall injuries by taking these preventive measures:

>> Clean up spills immediately (spilled or dropped food, grease, oil, and water can be extremely dangerous).

>> Use nonslip matting on the floors.

>> Keep the aisle clear at all times.

>> Remove tripping hazards, such as cords and hoses, by storing them properly.

TIP

Wearing appropriate footwear is a useful way to avoid falls, too:

>> Wear sturdy shoes with slip-resistant soles and low heels (no leather soles, open toe, platform, or high heels).

>> Keep shoes laced and tightly tied; you can easily trip over an untied shoelace!

>> Look for a tread that channels liquid out from under the shoe to prevent hydroplaning.

Driving accidents

Learning some basic truck driving safety tips can help you get to your next destination safely. Food trucks are powerful vehicles that can be potential hazards if not handled properly. You can avoid injuring or even killing yourself or others on the road by following these suggestions:

>> **Be aware of your blind spots.** Other drivers may not be aware of the areas you can't see while you're driving your truck. Watch out for vehicles in these blind spots. Blind spots represent danger areas around your truck where crashes are more likely to occur. One-third of all crashes between trucks and cars take place because of blind spots.

>> **Drive slowly in work zones.** Watch out for road construction and stay alert. Work zone crashes are more likely to happen during the day. Almost one-third of fatal crashes in work zones involved trucks. Take your time going through work zones and give yourself plenty of room.

>> **Always leave enough space between you and the vehicle in front of you.** If you hit someone from behind, you're typically considered at fault, regardless of the situation. Because of their weight food trucks require more stopping distances than other vehicles. Take advantage of your driving height and anticipate braking situations.

>> **Buckle up for safety.** If you're in a crash, a seatbelt can save your life and those around you. A seatbelt keeps you in your seat and allows you to maintain control of your truck or bus. A major cause of automotive fatalities involves being ejected from the vehicle. Wearing seatbelts is the single most effective way to save lives and reduce injures on the road.

>> **Use a second vehicle.** Each passenger in your truck must wear a seatbelt. This means that if you require a staff of six to operate your truck and you have only two seats with seatbelts, the additional staff members must follow the truck in another vehicle. Following this procedure will help prevent your employees from getting injured.

>> **Use a spotter.** Because of the size of your truck and because most of the spots you'll be parking in weren't designed with your truck in mind, have one of your employees assist you in parking. This person can help you avoid hitting someone or something that's hidden in one of your blind spots.

>> **Drive defensively.** Avoid aggressive drivers. It's estimated that each year, two-thirds of all traffic fatalities are caused by aggressive driving behaviors. Keep your distance and maintain a safe speed. The only thing speed will increase is your chance for a crash.

Stocking your food truck's first-aid kit

REMEMBER

Most municipalities require your food truck to carry a first-aid kit on board to help those who may be injured at your food truck. Basic first-aid kits typically carry the following supplies:

>> Adhesive bandages

>> Antibiotic ointment

>> Antiseptic wipes

>> Burn gel

>> Eyewash

>> First-aid tape

>> Gauze

>> Nonstick pads

>> Sterile eye patches

WARNING

Some first-aid kits may also carry over-the-counter medications, such as pain relievers and antihistamines. I recommend that you and your staff never give any of these medications to your customers (but feel free to treat customers with other items in your first-aid kit). It may seem like a wonderful customer service; however, if a customer has an adverse reaction to one of these medications, you'll be the responsible party.

The amount and frequency of first-aid training you must give your employees is determined by which state you operate in. For more information on the specifics of your state, check with the OHSA office at 1-800-321-OSHA or www.osha.gov.

Taking action in an emergency

Do your employees know what to do in case of an emergency? What if there's an explosion, a fire, or another type of emergency in or around your truck? Your employees need to understand what their roles are in the event of an emergency.

REMEMBER

Whether an accident happens to a co-worker or one of your truck's customers, your staff needs to know how to respond. Here are a few steps you and your staff should take:

>> Take care of the injured individual immediately; try to reduce any discomfort and embarrassment the individual may feel due to the accident.

>> Treat the individual with respect by being courteous and helpful.

>> If possible, take the individual away from the area where the incident occurred.

>> If the injury occurs to a customer and he's alone, ask whether he would like to call someone or if you may make a call on his behalf.

>> Ask the individual to describe what caused the accident.

>> Let the individual decide whether he needs an ambulance or medical treatment. If he's unconscious, immediately call 911.

Keeping Your Truck Comfortable in All Temperatures

The part of the country that you call home determines the typical conditions you'll find to be the norm in your food truck. During the winter months in northern cities, your kitchen will help you and you staff stay comfortably warm. Trucks located in these same northern cities in the summer, along with trucks that are located in predominantly warm climates year-round, have the most problems keeping their truck's kitchen cool.

WARNING

Keeping cool when temperatures reach record highs isn't just about comfort. When it's 100 degrees outside, it can be 120 degrees or warmer in your food truck. Dangerously high temperatures can result in heat-related illnesses ranging from heat cramps to heat exhaustion and heat stroke.

As it turns out, there are plenty of cheap and easy ways to beat the summer heat without beating up the environment or your wallet. Green isn't just cool: Cool is green. The following tips can help you keep cool at those times when the inside temperature of your truck becomes unbearable:

>> **Select a cool location when parking your food truck, if available.** A spot in the shade is ideal. Make sure any nearby trees or overhanging branches are stable and won't fall and damage your mobile kitchen.

>> **Set up the awning (if you have one) when you're parked.** The awning shades not only the service window but also the side of the food truck, and helps protect your customers and employees from the sun's sweltering rays.

>> **Make sure you minimize the heat load as much as possible.** I understand that you run a mobile food business and the kitchen is where you make your money, but don't generate heat unnecessarily. Turn off as many kitchen appliances as possible; lights, televisions, laptops, and other electronics also generate heat, so minimize their use, too.

TIP

If you're using a refrigeration unit, you absolutely need to keep this running. To limit the amount of energy the refrigerator uses and the heat it generates, make sure the coils on the back are clean and well maintained.

>> **Open the windows at night or any time there's a breeze.** This simple action creates a crosswind in the vehicle and can significantly help cool the temperature. Use small battery- or solar-powered fans throughout the vehicle to keep air circulating.

>> **Cover the windows of the truck with blackout curtains or windscreen covers.** These keep the sunlight and heat out.

>> **If cooking outside is an option in your area, do so.** Using the oven or grill heats up the small space inside a food truck in no time.

>> **Dress appropriately.** Wear loose-fitting clothing — but not so loose that it becomes a fire hazard while you're cooking — especially clothes made of cotton, to draw moisture away from your body. Dress for the heat by wearing shorts and, by all means, choose light instead of dark-colored clothing. Dark clothing attracts heat, leaving you hot and steamy.

>> **Wet a towel with cold water and wrap it around your neck.** The towel cools the passing blood in your veins, thereby cooling the body's temperature.

Speaking of wet towels, jump in a cool shower to cool down when you've just had enough. This is a great practice just before you go to bed, too. It removes the sweat from your body and opens the skin's pores to allow the body to cool.

Fueling, Maintaining, and Repairing Your Kitchen on Wheels

Your food truck is the heart of your business as well as the largest investment you'll make in getting started. As you find out in the following sections, fueling it, maintaining it, and understanding what to do to keep yourself and your staff safe while you're in it are keys to the ownership of a rolling bistro.

Keeping your fuel costs down

One of your regular expenses as a food truck owner derives from the fact that your kitchen has wheels, and you must bring your food to your customers. Your food truck needs fuel to complete this task. I've polled many food truck operators and have found that most of them spend between $250 and $500 a month to fuel up their trucks. With fuel prices in flux throughout the year, determining how much to set aside can be difficult, but unless your truck has a permanent location right next to your commercial kitchen, it's a sum that must be accounted for.

Most of the trucks on the road today haven't switched over to electric or biodiesel-driven engines and are still running on standard petroleum products. For those in that majority, attempting to cut fuel consumption can be a bit like dieting: Your success depends on setting an attainable goal, implementing a plan to reach your goal, and then making sure you stick to your plan. Improving your fuel consumption is a lot like challenging yourself to lose those extra 10 to 20 pounds; it requires you to stay disciplined and, in many cases, rework your everyday habits.

TIP

Although you have no control over tax rates or the actual fuel prices, I provide a few steps you can take to help lower your overall fuel costs:

- **Be sure to have regular maintenance completed.** You'll use less fuel if you keep your vehicle tuned up (see the next section for details). Don't forget about your vehicle's wheel alignment, either; you can't maximize your gas mileage if the truck isn't driving straight.

- **Improve your driving habits.** An estimated 30 percent of fuel costs are determined by engine and truck speed, both of which are controlled by the driver. Continually revving and braking your food truck lowers your gas mileage. Try using the cruise control (if your vehicle has one installed) on the highway to help maintain a constant speed.

  Don't be a lead-foot driver. As a rule, each mile per hour above 55 reduces fuel efficiency by 0.1 mile per gallon. Not only will you save fuel and improve safety by driving more slowly, but you'll also avoid having to pay the fines for those pesky speeding tickets. Remember: You're not in a drag race; there's no need for you to drive like a speed demon when you're on the road.

>> **Keep an eye on your tires.** Maintain the correct inflation pressure. Find out the proper tire pressure the manufacturer suggests and keep it there. When your tires are under-inflated, they're less round and require more energy to begin moving and to maintain speed.

>> **Take the shortest route.** This idea may sound obvious, but it doesn't always happen. Go to an online mapping website and plan your route for the day. If you can, plan to avoid congested, high-traffic areas (in terms of vehicles, not foot traffic) that continually are filled with traffic snarls and stop-and-go driving.

>> **Get a good deal on fuel.** Saving a penny or two per gallon really adds up. The GasBuddy app and website (www.gasbuddy.com) can assist you in shopping around for the best prices in your area. Another way to save is to read your owner's manual to find out what octane level of fuel the manufacturer recommends for your vehicle. Don't pay for premium (91 octane) if your truck only requires regular (87 octane).

>> **Use your air conditioning less.** I know many in the food truck industry live in warmer climates, but air conditioning makes the truck consume more fuel, so shut it off when you can and use your vents instead.

Understanding the importance of regular maintenance

Too many food truck owners center all their attention on their food instead of their entire business. Your food is important, of course, but your truck is the platform for getting your food to your customers. If it isn't properly maintained, you may find yourself in a situation where you waste money not only by throwing away the food you've already prepared for the day but also by sinking in a lot of money to get your truck back on the road.

REMEMBER

You need to incorporate regular preventative maintenance into your recurring scheduled to-do list for your food truck. This maintenance not only helps to provide your truck with a longer lifespan but also keeps your business out of the shop when you're not planning on it. Unexpected trips to the mechanic can mean lost days of business as well as a lot of extra expenses for problems that could easily have been avoided by having regular checkups performed. Regular maintenance can be difficult to afford at times, but it's priceless when it comes to maintaining the good health of your vehicle.

Regular checks and replacements of the following items will help lengthen the life of your vehicle:

>> Air filter

>> Antifreeze

>> Brake fluid

>> Brake pads

>> Engine oil

>> Fuel filter

>> Oil filter

>> Power steering fluid

>> Tires

>> Transmission fluid

>> Wiper blades

Note: The condition and amount of each of these items will depend on the make, model, and age of your truck, so verify how often they need replacement from your vehicle's service manual or a local dealer.

Finding a mechanic

When it comes to finding a reliable automotive repair service shop or mechanic, you have various options in your local area. Choosing the right one for you depends on the type of vehicle you select for the base of your business as well as the proximity of the repair shop to your location.

TIP

Looking for an auto repair shop when you begin the process of purchasing a food truck is always advisable. Many mechanics can help you inspect the vehicles prior to their purchase. They know what problems should be avoided and what to look for to prevent you from buying a lemon.

Here are some tips to find a reliable automotive repair service for your food truck:

>> **Ask local food truck owners for their opinions.** This strategy is one of the best and most reliable options for finding an auto repair business. Many other food truck owners have already experienced the good and bad mechanics in your area, so why not hear what they have to say? You may be able to find a quality service in a very short time by using this tip.

>> **Expect the shop to have qualified professionals to perform any repairs or maintenance work.** Using an auto repair shop with a National Institute for Automotive Service Excellence (ASE) certification ensures that the shop and its mechanics have undergone thorough training.

>> **Find out whether the shop has technicians with certification from vehicle manufacturers.** Mercedes, Ford, Nissan, and GM are examples of manufacturers that offer technician certification. This certification indicates how serious the technicians are about their job and the service they provide. It also means that the technicians are up-to-date on the latest automotive technology.

>> **Keep in mind that bigger isn't always better.** A backyard mechanic can provide service that's as good as — if not better than — the service of a full-sized service shop.

>> **Ask for references.** This advice applies to all potential repair shops, regardless of whether they're big or small.

>> **Look for state-of-the-art equipment in the repair shop.** Without a well-equipped shop, complete in-house repair can't be guaranteed. Having to allow the shop to farm out work to another mechanic who does have the proper equipment can cost you more.

TIP

After you find a mechanic you like, show your appreciation by dropping off some leftovers or a goodie bag filled with your truck's delicious food once a month. Doing so will pay you dividends when you need them.

Knowing what to do in the event of a breakdown

REMEMBER

We all know that from time to time any vehicle may need to pull over due to engine or tire problems. Here are some important tasks to perform in case you have issues while driving your truck:

>> At the first sign of truck troubles, gently take your foot off the accelerator. Don't brake hard or suddenly. Carefully work your vehicle toward the shoulder, preferably the one on the right side of the road. If you're on an interstate, make your best attempt to reach an exit. Use your turn signal to inform drivers behind you of your intentions. If changing lanes is necessary, watch your mirrors to monitor the traffic around you closely.

>> After getting off the road, make your truck more visible than it already is. Put reflectorized triangles or flares behind your vehicle to alert other drivers; use your emergency flashers. If it's dark, turn on the interior lights in the cab and kitchen.

» When you have a flat tire, be certain that you can change it safely without being close to traffic. If that's possible, change the tire as you normally would.

To help prevent being stranded with a flat tire, check that you have a properly inflated spare tire onboard *before* you hit the road.

» When your truck's issue is beyond your ability to make repairs, get professional help. Wait inside the vehicle with the doors locked, and use your cellphone to call for help (make sure you keep the numbers of your mechanic and a towing company written down and stored in your phone). If someone stops and offers to help, open the window slightly and ask him to call the police. Don't try to flag down other vehicles unless it's a marked police cruiser. Raise your hood and tie something white to the radio antenna or hang it out a window so the police or tow truck operators will know help is needed.

Wait for a uniformed police officer or other emergency personnel. All interstate highways and major roads are patrolled regularly. Some highways have special call boxes available.

» Don't stand behind or next to your vehicle. If the truck is in the roadway, stand away from the vehicle and wait for help to arrive.

WARNING

» Walking on an interstate is never advisable. However, if you can reach a source of help on foot without jeopardizing your physical or personal safety, try the direct approach by walking. Keep as far from traffic as possible and walk on the right side of the roadway. Never attempt to cross a multi-lane, high-speed roadway.

Chapter 14

Evaluating the State of Your Food Truck Business

Whether you've run a food truck for years or are just now starting one makes no difference; you need to understand how to determine whether your mobile food business is actually succeeding. Sure, you see constant lines at your service window, and your sales keep increasing, but some unseen circumstances can hit your bottom line — and hit it hard. Recognizing those circumstances and then making the proper corrections can mean the difference between true success and utter failure of your business. In this chapter, I show you how to interpret key indicators for your food truck, even if they currently look like a jumble of numbers on a spreadsheet.

As important as these metrics are to your business, you can't properly manage a business on the visible numbers by themselves. In this chapter, I also explain how to listen to and use all the complaints and suggestions you receive from your customers, employees, and even food critics so you can improve your truck's operations.

Investigating Key Performance Indicators

The old business adage "You can't manage what you don't measure" still holds true today. You can't manage for improvement if you don't measure different aspects of your business to see what's improving and what isn't. Remove the guesswork from managing your business by checking the numbers that tell you what's really happening. If you find problems, you can find them quickly and can take corrective action promptly. If you're having success, you can see what to do more of to maintain and grow that success.

So during the process of evaluating your food truck business, you'll regularly collect data (measurements), determine how they'll be conveyed as a standard (metric), and compare them to a benchmark to evaluate your truck's progress. These tools are often referred to as *key performance indicators* (KPIs).

REMEMBER

KPIs are quantifiable measurements that reflect the factors you've deemed critical to the success of your business. They differ from business to business. For example, an experienced food truck owner may have the percentage income that comes from return customers as one of her truck's KPIs. On the other hand, a new food truck owner, who doesn't have return customers yet, may be more interested in measuring which of his menu items is his highest-selling food option. (See Chapter 3 to read up on developing your food truck "battle plan.")

So how do you decide what to measure for your mobile food business? In the following sections, I provide a whole host of items you can choose from, and I explain how to use them effectively.

TIP

For a slew of other performance indicators covering almost every business aspect imaginable, check out KPI Library (`www.kpilibrary.com`); access to these KPIs is free. More than 6,500 different metrics at this site cover a wide range of industries. Take a look at its management, financial, and operational metrics to find some ideas that are helpful for measuring and growing your successful food truck business.

Listing the most useful KPIs

Many aspects of your mobile food business are measurable. That doesn't make them keys to your food truck's success. In selecting KPIs, limiting them to the topics that are essential to reaching your business goals is critical. Also, keeping the number of KPIs you follow small enough to keep the staff's attention focused on achieving the same KPIs is important.

TIP

The specific number of KPIs you select to track depends on the size of your business and how much time you can put into managing and trying to meet or exceed these metrics. If you're just starting out, you may want to limit your KPIs to two or three; if you're a seasoned truck owner, though, you may consider a range between four and six.

Some key metrics related to your food truck business include but aren't limited to the ones in the following sections.

Sales and kitchen indicators

These indicators center on your bottom line. Your sales and food costs will determine whether your truck is succeeding financially. Because I recommend that new food truck owners monitor fewer KPIs than experienced truck owners, this section is where you should spend most of your time focusing.

>> **Food cost percentage:** How much is your typical food bill? You usually calculate your food cost as a percentage of your total business expenses. You measure it by adding your food purchases for the week and comparing those figures to your weekly food sales. Depending on the type of cuisine you serve, this number can range from 25 to 35 percent. If your food costs are higher than 35 percent, flip to Chapter 8 to figure out how to get your costs in or below this range. (**Note:** People who choose the route of operating a franchised concept food truck will have a lower food cost due to the buying power and cost control systems the franchisor can bring. See Chapter 2 for details on franchising.)

>> **Weekly sales:** This number is one of the standard sales-related numbers that everyone looks at. As you may expect, weekly sales can vary widely from one truck to the next. The key number to look at is any change you find from week to week and how it compares to previous years.

>> **Sales per head:** One of the most used performance indicators is sales per head, which you calculate by dividing your total sales by the number of customers you serve. To do this, you must make sure your point-of-sale system (see Chapter 12 for info on this topic) or your service staff are properly accounting for the number of people each receipt covers, because many receipts may involve the purchases of two or more people. You can calculate your sales per head at different times or shifts throughout the day. For a more detailed understanding of this metric, you can track your sales per head each week or month to look for reasons for positive or negative trends. For example, your sales per head may trend downward when you run discount specials.

TIP

You can separate your sales into smaller groups, such as food, dessert, and beverage sales per head. By doing this, you can find out how certain menu items appeal to your customers and how well your staff is selling them. You can also use these numbers as a basis for an employee bonus system.

>> **Inventory value:** How much food is being regularly stored back in your commercial kitchen? It should be less than a week's use, but it can get out of control if you're storing food by freezing or *cryovacing* it. (Cryovacing is the process of removing excess oxygen from a food storage bag where the bag is heat sealed to make it airtight.) (Flip to Chapter 10 for tips on building your inventory system.)

>> **Best (and worst) selling items:** Check the weekly sales from your receipts or point-of-sale system to help you determine which menu items are consistently selling out or taking up space on your menu board.

Staff indicators

If you have more than a couple of employees, the following staff indicators will help you keep track of how your employees are impacting your business. If you choose to use only one indicator in this category, I suggest you use the total labor cost indicator, especially if you're a new food truck owner, because it centers on how your staff impacts your food prices.

>> **Total labor cost:** Total labor cost is one of the largest expenses you'll incur as a food truck owner. Hence, the reason you must consistently keep track of it. Similar to food cost (see the preceding section), the labor cost should range from 25 to 35 percent of your total expenses. (If it's higher, it may be time to adjust the number of employees you maintain on your staff.) Total labor cost includes salary or hourly wages, benefits, insurance, retirement, and bonuses that you pay to yourself and your employees.

TIP

One way to lower your total labor cost is to have fewer workers on hand during slow times.

>> **Labor hours:** How many hours do your employees work during a certain time frame? You can compare these hours against your sales to measure the productivity of your staff. (Check out Chapter 11 for an introduction to staff scheduling.)

>> **Turnover:** Industry professionals say that high staff turnover is part of operating a food service business, but it doesn't have to be for you. Count the positions you employ, and then divide this number by the number of people you've employed during a certain period of time. For example, if you have six staff positions and you've employed ten people in the last year, your staff turnover is six-tenths or 60 percent. (Of course, lower turnover is better for your business. I show you how to reduce your employee turnover in Chapter 11.)

Customer indicators

You can measure customer satisfaction in different ways, such as feedback forms, social media, and other such methods that are hard to quantify. (You discover how to handle customer feedback later in this chapter.)

The National Restaurant Association estimates that three-quarters of most food service business sales come from repeat customers. The most successful food trucks aim to get at least 50 percent of their customers to visit their service window at least once a week. You can have your staff mark order tickets to confirm that an order is from a repeat customer. However, if your service window employees don't specifically ask each customer whether they've visited your truck in the past, this trend can be difficult to track.

TIP

Ask customers for email addresses to provide them with special offers for returning customers. This type of marketing costs you considerably less than having to advertise and market for a new customer. (Flip to Chapters 15 and 16 for details on marketing, public relations, and social media.)

Marketing and advertising indicators

This list of indicators is more important to food truck owners who actually spend money on marketing. Many new truck owners start up without putting any funding into this area, and thus don't need to track this data. When you determine it's time to invest in marketing or public relations, I suggest you start tracking, at the very minimum, the costs involved in your campaigns to help you determine whether continuing with future campaigns is worth your time and money.

>> **Marketing and public relations (PR) costs:** These costs are the total value of what you spend, measured against the response you get. This metric can be a difficult one to measure, but it's worth investigating. For example, you may run a coupon in a local newspaper that's distributed in your market. You track the number of customers who use the coupon for this campaign. Subsequently, you can determine whether it generated enough sales to justify using this medium again.

>> **Response rates:** How many people responded to different marketing or PR campaigns and what effect did they have on your bottom line?

>> **Sales inquiry conversion rate:** This metric is the number of information requests that turn into actual sales. For example: If ten people asked for information about your catering service and these inquiries resulted in two catering jobs, the sales inquiry conversion rate would be two-tenths or 20 percent. You can use this data to find out why these people converted into customers. Was it the quality of your promotional material, your pricing, or the makeup of your menu?

>> **Press mentions:** Keep your eyes open for mentions in media platforms, such as newspapers and TV, and see how they affect your sales. You may find that any press (even if it's bad) boosts your sales.

TIP

To create opportunities for positive media coverage for your truck, try partnering with a local charity or becoming involved in a high-profile community event. Check out Chapter 15 for more ways to get word of your truck out to the media.

Putting KPIs to use

REMEMBER

After you've chosen your KPIs, what should you do with them? If a KPI is going to be of any value to you, you must have a way to accurately define and measure it. Saying "get more repeat customers" is useless without a way to distinguish between your new and repeat customers. Or saying "be the most popular food truck in town" won't work because you can't measure a food truck's "popularity" or compare it with your competition in a non-subjective way. Instead, say "get more customers," knowing that increased customer numbers will also increase the number of return customers; or say "increase number of sales" to help you determine an increase in popularity through your bottom line.

You can use KPIs not only as a management tool but also as a figurative carrot for your employees. KPIs give people in your business a clear picture of what's important to you and what they need to do to meet those goals. Share your metrics with everyone on your staff. Not only do you and your managers (if you have them) need to know, but your kitchen and truck employees need to know as well. Effectively motivating your staff to progress in the areas that need improvement can be difficult unless they're made aware of what needs to be fixed.

TIP

Post team (shift) and individual results on the truck or in your office to motivate employees. Make sure you use charts and graphs (which you can create in a user-friendly program like Microsoft Excel) to visually communicate these metrics in a way that won't confuse them.

Review and use KPIs to guide your decisions. With your KPIs in place, you'll be able to tell which strategies are working and which aren't. If you make a change, you use the metrics to tell you whether the change improved things. When the metrics show improvement, be sure to share that accomplishment with everyone, and don't forget to reward employees who are responsible for that success, even if it's with just a pat on the back.

Evaluating and Using Feedback

Whether your food truck is in a sales slump or your receipt totals have been off the charts, you know that this trend can change as fast as it began. For that fact alone, you need to constantly check the pulse of your mobile food business to find out whether your customers and employees are happy with your food and service. If they aren't, it's time to make some changes to create happy, loyal, long-term customers and employees who are the key to your company's success. The best way to evaluate how your business is doing is to gather feedback from your customers and employees. You can do this in several ways, from asking questions verbally to distributing surveys.

As a food service provider, you'll also have to deal with feedback that you don't ask for. Professional and amateur food critics are everywhere, and knowing how to prepare for their write-ups is important to keeping a good light shining on your food truck.

The following sections help you sort through all this feedback and determine how to react to it properly.

Paying attention to customer feedback

The best judge of whether you're providing a first-class dining experience is always going to be your customers. Customer feedback is often given immediately, which allows you to act on it quickly. People like when you ask for their opinion, and you need this information for your business to grow.

By requesting customer feedback, you're able to discover what you're doing well, generate new ideas based on customer comments, and identify weaknesses or areas that need improvement. In the following sections, I look at the methods of customer feedback, their value, and how to use them.

Employing online feedback methods

Thanks to the rise in social media (see Chapter 16 for details), you have more opportunity than ever to discover what your customers want. In fact, your food truck's online persona will likely help widen your customer base and increase your sales as more new and returning customers discover your presence on the web. Online customers can serve as focus groups, temperature gauges, and brand ambassadors for your business.

TIP

Adding a feedback application to your website is relatively inexpensive and easy to install. These applications can offer analytics that analyze feedback data, organize the feedback into a specific inbox, and categorize feedback by type (complaints, questions, and suggestions). Automatic replies to these submissions are available, but I suggest that you send customized or even personal replies that include an acknowledgment of the issue, a reason (as opposed to an excuse) for the problem, and a promised action. A couple of inexpensive but effective feedback applications to investigate are UserEcho (www.userecho.com) and UserVoice (www.uservoice.com).

TIP

You should answer unsolicited online feedback as quickly as possible, ideally within 24 hours. You can deliver a simple thank-you note and a return compliment quickly and sincerely, but you should handle complaints with an eye on restoring the person's trust in you and your truck. For full details on how to handle these complaints, check out Chapter 17, where I discuss how to convert these unsatisfied guests into repeat customers.

In addition to unsolicited feedback from your website and social media platforms, you can send survey links through Facebook, Twitter, and email newsletters that direct customers to your website. Surveys should be between five and ten questions that relate to areas of food quality, customer service, or help in determining new locations to park your truck. A simple way to conduct a quick survey on only one question is to send the question to your social media fans and followers. This way, the question not only reaches your targeted market, but it also allows you to interact with them as they submit their responses. For more information on social media interaction, see Chapter 16.

Opting for print surveys and comment cards

TIP

Print surveys seek specific information that you can analyze over time. Using this medium allows you to know which changes have impacted customer satisfaction and lets you put the survey right in the hands of the customer as opposed to referring the customer to your website to fill out an online survey. Consider conducting short, simple surveys. Pick one key issue to focus on — such as food quality or customer service — and ask five to ten questions about it. You'll have an easier time quantifying your results if you ask customers to rate their answers on a scale of one to five.

Comment cards, on the other hand, may provide only broad opinions, which, while valid, can't be used to trend changes in customer opinion. Still, they're a simple and direct way to solicit feedback. Keep your cards simple, but be sure to ask for names and email addresses.

TIP

Make it worth the survey participant's time to help you. With each print survey or comment card you hand out, offer customers something of value, which may lure more customers to complete your surveys. Enter the names of everyone who takes the survey into a contest or drawing for a free menu item to encourage customer participation. (Not all customers are interested in receiving discounts or incentives to share their ideas with you, though. They feel that their reward is having their opinion heard and their suggestions incorporated into your business operations.)

Talking with customers face to face

The simplest way to find out what people want from your business is to ask them while they're at your truck. You or your service window staff can ask questions, such as, "Is there anything else I can help you with?" or "Is there any way we're failing to meet your needs?" Pay attention to what your customers say and record it in a notebook kept near the service window to analyze later.

TIP

While you need to listen to your customers, you also need to read between the lines. Even though customers may say they're happy, does the tone of their voice really reflect it? Pay attention to the questions customers asks. Track how often customers ask the same or similar questions. If you know that a certain question always leads to more questions, you can manage customers' expectations by developing a response that answers the initial question and answers the follow-up questions.

Encourage your service staff to build strong relationships with customers so customers feel free to share how they feel about the service. They can give both general and specific observations (for example, customers may have mentioned that they liked the quality of one menu item but haven't been as happy with the quality of another). Employees can be a valuable asset when they're given the knowledge and support to address customer concerns, and customers are more likely to give feedback to someone they believe is able to act on it.

TIP

Use direct customer feedback as a tool to evaluate employee performance by asking specific questions: "Was your server knowledgeable, polite and friendly?" The responses you receive will identify who needs more training and who is performing well.

Sifting through customer feedback and making changes

When you've finished gathering your feedback, take the time to read it carefully and tabulate the results. You can follow these steps:

1. **Read through the comments a few time and then create categories for the different types of comments.**

   Typically, these categories include food, speed, customer service, location, and pricing.

2. **Create separate lists for positive and negative comments in each category and then review the comments again, this time marking "positive" or "negative" for each comment.**

   Because people often comment about more than one thing, consider breaking each comment into parts and marking each part of a comment. For example, "I had to wait too long to receive my food, and the server was rude," could be coded in both the speed and customer service categories of your negative comments list.

3. **Look for patterns.**

   If you see many of the same things identified as issues in the quantitative portion of the survey report, cross-check with the comments because they may provide you with more specific info about how to fix the problems. If you see a lot of references to individual employees, consider including employee names in both the positive and negative comment coding sheets and then mark in the appropriate column each positive or negative mention of an employee.

Chances are you'll see a number of expected responses, which should serve as a reminder that you do know what needs to be addressed, but be prepared for some surprises, too. When coming up with solutions to the issues you uncover through customer feedback, think in stages:

1. **Consider the topic and gather input for change from your staff.**

   For example, if you receive complaints on the speed of your service, first observe and time your staff to find out how long creating and serving particular menu items are taking. If you find the complaints to be legitimate, you may need to work with your staff to improve on your food preparation times. In many cases, you can increase the timing in the truck by adding additional prep work at your commercial kitchen.

2. **Define the plan for change and check whether you have the budget to implement it.**

   To continue the preceding example, you may find out that one of your staff members needs some additional training to get him to the speed necessary to keep your customers happy. Set time aside for yourself or another staff member to work with this employee to improve his cooking speed without taking away from the menu items produced. If you have the time to do this while the truck is in a slow period, you'll find that you don't need to take away time or budget to accomplish this task.

3. **Benchmark the success or failure of the change with metrics over a reasonable period of time.**

   Use a KPI, which I discuss in the earlier section "Investigating Key Performance Indicators," to help you measure your changes, especially those related to pricing.

It's amazing to me how often companies neglect to get back to customers even after they've implemented changes. When you make a change that's customer-driven, contact the customers who were part of the feedback process. This step is critical, because customers will be encouraged to give even more input if they know they're being heard.

REMEMBER

Analyze all the data you receive and put it to good use. Only then will you have the information you need to keep your company strong and profitable for years to come. If handled right, the communication between you and your customers can become the lifeline of your mobile food business. To establish and maintain a healthy flow, customer feedback must result in change your customers can see. Change is the most powerful currency to reward your constructively vocal customers.

Listening to employee feedback

One of the most overlooked duties you have as a food truck owner is an obligation to your employees. Frequently, food truck owners get caught up in getting things done and tend to forget that they need to be there for their staff. One thing you can do to help alleviate some issues you may run into is to gather feedback from your employees and truly listen to what they say.

The first step to getting feedback from your employees is easy: You ask them for it. However, don't walk up to them and ask, "What would you change about the company?" because this style isn't very productive. If you approach employees in that manner, you're likely to receive a lot of complaints as opposed to constructive suggestions. Instead, formally survey your staff to let them know exactly what type of answers you're looking for and what you intend to do with that information. The vast majority of U.S. companies are now surveying their employees to gauge their job satisfaction and assist in the creation of internal policies.

When done properly, an employee survey tells your staff that their input and concerns are important, which creates better morale and stronger loyalty to you and your business. Ask your employees to write down three things they feel are positive and a brief explanation on how they see them executed and three things they feel could use improvement and a brief description on how they'd implement improvement.

REMEMBER

Preserving employee anonymity when conducting your surveys is very important. If employees' identities are tied to their responses, they may feel threatened, especially if their opinions differ from yours. As a consequence, they may choose not to participate, or their responses may not reflect their actual opinions.

So what should you do with this information after you receive it? This step is the most important part of the process: *Read each and every response.* Put together your own list of the points presented in the survey, starting with the most common and working down to the least common. If you have common solutions, list those also. Next, you must carefully consider each of your employees' responses, analyzing whether they're practical, cost-effective, and fit into the concept of your business. If a suggestion is a fit or if you can modify it to get a usable idea, try it.

Whatever the findings, make sure you hold a staff meeting within a week of analyzing the survey results. Explain what suggestions were made and how you plan to implement them. If a suggestion isn't going to be acted on, inform the staff of the suggestion and your reasoning behind the lack of or delay in action on it.

WARNING

One of fastest ways to destroy the morale of your staff is to ask them for their opinions and then ignore their answers. When employees are asked for their opinions about their workplace, they expect to receive some type of response. If no response or comments are received, they'll assume that their feelings, opinions, or solutions have been ignored.

Dealing with food critics

In the mobile food industry, a bad review from a local food critic may seem devastating, but it's never the single factor that makes or breaks a business. A bad review isn't likely to close down your food truck any more than a good review makes it the "it" place to dine at. If this were true, food critics would have the power to fill their cities with the types of food trucks or restaurants they personally prefer.

Food critics are critical, biased, and opinionated — that's their job! Critics go to dining establishments searching for imperfections. Even if critics love your food, there's a good chance they'll point out your slightest mishaps with brutal honesty.

Every customer is a potential food critic. Professional food critics like to remain anonymous, so you may not know when one walks up to your truck. Furthermore, with the increasing popularity of online review sites, like Yelp (www.yelp.com), any customer with a smartphone or access to the Internet can become a food critic (see Chapter 16 for more information).

Good public relations strategies can convince food critics to visit your truck, but when they're there, it's up to you to impress them. Your work begins the moment a food critic arrives at your truck.

The best way to recognize a professional food critic is simply to keep up-to-date with the names and faces of local and regional reviewers and make sure your staff does as well. If you spot a food critic in line at your food truck, there's no need to give him a hard time. Instead, use it to your advantage and let him know that you're available to fact-check information before he submits his review.

If a food critic is eating at your food truck and begins to critique or complain about the food or service, accept the criticism and do what you can to fix the problem immediately. The worst thing you can do is become defensive. But if you fix the problem, you may win some points with the critic for superior customer service.

Before he leaves, ask the food critic to let you know several days in advance when the review will appear online or in print to give you enough time to prepare for a rush that could result from a positive review (plus you may want to pick up a few copies of the article for your scrapbook).

Take advantage of each review you receive from a food critic to help you modify your food truck's food and operations. If you receive a fantastic review on a menu item, make sure all your other menu items match or exceed the quality of the item that received praise. At the same time, take any negative reviews as learning points. If your service is criticized, look at ways to improve it as soon as possible. If a food item is cut down by a critic, make sure you get additional opinions from chefs or other food truck owners. If you get a consensus on the bad food review, take a look at ways you can improve that item, such as the quality of ingredients or how it's prepared. If nothing with fix it, pull it from your menu immediately.

Focus on the positive media attention you receive. Frame positive newspaper and magazine articles and display them in your truck and post them on your website.

5
Generating Buzz and Growing Your Food Truck Business

IN THIS PART . . .

Marketing your truck through the tried-and-true methods of public relations (PR) and promotions

Getting familiar with the new reality of PR in the mobile food industry: social media

Using popular software applications to help build and retain a customer base

Considering the future of your food truck, from rebranding and expanding to selling

Chapter 15

Mastering Food Truck Marketing and Public Relations

Your food truck may ooze the exact atmosphere your concept dictated, and it may have a unique, out-of-this-world menu, but if nobody knows about it, it's likely to fail. If you want your mobile food business to thrive, you must promote it. Hoping your family and friends will keep your service window busy until the rest of your community finds out about you just isn't enough.

In this chapter, I cover the aspects of marketing and public relations that allow you to concentrate on getting people to your service window in a number of different ways. After that, it's up to you to keep them coming back for more. (Not to worry; Chapter 17 covers that.)

Defining Your Marketing Message

The foundation of your food truck marketing plan is your marketing message. This message must concisely communicate what you want people to remember about your truck and stick to that point. To develop a successful marketing message, you must have a firm grasp of what you want to say, whom you want to say it to, how to reach these individuals, and why you've chosen to do so. If you don't have an understanding of these issues, your message will be incomplete or miss your target altogether.

In the following sections, I explain how to focus on your target customers and use a few easy steps to create a marketing message. After you develop an effective marketing message, you can use it in all areas of your marketing execution (as I explain later in this chapter).

Doing your homework on your target customers

In Chapter 3, I cover how to research your desired target customers in your market. By defining your target customers, you can identify the specific characteristics of the people you believe are most likely to visit your food truck. These characteristics are sometimes called *demographics.* The following are some of the common characteristics you can use to classify your target customers:

>> Age

>> Gender

>> Income level

>> Buying habits

>> Occupation or industry

>> Marital status

>> Family status (children or no children)

>> Ethnic group

>> Religion

Crafting your marketing message step by step

REMEMBER

Narrowing down your target customers (see the preceding section) makes it easier to craft a message for that group of individuals. How do you do that? Always create marketing messages that feature the customers and their needs, rather than your truck. Your customers want to know what's in it for them, so you need to put yourself in your customers' shoes. Listen and discover what their wants are; then align your message accordingly. Follow these steps:

1. **Determine the problems that your target audience is experiencing.**

   The first secret to crafting a marketing message that will make prospective customers listen is to identify their problems and the results of those problems. Maybe the restaurant in your area that's been the market's only source for Mediterranean food has lost its focus, and the quality of its food and service has suffered. You can provide an answer to this problem if you're planning to open a Greek or Lebanese cuisine food truck.

2. **Present your food truck as the solution for the proverbial pain and suffering that your community is feeling as a result of the problem.**

   Identify all the benefits you'll provide and how those benefits will take away this pain. Also show how your solution is easy to implement, because we live in a society where people don't want to jump through too many hoops to have their issues resolved.

   For example, your message could say something like this: "The Napa Shawarma Truck provides a new option for diners who love Mediterranean cuisine. We serve fresh, high-quality Lebanese dishes with the highest standards of customer service."

Here are some pointers to consider when developing your marketing message:

>> **Be concise.** Don't include everything there is to know about your business in your marketing message. What makes you different from everyone else in your market? Your uniqueness differentiates you and prevents you from becoming "more of the same."

>> **Be consistent.** Don't confuse people with too many ideas, and don't change your message frequently. A consistent message is easier to remember. If you want your message to be heard, you must repeat the same message time and time again.

>> **Deliver on your promises.** Never guarantee something in your marketing message unless you're absolutely positive you can deliver on that promise every single time. Establishing expectations in your community and then failing to live up to them will harm your reputation quickly, and news of bad service travels fast.

Here are some examples of marketing messages that follow these rules:

The Mangia Mobile is a food truck that caters to diners who love Italian cuisine. We serve classic Northern Italian dishes in a unique mobile setting.

Jim's Food Truck is a casual and friendly mobile eatery, serving lunch and dinner with an ever-changing menu, including items developed by our customers.

Arepa Arepa is an eclectic rolling kitchen, spotlighting small plates of cuisines from around Latin America. We serve fun, exotic food in an upbeat, energetic atmosphere that caters to foodies.

Communicating Your Marketing Message with Public Relations

After you've developed your marketing message (see the preceding section), you need to determine how to share it with your community. Three of the most common methods of message promotion are public relations (PR), advertising, and social media. (Due to the importance of social media in the mobile food industry, I dedicate an entire chapter to this topic; see Chapter 16 for the scoop.) Using PR in particular to market your food truck gives your targeted customers the ability to become familiar with what your business is all about before you even hit the streets.

WARNING

Advertising is a way to get your marketing message to a select audience, but, unlike PR, advertising is something you typically pay for. Advertising hasn't proven to be a sustainable marketing strategy in the mobile food industry as it has in other industries. Findings indicate that advertising rarely pays off, especially when the goal is to acquire new customers. Along with being disruptive, advertisements lack credibility. No doubt about it: Advertisements just can't compete with the power of PR and getting positive (and free!) media coverage.

Public relations means a lot of different things to a lot of different people. *Webster's New World College Dictionary* (Wiley) defines *public relations* as "relations with the general public as through publicity; specifically, those functions of a corporation, organization, etc. concerned with attempting to create favorable public opinion for itself." For you, the basic purpose of public relations is to shape and maintain the image of your food truck business in the eyes of anyone who will ever form an opinion about it. The main goal of your public relations strategy is to enhance your company's reputation.

The food truck industry is extremely competitive. You need to have an edge that makes your business stand out from the crowd, something that makes it more appealing and interesting to both the public and the media. The public is your current and future customers, whereas the media is partly responsible for selling your brand. Your PR efforts help you give the public and the media a better understanding of who you are.

In the following sections, I describe two options for putting together your PR efforts: doing PR yourself and hiring help. (I discuss two types of PR tools — press releases and websites — later in this chapter.)

WARNING

Although PR is one of the most powerful ways to promote your business, it also has several disadvantages that you need to be aware of:

>> **Coming up with an interesting press release isn't always easy.** Lucky you; I discuss how to create a press release later in this chapter.

>> **Measuring the success of a PR campaign is difficult.** Although some people may use an increase in sales as a way to measure the campaign's success, it's hard to determine whether the campaign is the sole reason someone came to your service window.

>> **Selecting the appropriate media may be challenging.** Deciding who to pitch your stories to can prove problematic if you don't have access to the readership demographics of your local media.

>> **Controlling the interpretation of your press releases is tricky.** When you distribute a press release, it falls into the hands of many journalists, who may use it to create a story that's inaccurate, incomplete, or misleading, thereby damaging your reputation.

Going solo

Many start-up food truck businesses don't have a budget for PR at the outset, so they take the responsibility for PR on themselves. You can take the following steps to get off on the right foot (and establish a foundation to build upon if you later have the ability or desire to hire a PR agency — see the next section):

1. **Understand what makes news.**

   This process can involve reading the local publications you want to appear in so you can see what type of story makes the cut. If you want to achieve television or radio coverage, research the programs you'd like to appear on.

2. **Apply your marketing message and determine what newsworthy information you have to share that would interest readers, listeners, or viewers.**

   For example, are you launching a food truck that will be the very first of a specific type of ethnic cuisine to be offered in your community? Have you just secured permitting in a city in which you'll be the very first food truck? Is your business doing a lot of charity work in your community? These types of topics are appealing leads to the media, and by talking with relevant journalists, you may secure a few column inches or air time to promote yourself and your mobile food business.

   PR is all about getting closer to your audience by amplifying your marketing messages and inspiring others to tell your story. You can get your message to relevant journalists via press releases, your website, and other social media platforms.

   TIP

   When you read your target publications, you're likely to see profiles that introduce you to a person or business. This type of article represents a great opportunity to explain who you are and why you've started your business. Track down the editors of these publications to see whether they'd be interested in writing a profile featuring your food truck. This option is much better than placing an advertisement because you can share more of your story, and no cost is involved.

TIP

Stories that are of interest to your customers but don't make good news stories are perfect for your website. You can also tweet links to updates and any coverage you manage to secure to make your online presence work even harder. I discuss the building of a compelling website later in this chapter; I talk about the use of Twitter and other social media platforms in Chapter 16.

Getting some help

Owning a food truck can seem like a 24/7 operation where some business tasks simply must be farmed out to consultants to be completed. Read through the following reasons why some food truck owners select this route to help you determine whether hiring a PR agency is the right avenue for you:

>> **They don't have enough time to devote to it.** PR requires more than flipping an "on" switch and walking away. PR continues to benefit you only if you put more effort into it. Just like other marketing functions, consistent, strategic, and measurable PR is something that needs to be planned for and executed over a long period of time.

>> **They want to maximize their launch.** Most business owners understand the importance of their initial launch to the success of their business. PR is much more than just writing a press release and sending it out via a wire service. Having a partner who can maximize your media relations, events, and other PR-related activities in conjunction with a major press release can help you successfully launch your truck.

REMEMBER

If you plan on utilizing an outside agency for your launch, you need to make sure you have a system in place to continue all the energy and momentum you've built after the launch is over. The worst thing you can do is launch your truck with a huge amount of fanfare and then fade away without maximizing what you and your agency spent months developing.

>> **They're in a crowded market.** Food truck owners who are trying to compete in large, well-established, or crowded markets may see some benefits to hiring an outside PR agency. A good agency can develop a strategy that focuses on your company's strengths and makes you stand out from your competitors.

TIP

Find out about agencies that have experience within the restaurant or food truck industry by asking fellow food truck or restaurant owners for recommendations. Look at press releases issued by other food trucks to see who represents them. After you identify a few agencies that seem appropriate, take a look at their websites or call and ask for general information about their services, including a complete or mobile food industry related client list. If you plan to get the word out about your opening, hire an agency about a month before you plan to hit the streets.

TIP

If you have a limited budget, consider hiring a marketing intern from a local college to do the PR work for you. In most cases, interns will work for a low price or for free.

Putting Together Press Releases

One of the best ways to promote your mobile business is to issue press releases to your local media. You can distribute most of your press releases by email or through online distribution services, such as PRWeb (www.prweb.com) or PR Newswire (www.prnewswire.com), to editors at newspapers, magazines, radio stations, and television stations. Using distribution services may lead to your news getting syndicated by all your local or regional media outlets.

REMEMBER

If you plan to regularly send out press releases, you must be aware of the standard format that these media sources use and accept. Include the following elements in every release you write:

>> **Title or headline:** Use headlines (like those you see in newspapers and magazines) to attract the reader's attention. The headline is the first single line of text in the press release and tells what the press release is about, so it should be descriptive but not too long (try to limit your headline to 100 characters). Capitalize the first letter of each word and lowercase the rest.

A striking headline must communicate your subject matter instantly and convey why the content is new and interesting. It must grab the reader's attention by creating curiosity while specifically defining the information provided in the rest of your press release.

>> **Date and place:** Note the release date and the originating city of the press release.

>> **Introduction:** Highlight the importance of the news in this paragraph, which usually contains three or four lines. The introduction generally answers who, what, when, where, and why.

>> **Body:** Provide further explanation, statistics, background, or other details relevant to the news in the subsequent paragraphs, which comprise the body, or bulk, of the release. The body is a good place to share some personal quotes.

>> **Boilerplate:** Include a short, standard "About" section that provides background on you or your company. You can use your Twitter bio as a template

and simply expand on it. But don't make it too long; this section should be only one or two paragraphs.

>> **Contact information:** Don't forget to give your name, phone number, email address, mailing address, or other contact information (such as your website URL or Twitter account) so editors can track you down.

>> **Ending:** Insert a line with the characters "###" centered on it to indicate the end of the press release.

Check out the sample press release in Figure 15-1, which provides a story with quotes that journalists can use as the background of a longer story.

Mobile Cuisine Food Truck Launches in Chicago

Online magazine brings a new twist to the mobile food industry and the streets of Chicago

(CHICAGO, IL) Aug. 1, 2016 — Chicago foodies can now find a new food truck, Mobile Cuisine, that will provide them with gourmet menus from local Chicago chefs. The Mobile Cuisine Food Truck will launch in the Chicagoland area on Wednesday, Aug. 1, driving throughout the city morning, noon, and night, offering daily deals, and tweeting its location. The first stop of the food truck will be from 11 a.m. to 1:30 p.m. Wednesday, Aug. 1, in the Chicago Loop at the intersection of Monroe and Dearborn.

Created by Richard and Hannah Myrick, owners of Mobile Cuisine Magazine (*the* online resource destination for the mobile food industry at http://mobile-cuisine.com), the truck will offer a wide range of delicious made-to-order menu items for prices ranging from $3 to $10. Mobile Cuisine will serve lunch, dinner, and late-night meals throughout Chicago.

Menu items include a range of gourmet meals from sizzling Kobe beef sliders to tacos that offer a spin on almost every ethnic cuisine possible. Mobile Cuisine also offers favorites such as duck fat French fries and a wide variety of decadent "cake pops" if it's dessert you are looking for.

"We are thrilled to be opening a food truck that will cater to all types of cuisines the foodies of Chicago are looking for. We've covered the food truck industry for years and finally have been able to start a truck on our own," said Richard Myrick. "We know people in the Chicago area know good food, and that's why we've chosen this as the place to launch our truck."

About Mobile Cuisine

Mobile Cuisine, a Chicago-area food truck, brings local food enthusiasts street food with a gourmet twist. Mixing fresh, high-quality ingredients and unique flavors, Mobile Cuisine was created to bring high-quality meals without compromising taste and value. Mobile Cuisine travels six days a week throughout the Chicagoland area, providing food to consumers in areas such as universities, businesses, and festivals.

For details on the truck's location, as well as for more information on featured specials, follow the truck on Twitter, @MobileCuisineFT, and "like" the truck on Facebook, www.facebook.com/MobileCuisineFoodTruck.

###

FIGURE 15-1: A sample food truck press release.

TIP

Here are a few handy guidelines for writing a press release:

>> Write the news for journalists and media, *not* as articles or stories; if you do, a good chance exists that they'll be rejected by the media. Unless you're submitting your press release to be reprinted word for word, many journalists use the data and quotes from the press release to add to a story that they write themselves.

>> Keep it short (five paragraphs at most in the body of your press release). If you write more than that, you risk losing the interest of the reader and you risk the press release being too long to reprint by some publishers.

>> DON'T WRITE PRESS RELEASES IN UPPERCASE. Copy editors won't use a press release in this format and won't rewrite the press release to eliminate your all-caps text.

REMEMBER

This is just a general set of guidelines for press releases; for more detailed information, I suggest you pick up a copy of the latest edition of *Public Relations For Dummies*, by Eric Yaverbaum, Ilise Benun, and Richard Kirshenbaum (published by John Wiley & Sons).

Creating a Compelling Website for Your Food Truck

With the majority of your potential customer base being tech savvy, the creation of a website to market your mobile food business is an absolute necessity. Food truck customers treat the Internet as their directory to find good places to eat.

A well-designed website (such as the example in Figure 15-2) is very important for branding your business and ensuring that your food truck is considered a legitimate dining option. When customers hear about a food truck, in most cases, the first thing they do is jump on the Internet to find out more about it. Your website is a portal into your business; customers will use it to determine whether they're interested enough to track your truck down. If customers like what they see, you can expect them to hunt you down very soon. If you don't have a website, chances are these people will never make it to your truck.

In the following sections, I list the traits and essential building blocks of a good food truck website; I also help you get a handle on search engine optimization so you can drive as much traffic to your site as possible.

FIGURE 15-2:
A sample food
truck website.

Courtesy of Dave Danhi

Recognizing the traits of a good website

Your site doesn't have to be extravagant, but it should have these important characteristics:

>> **Easy to remember domain name:** Choosing the right domain name (also known as your web address or URL) for your website is important. It pays to spend a little time thinking about your options. If possible, register your domain name before you start your food truck website.

Your domain name can range from a minimum of 3 characters up to 67 and include lowercase letters of the English alphabet, numbers from 0 to 9 and hyphens (-). However, it may not begin or end with a hyphen and other symbols, including the ampersand (&) and apostrophes.

To make your website address easy to remember, try to use your food truck name or the truck name with *foodtruck* after it. Also, if possible, use a `.com` extension at the end of the URL rather than `.net` or `.biz`, because the `.com` extension is the most common and easiest to remember. You can use domain sites such as Whois? (`www.whois.com`) to see whether your preferred domain name is already taken.

>> **A strong visual design:** I don't know about you, but if I go to a website that's not visually pleasing, I typically navigate away from it quickly. A clean and

simple design is usually all you need. Bells and whistles are nice, but not necessary. The key is to make your site stand out from your competitors'.

>> **The information customers seek most:** The main reason potential customers will come to your website is to find out where you're normally located or how to contact you. You'd be amazed at the number of food truck websites that either make this information difficult to find or don't bother to post it at all.

>> **Up-to-date content:** If you're not going to keep your website updated, it may be best not to have one at all. Managing your customers' expectations is essential in this industry. For example, when you change your menu, update your site. If a customer takes the time to show up at your truck only to find out that the menu item he was planning to order was removed weeks ago, well, you haven't gotten off to the best start.

>> **A reflection of your brand:** Your website is a direct reflection of your concept, so make sure you use it to tell the world what makes your truck special. If your truck is wrapped in tones of red, your website should reflect that in the design. If your concept revolves around organic food, put that on the home page.

>> **An absence of technical difficulties:** The Internet makes recovering from an error message or broken link very difficult. Once a visitor encounters an error, that's it; that interaction is unrecoverable at that point. As opposed to running into the same situation at your truck, the web gives you no ability to react quickly or even offer an apology. These errors can easily translate into lost customers.

>> **Speedy access:** The speed at which your site allows the downloading of information and the ease with which visitors can navigate around your site are key factors to keep in mind when building your website. How quickly can users find what they're looking for? Provide a search function and make sure it provides relevant results and links throughout the site.

If you're lucky enough to have the proper knowledge or a staff member who does, you can build your site yourself. If you're like most folks, though, you'll have to hire a website designer to build it. A fully functional website with many custom features can cost you as much as $3,500.

TIP

You may also be able to get a local art student or web designer to build your site for you for about $1,000. Another option is to check out Elance (`www.elance.com`), where you simply give your project specs to find a number of freelance developers willing to do the work for your price. If you go this route, though, do your due diligence and ask for referrals and examples of other sites they've developed.

Identifying the essential components

The goal of your food truck website is to attract customers and provide them with information about your products and services. All too often, I see poorly designed websites that lack the key ingredients needed to successfully convert visitors to customers. Use the following elements on your website to maximize your chances of converting the site's traffic into paying customers.

An effective home page

REMEMBER

Your home page is the most important page on your website because it gives your visitors their first impression of your business. Within seconds of arriving at your home page, visitors will decide whether it's worth their time to browse through the remainder of your site. What should go on your home page?

>> **A prominent photo:** Pick a great image of your truck, your logo, or perhaps your signature dish.

>> **Some well-written text to complement the photo:** This text should tell people what you and your food truck are all about and how it differs from other dining experiences the visitor may have had. Make it short and compelling; if it's too long, people simply won't take the time to read it.

For example, if you have a photo of one of your signature dishes, your text can say something like, "Our carne asada tacos (grilled marinated steak) have helped make us famous on the streets of Chicago."

TIP

In addition to this main image and compelling copy, you need to provide visitors a call to action. A call to action can be a link or a button that encourages the person viewing your home page to click to another page. Here are some examples:

>> A link to your menu or weekly specials

>> A button to share your home page with friends or family

>> A link to a landing page that provides info about your catering services and the ability to request more details about them

A map and a Twitter feed

Don't make it difficult for people to find where your food truck is located. Instead of simply listing your business mailing address, display an easy-to-read map and directions.

TIP

The easiest and quickest way to display a map to your food truck is to use Google Maps (www.googlemaps.com) and embed the visual on your website.

Due to the mobile nature of your truck, you'll also want to include a feed that displays your most current Twitter messages. This feed allows a guest on your site to track you down or at least get an idea of your most frequented locations. (Flip to Chapter 16 for full details on using Twitter to your advantage.)

Your menu with some photos of your food

Your menu is the main marketing tool on your website and your opportunity to make your visitors' mouths water; don't forget to include some enticing pictures of your dishes.

WARNING

The key to adding your menu is to make it accessible. All too often, I see food truck owners provide a downloadable PDF copy of their menu. These PDFs can take a very long time to load, especially for people who are trying to view your menu from their mobile phones. PDFs also provide no search engine optimization (SEO) benefits for your website. (I discuss this topic later in this chapter.)

My advice is to take the extra time to create a dedicated menu page on your website. Make sure it includes descriptions of the food along with photos of these menu items. For tips on acting as your own photographer, check out the nearby sidebar "Capturing eye-popping photos of your food."

A list of your days and hours of operation

Showing your hours of operation and the days you have your truck hit the streets saves your customers the time it takes to monitor your daily Twitter updates if they're not Twittaholics. By adding your days of operation, you also allow your customers to plan their schedules so they can meet your truck when you're in their area.

A photo gallery

People love to see the fantastic designs food trucks have been wrapped with. They also like to see what the food looks like before they decide to eat at a particular truck. For this reason, I always suggest that food truck websites include a photo gallery (in addition to the photos on the home page and with the menu). Hire a professional photographer or have your staff get some pictures during a food truck event or during one of your busy times to capture the visual portion of your food truck's atmosphere. You can then display the photos on your website in a simple photo gallery.

A blog

Many food truck businesses today use blogs on their websites to communicate with their current customers, potential customers, and the general public. Social media sites like Twitter are considered *micro* blogging sites, but if you want to share your thoughts in more than 140 characters, a blog is the way to do it. Adding a blog to your website has many advantages; here are a few of them:

>> **Developing a casual dialogue with your customers:** A blog allows you to speak casually to a wide range of people, including your customers and potential customers. Through a blog, and through blog comments, you can create a casual conversation that builds real relationships.

>> **Communicating quickly:** A blog allows you to provide up-to-date information to your customers quickly and easily. Updating your blog is much easier than updating your website, and it requires no special technical skills.

>> **Increasing search engine visibility:** As you blog about topics such as events you'll be attending or new menu items you plan to add, you increase the visibility of your business in search engine results for these topics.

>> **Sharing multimedia content:** With a blog, you can easily embed other types of content, such as videos and podcasts.

>> **Making you the expert:** A blog allows you to showcase your knowledge about the mobile food industry. As other people discover the benefit of your knowledge, you'll be seen as an expert in the field.

Creating a website people can find with search engine optimization

Search engine optimization (SEO) is a technical term for techniques used to make it easier for search engines such as Google, Yahoo!, and Bing to find your website. These search engines are the primary means by which many of your potential customers will find out about your food truck. By increasing your search engine ranking, you raise your site's popularity and influence. And the greater the number of people who visit your site, the more often (and even higher-ranked) your website will appear in search results and the more likely you'll be to outrank the millions of other websites out there (including your competition).

Although an entire profession is dedicated to assisting website owners in accomplishing this task, I cover some of the basics here to help you maximize your website's visibility on the World Wide Web. Try the following steps to improve your site's search rankings, and watch your site jump ahead of your competition:

1. **Develop a list of relevant keywords that relate to your food truck business.**

   Think about these words and phrases in terms that someone may use to search for a restaurant or food truck serving a particular style of food. Do you plan to have a rolling hamburger joint? Then start your list with terms related to hamburgers and food trucks.

CAPTURING EYE-POPPING PHOTOS OF YOUR FOOD

If you visit any bookstore and head to the culinary or cookbook section, you may be overwhelmed by the number of books that are filled with beautiful food photography. In some cases, these images become the true focus of the book, with the recipes or stories taking a back seat.

Earlier in this chapter, I state that an effective food truck website should include photos of the food on your menu. To assist you in adding quality photos to your website (or any marketing materials) without breaking the bank, check out these tips for nonprofessional food photographers:

- Because your food is typically served in disposable packaging, make sure you either buy or borrow some suitable dishware to display your food for these photos.

- The way the food is placed on the plate is as important as the way you photograph it. Pay attention to the balance of color, texture, and the forms the food takes when designing your shot.

- Keep some vegetable oil on hand during your photo shoots. Brush it over the food to make it glisten.

- Having steam rise off your food can give it that "just-cooked" appearance, but this can be difficult to achieve naturally. Food stylists suggest adding steam via a number of artificial techniques, including placing microwaved, water-soaked cotton balls out of the shot.

- Treat the food you're photographing as you would any other still-life subject and ensure that it's properly lit. One of the best places to photograph your food is by a window where there's plenty of natural light. This light helps to keep your food looking natural. You can supplement the natural light with a flash to cut down on shadows.

- Don't make the common mistake of taking shots that look down on the food. You get a much better shot by photographing food from below plate level or slightly above it.

- As you know, food doesn't maintain its appetizing appearance very long after it has been served. You need to take your photos soon after the food has been finished — before it melts, collapses, or changes color. Be prepared and know what you want the image to look like before the food shows up for its photo shoot. One way to do this is to have the shot completely set up with props before the food is ready and then substitute a stand-in plate to get your camera exposure right. When the food is ready, you just switch your stand-in with the star.

2. **Create a list of keywords related to your location.**

   Does the city you plan to work in have a nickname? Add the proper city name, its abbreviations, and its nicknames.

3. **After you create your lists, determine which keywords are primary terms and which ones are secondary.**

   A *primary keyword* is the main keyword you want your website to rank for and should be placed in your header, footer, and primary titles used on the site. A *secondary keyword* is placed in your content or is used to support your primary keywords.

   For example, in the phrase *Middle Eastern Food Truck Business in Los Angeles,* the primary keywords are *Middle Eastern food truck,* and the secondary keywords are *business in Los Angeles.*

4. **Use these lists to place keywords throughout the text of your website.**

   Proper keyword placement maximizes your SEO efforts. Placing your selected words and phrases within your website's content enables the search engines to establish your relevancy to them, which results in a higher ranking for you.

   Within your content, use your primary keywords in titles and sprinkle secondary keywords throughout the body of the content. The best placement within the content is in the opening and closing paragraphs. Using keywords in the opening paragraph helps you immediately establish relevance, and closing out your content with keywords serves as a reminder of the terms' relevance.

The more information you circulate through your site to the Internet, the greater your exposure will be. Search engines love fresh, new content and seek it out. If you have lots of relevant content online, you'll attract many more search engine visitors.

TIP

There's no greater way to provide fresh, updated content on a regular basis than to have a blog on your site (which I discuss earlier in this chapter). Because blogs are updated on a regular basis, they're able to attract a lot more search engine attention.

TIP

Sound complicated? No worries! Check out the latest edition of *Search Engine Optimization For Dummies* by Peter Kent (published by John Wiley & Sons) to get an even better understanding of SEO and how you can maximize its use on your food truck website.

Chapter 16

Handling the Art of Social Media

I n the past, word-of-mouth communication involved one person telling another whether an establishment's food was good or bad. Now, thanks to Twitter, Facebook, and Instagram (along with other websites), a social network of connections around the world has brought many more people into the fold. Between retweets and rating services, a customer can deliver a good or bad review of your food truck to literally tens of thousands of people before he even gets home. If a few connected people say your food quality isn't what they expected (or, in a preferable scenario, exceeded their expectations), one or two meal services can alter the perception the entire community holds about you. You need to be a part of the conversation so you know what's being said about you.

In this chapter, I describe the importance of social media to your food truck business, and I show you how to use a variety of social media platforms.

Sounding Off on the Importance of Social Media to Your Food Truck Business

Do you remember the days when we worked from 9 to 5 and reserved our nights and weekends for family and friends? Those days are long gone. Today, the

Internet has reshaped our world beyond anything we could have imagined. People now use their computers 24/7, not only for work but also for entertainment and communication.

The growing popularity of the World Wide Web has given computer developers a huge canvas on which to create social networking sites. These websites can be used by anyone with a computer or smartphone to post personal information, pictures, videos, music, and messages. Websites such as Twitter and Facebook allow much easier interaction among individuals and businesses than ever before.

If you have a smartphone with Wi-Fi or LTE access, social media platforms, such as Twitter, Facebook, and Instagram, allow you to share your upcoming locations, menu updates, and any other pertinent information with your followers while your food truck is parked.

Most food truck operators contend that if social media can provide them with a free method to connect with customers and increase sales, they'd be missing an important opportunity if they didn't at least find out what it's all about. Social media expands the pool of potential customers for your food truck business far beyond what you could have expected to gain in the past. You're no longer restricted to paying for high-priced advertising campaigns or relying on individuals to stumble across your truck as they're walking around your community.

Social media also allows you to have more personal conversations with your customers than email interactions do. Unfortunately, social media gives you more opportunity for social gaffes or missteps, too. Perhaps for that reason, some people still feel that these tools lack dignity or are merely toys for business owners who are desperate to speak with anyone.

On the contrary, these social networking tools are just the beginning of a trend that leads to ways of finding and interacting with others that exceed your expectations. In any case, you can't dismiss these tools without risk. Being unwilling to use social networking in your marketing plans is like being unwilling to speak with your customers and is almost guaranteed to give you the same results. The turn these tools are taking is exciting, but at the same time, business owners have to navigate them wisely and deal with the fading social boundaries these tools have crossed.

Talking about Twitter

Twitter got its start on March 21, 2006, when Jack Dorsey published the first Twitter message at 9:50 p.m. Pacific Standard Time (PST): "Just setting up my twttr." As of 2016, Twitter has over 300 million users who post over 500 million tweets per day.

Many food trucks are very active on social media platforms, especially Twitter, where you can witness an incredible amount of dialogue between food trucks and their customers. Twitter (www.twitter.com) is a social community that can help build brand awareness and reinforce your connection to a wide audience. Not only does it allow you to share basic information like your locations and menus, but it also gives you the ability to engage customers with mentions, replies, and retweets (I explain Twitter terminology in the next section).

Twitter is a free marketing tool that's easy to learn and takes only a few minutes a day to use. Getting followers can take time, but putting forth the effort is well worthwhile. The best part is that customers love it and build on the conversations you begin and participate in.

TIP

Keep tabs on what other food trucks and customers are saying. Their conversations can serve as a great source of ideas and inspiration.

In the following sections, I provide a brief introduction to basic Twitter terminology and tell you how to write a great Twitter bio. I then show you how to send Tweets that represent your food truck business well, and I also explain how to resolve any negative customer comments you receive on Twitter.

Getting a handle on Twitter terms and functions

Maybe you already have a Twitter account and are familiar with the fundamentals, in which case you can feel free to skip to the next section. If, however, you're new to Twitter, the first thing you need to do is set up an account. Just follow these steps:

1. **Go to www.twitter.com.**

2. **Enter your name and email and create a password, and then click the Sign Up for Twitter button.**

   Be sure to use a general business email so you can allow other staff members to use this account and not risk them accessing your personal email.

3. **Create a username.**

   Because you're using this Twitter account for brand management for your business, I recommend using your food truck name or website domain name minus the .com.

4. **After reading the Terms of Service, click Create my Account.**

Your next step is to create a bio (see the section "Writing a Twitter bio that works"). After that, you can start tweeting — see the section "Sending tweets" for the lowdown on this process.

REMEMBER

Before you send out your first Tweet, however, make sure you're familiar with these common Twitter terms and functions:

>> **Tweet:** A *tweet* is a 140-character post that's intended to be read by individuals who "follow" your account. Tweets can be directed to individuals but aren't private and can be seen by anyone who has a Twitter account.

>> **Retweet:** The common and accepted practice of sharing someone else's tweet with your followers is referred to as *retweeting.* To give credit to the original author, you just put "RT @the-original-tweeter's-name" in front of the original poster's tweet and post away. (*RT* stands for "retweet.")

>> **Direct message:** The *direct messaging* (DM) function allows you to send a private, 140-character message to another user. Think of it as an abbreviated email. The only criterion for using this function is that you may send a direct message only to Twitter users who are also following you.

>> **The @ sign:** To create a reply or to speak with someone on Twitter, you place an @ sign in front of his Twitter name. If you're posting a reply, the @ sign must be the first character of the tweet. To see replies to your tweets, click on @Replies from your *profile* (your Twitter home page after you've signed into your account).

>> **The hashtags (#):** If you're tweeting about a popular subject (for example, food trucks or Los Angeles), putting a hashtag (inserting the # sign) in front of the subject makes it easy for others to find your tweet. Making it possible for users to find you is the first step in getting them to follow you.

TIP

Twitter is a complex subject, making it impossible to cover all the ins and outs within the confines of this book. For in-depth how-to information, check out the latest edition of *Twitter For Dummies,* by Laura Fitton, Michael Gruen, and Leslie Poston (John Wiley & Sons). To expand your horizons even further, consult *Twitter Marketing For Dummies,* by Kyle Lacy (also published by John Wiley & Sons).

Writing a Twitter bio that works

Many food truck owners forget that without a good Twitter biography, being found and followed by people who are interested in what your food truck Twitter feed has to say can be virtually impossible.

ENGAGING CUSTOMERS WITH A RECIPE CONTEST

Thomas Kelly and David Schillace, owners of Mexicue in New York City (www.mexicue.com), are very active with their followers and run seasonal contests for their fans. In the fall of 2011, they ran a recipe contest focused on one seasonal ingredient: butternut squash. Kelly and Schillace reached out to their fans on Twitter, Facebook, and their website to get the word out. The winner of this contest submitted a recipe for a taco with butternut squash, cilantro lime cream, tortilla strips, spicy slaw, and cotija cheese. The creator of the winning seasonal recipe wins a $50 gift certificate to Mexicue and a messenger bag. The second and third place prizes are $25 and $10 Mexicue gift cards.

This seasonal contest allows Kelly and Schillace to engage the community and allows aspiring chefs to create recipes for the opportunity to be featured on the Mexicue menu.

Some may argue that writing a 160-character bio is hardly rocket science, and that's true. However, the number of blank or poorly written bios I've found that were created by established food truck owners still baffles me. For some folks, creating a clear description that's interesting — and possibly even funny — isn't an easy task.

Even if you've already set up a Twitter account for your food truck business, take a moment to look at the Twitter bio you use for your food truck and ask yourself these questions:

>> Will someone reading my bio want to follow me?

>> Is that follower the kind of person I want to attract?

Users won't follow you if they don't know who you are, and they won't know who you are if you don't tell them — clearly and concisely. This is where your Twitter bio enters the picture. In the following sections, I provide the dos and don'ts of crafting Twitter bios.

Trying tips for great bios

The main point of your Twitter bio is to help others determine whether they want to follow you based on your mutual interests. People like to follow food trucks that

>> Are in their location

>> Serve a cuisine they enjoy or want to try

>> They can learn something from

Now the big question: What should you put in your bio to attract the right audience? To find the answer to that question, consider the following: What defines you? If someone asks you what your mobile food business does, how do you typically reply? Your reply is your bio, in a condensed form. Here are some guidelines to keep in mind:

>> **Include keywords.** If you want to be found on Twitter search or by the numerous Twitter apps that group people by interest, including relevant keywords in your profile is absolutely imperative. If your goal is to market your food truck locally, you may want to list your location plus your business and cuisine style as part of your Twitter bio. A good example of this is "NYC's go-to food truck for Asian fusion." As you can see, this message tells anyone reading it that this food truck is in New York City and serves Asian fusion cuisine. Search engines are also likely to find this Twitter profile in searches that utilize the keywords *NYC food truck.*

>> **Add a dash of personality.** Your personality is what makes you interesting to others and differentiates your truck from the others in your area. Don't be afraid to show off your personality in your bio; when done tastefully, it will unquestionably amplify it. Here's an example:

   • *The Grilled Cheese Truck: Chef driven grilled cheese . . . 'cause that's how we roll . . .*

   • *We'll tweet it daily!* | www.thegrilledcheesetruck.com

>> **Use short phrases.** Use phrases rather than complete sentences. This practice saves space while still conveying the same message. For example, instead of saying "I have 15 years of culinary experience," write "culinary veteran."

>> **Employ symbols.** I like using the pipe symbol (|) to separate key terms because it saves a bunch of space and makes a clear visual breaking point in your message. Alternatively, you can use a comma or a semicolon.

>> **Take advantage of abbreviations.** To save additional space, make sure you use abbreviations that the mobile food industry or your local foodie population understands. For example, say "GFT" instead of "Gourmet Food Truck."

You don't have to use all these suggestions; just stick to the ones that feel comfortable to you. Determine what defines you best and construct your bio, using that information. Think of your food truck bio as a concentrated version of your tweets.

Here are three food trucks bios that explain who these trucks are and what they sell:

>> *We're an Organic Vegan Food Truck from Orange County using local produce and top quality, organic ingredients. Gluten-free & Soy-free Options!*

Orange County, California | www.seabirdstruck.com

>> *Rickshaw Dumpling Truck: Tasty, healthy Dumplings on the go! Less than 300 cal for an order of 6 dumplings. Available for private events: call 212-796-6090 x4102*

New York City | www.rickshawdumplings.com

>> *We are the DMV's area truck! We specialize in authentic Venezuelan cuisine! Voted Best New Food Truck, Food Truck of the Year, Best South American Fare!*

DC and Arlington | www.arepazone.com

Steering clear of bio no-nos

WARNING

Here are a few things you definitely want to avoid when you write your food truck's Twitter bio:

>> **Don't leave the bio blank.** This one is self-explanatory.

>> **Don't use more than 160 characters.** Bios that are cut off mid-sentence appear both sloppy and unprofessional.

>> **Don't write something in the bio that has nothing to do with your food truck (for example, a popular quote).** You're limited on what you can write, so don't waste the space on text that doesn't describe your business.

>> **Don't mix languages unless your audience understands both.** Never risk confusing someone who finds your bio. By using multiple languages, people may think that you're not in their area and won't bother reading further to find out where you actually are.

>> **Don't write your bio in alternating caps.** BeSiDeS lOoKiNg UnPrOfEsSiOnAl, it can be difficult to read.

Sending tweets

Tweeting isn't difficult, but just as with any other conversational medium, if you want to look professional, you need to follow certain forms of etiquette. I cover these rules in the following sections.

REMEMBER

People enjoy Twitter because they get a lot of great information packaged in a concise and creative way. The key to using Twitter successfully is to avoid over-thinking every post. Be sure to have fun and experiment with new ideas. Much of the allure associated with food trucks is a result of their creative personalities. They emit a fun aura, from the trucks' names to their packaging (the paint job) to the attitude they communicate to their followers.

Considering the content

You may be wondering what to say. A good rule to follow is to keep it short and sweet. Generally, if you can't get your point across in 140 characters, you'll end up running over into multiple tweets, which misses the point of Twitter. Each tweet should be a stand-alone statement.

REMEMBER

Don't tweet about only yourself and what you're trying to get people interested in, whether that's your next location site or the fact that you're giving something away for free. Sure, you need to ask followers to check out your location, website, Facebook, and merchandise, but make sure those details aren't the point of every tweet. I suggest something close to a four to one ratio of promotional tweets to general discussion messages. What's the difference?

>> **Promotional tweets:** Everyone knows that you have a commercial interest and are trying to sell something. Food trucks are always tweeting about their offerings. How you do it is what's important. Be creative when you talk about your products or services and avoid becoming a promotional broken record. Tell people about what you're doing when you're parked at a sales location, testing a new menu item, or designing a new T-shirt; talk about what's happening with local laws regarding the mobile food scene in your area; and so on.

>> **General tweets:** General discussion can be pretty much whatever you want it to be. Generally, you don't need to tweet about your everyday functions such as eating, sleeping, or worse. But every rule has exceptions, so if you're unsure about a topic, test it out for yourself. If you really want to be open with your followers, tell them about yourself: the music you listen to, which local restaurants you like, where you hang out, and what you do when you're not working in your truck. What common interests are you likely to share with your fans? This type of sharing garners a real sense of kinship with your followers and helps your following grow.

TIP

People commonly use Twitter to share links. You have only 140 characters to work with, so instead of sharing a long URL (Uniform Resource Locator), use one of several URL-shortening services to shrink that link. I prefer to use the one at www.tinyurl.com. You can share links to direct people to your website or interesting articles you may have just read about the mobile food industry. People also love sharing their photos with the world, and some even break news with them.

WARNING

Be careful of clicking on malicious links. A lot of hackers on Twitter try to get influential people and businesses like you to click on a link and log into a site that looks like Twitter. If you're not familiar with someone sending you a link, avoid clicking the link to prevent any problems.

Determining the right frequency

How often should you tweet? Regularity is the key to success with all online activity for your truck. Most of your messages will be based around your location, but some will be personal, some will ask questions, and others will contain links. To gauge what to talk about, how often, and when to change the topic, think about how you talk to people you hang out with and imitate those patterns.

TIP

Discerning how much is too much can be difficult. If you feel like you're detailing every little event and your followers aren't growing organically or responding, you're probably overdoing it. You can start with tweeting every time your truck stops at a new location to operate. Then, you can tweet about 30 minutes before you plan to leave that location. These instances are a good place to start, but keep an eye out for people attempting to contact you through their own tweets. You can use their messages to start up a conversation that the rest of your followers can watch.

Engaging with your followers

REMEMBER

Twitter isn't all about you; it has to be about your customers, too, and the conversations you have with them. That's what the @ function is for (see the earlier section "Getting a handle on Twitter terms and functions"). When someone wants to comment on something you've tweeted, he'll usually use @ to reply. This reply appears in your stream and the public stream of anyone following you and/or the replier. This feature is cool; it means that people who may not already be following you can see that you're getting reactions, and they may end up coming over to your full feed to see what you're all about. Thus, the word about your food truck spreads.

TIP

Posting @ mentions of some of your favorite customers is akin to a DJ giving you a shout-out on the radio. It's exciting and customers love it. Find out the Twitter handles of your customers at certain locations and be sure to give them shout-outs. They're the connectors who will often share your location with others, especially others who aren't on Twitter.

Your tweets also create conversations that show you're an interesting person. These exchanges foster genuine relationships with followers and potential customers. And that's just when people come to you — it works even better the other way around, that is, when you jump into a topic that someone you're following is talking about. Be involved; have an opinion and bat it back and forth.

Look at what some of your followers tweet about, read their bios, and take a look at their linked websites to find those whom you genuinely want to talk with and find out more about.

Don't overdo the @reply function. If you find you're jumping into conversations and aren't getting a response or are sending too many short ("I agree" or "That's funny") replies, then you're overdoing it. Not only does this behavior make you look too needy and shallow, but the level of noise and interruption you're putting into your followers' streams may lead them to unfollow you.

Don't ever send someone you follow an @reply with a message to check out your site. Doing so is similar to shouting — it's rude, and it turns people off. Engage them another way first. Get involved in their discussions and add your thoughts. When you follow this route, people are far more likely to check you out on their own.

Dealing with negative Twitter comments

Twitter has shown its worth to the mobile food industry as a near-perfect tool to reach food truck followers quickly. But just like anything else in your personal or business life, this fantastic social media tool can have a negative side. As quickly as you can notify your followers about your future parking locations, so can comments from individuals with complaints be shared on your Twitter feed for the entire world to see.

So what do you do you when the world has access to negative comments that are made about you, your food, your truck's service, and ultimately your brand? You must deal with it. Here are some tips to follow when you run into one of these situations:

» **Don't take complaints personally.** This tip must be considered an absolute. If you ignore this advice, you may adopt an immediate defensive mentality, and it'll show up in your response. Replying in this tone may give you temporary solace; however, this attitude may also lead to more negative feedback and a loss of potential customers. Unless the situation demands immediate attention, spend a little time putting together a well-thought-out response.

For example, if a customer complains about your service, instead of jumping in without all the facts, you can explain to him that you'll get back to him shortly. Doing so gives you time to gather all the background information from your employees or at least enough time to come up with a well-planned response.

» **Remember that everyone wants to be heard.** You can't solve an issue unless you fully understand the situation from the customer's viewpoint. Let the upset customer or follower know that you want to hear about what happened to make him give you negative feedback. Ask him to contact you directly via email, because a limit of 140 characters doesn't allow for detailed explanations.

» **If the issue is resolved, ask the complainant to spread the word.** If the person with the complaint leaves your conversation happy, ask him to tell the world. Nothing is wrong with asking him to go back to Twitter and state that you've dealt with the issue. Think of it as asking for a letter of recommendation from a client. Don't toot your own horn — let your public do it. A third-party recommendation always goes much further than self-promotion in the landscape of the social media world.

Paging through Facebook

As most mobile food vendors discover early in their careers, social media can be the best way to build your food truck's national and local brand recognition. Facebook (www.facebook.com) is one of the strongest online branding tools at your disposal. With Facebook presently maintaining a population big enough to make it the third largest country in the world, you want to make sure you have a strong presence on the site. In the following sections, I explain how to establish and use your food truck's Facebook page, how to avoid having your page banned, and how to use Facebook ads.

REMEMBER

Making the most of your social media marketing efforts on Facebook helps you build your brand and establish your reputation. It also helps you keep an ear to the ground for what's being said about you and your food.

Setting up and using your Facebook Page the right way

You may already use Facebook for personal reasons, such as keeping up with friends and family, but the idea of running a business page on the world's largest social network may still seem a bit intimidating. Where in the world do you start, and how much work will it take? Don't worry! In the following sections, I explain how to start your food truck's page, add basic info, and take advantage of some fun Facebook features.

Starting the page and classifying your business

The first step in starting a new Facebook page for your food truck is to go to www.facebook.com and click Create a Page for a Celebrity, Band or Business (you'll find the link under the Sign Up button for personal accounts).

The next step is choosing how to classify your new food truck business page. Facebook provides you with six different classifications for creating a page:

>> Local business or place

>> Artist, band, or public figure

>> Company, organization, or institution

>> Entertainment

>> Brand or product

>> Cause or community

TIP

I always suggest food truck owners select the local business option unless they have trucks in more than one area of the country (in which case, I recommend choosing company or organization). This classification helps your page rank higher in more searches and provides relevant information fields on your food truck page.

After you make this selection, choose the category your food truck fits in (such as restaurant/café or food), and fill out your business name. The business option also asks for further information on your location, such as your address and phone number. After adding this information, check the "I Agree to Facebook Pages Terms" (of course, after you've read them) and click the Get Started button.

WARNING

You can't change your category and name after you create your page, so choose wisely; otherwise, you'll have to delete the entire page and start over.

Adding details about your food truck

After you start a page and classify your business (see the preceding section), the next step is to complete your page's basic information. Upload a photo that you want to be the first image new visitors see when they find your page. Ideally, this image should be your truck's logo or a picture of your truck (flip to Chapter 7 for basics on creating a logo).

Facebook will then ask you to invite your friends. You can do so by allowing Facebook to add people you've listed as contacts in your email provider, such as Gmail, Yahoo!, or Hotmail. Uncheck the options to "share this page on my wall" and "like this page." You don't want your page popping up in your friends' or family's news feeds until you're done creating it.

Your next task is to fill in your basic information. Add your website's URL (check out Chapter 15 for details on creating a website) and a brief biography about your truck in the About section. Make sure you focus on your food or your business philosophy in this section. If you've already created a Twitter bio (described earlier in this chapter), you can use that same blurb in this section as a short introduction about your truck.

Now click Edit Info and add the information you feel is most important for your visitors to know about your truck. As a local mobile food business, you likely want to add the days you're open as well as your hours of operation. Be sure to also fill in a description. The description differs from your About section in that you can share more in-depth information about your business. Be sure to add an email address and spend time adding pictures to the photos tab. This section is the place to share images of yourself, your food, your truck, or even guests who have been to your truck.

Making the most of special features

Make sure you take advantage of the various features Facebook business pages have to offer. Clicking on the Get Started button under your default image displays multiple steps you can take to make the most of your page. Here are four I feel are worth your time:

>> **Invite your friends:** When you invite your friends and family who you're already connected with, your posts show up in their timeline, which exponentially increases the number of people that see your updates.

>> **Post status updates:** By posting status updates, you're able to stay in constant contact with your friends and those who "like" your page. You can post your truck's schedule and location and any changes that take place

during the day. You can share interesting stories that occur at the truck or even correspond with people who "like" you if you get a slow moment in the truck.

>> **Promote this page on your website:** Social media is best used when it's shared among all your online platforms. This function provides you with a graphic link that allows those who visit your website to visit your Facebook page, "like" it, and even help share your information with their friends.

>> **Set up your mobile phone:** By selecting this option, you're able to use your smartphone to make Facebook updates, post comments, and track all the activity taking place on your business page, even when you aren't sitting in front of a computer.

TIP

To measure how all your Facebook efforts are panning out, make sure you take advantage of Facebook Insights by clicking the View Insights tab on the right-hand side of your Facebook page. This feature allows you to see how many people have become fans of your page or, in Facebook terms, "liked" your page. You can change the time frame to compare how many "likes" you received on one day versus another.

SPREADING THE WORD ABOUT A SWEET BREAK

If you've ever stayed at a DoubleTree hotel, you know its trademark: Every time a guest checks in, he receives a warm chocolate-chip cookie, which amounts to more than 21 million cookies annually. To celebrate the 25th anniversary of this tradition, in 2011, DoubleTree created a food truck (dubbed the CAREavan) and embarked on a 10-week, 10,000-mile, 50-city journey to deliver hundreds of thousands of smiles to weary workers, tired travelers, and local charities across the country through the pleasant surprise of a sweet, chocolate-chip-cookie treat.

DoubleTree used every possible social media channel to get the word out about the truck. Its Facebook page featured a live map of the truck's whereabouts. It held a Twitter contest, where select followers who used the hashtag #SweetBreak were awarded 250 cookies to share with their co-workers. DoubleTree even integrated YouTube and Foursquare into the celebration by posting short commercials on YouTube and listing the special at all DoubleTree locations around the country on Foursquare during the promotion.

Avoiding having your account banned

Outside of Twitter, Facebook is the primary means that food truck owners use to market their updated locations and expand their reach into their local foodie communities. One problem that some of these owners are starting to face is having their profiles banned from Facebook, and, unfortunately, this trend shows no signs of slowing down.

Imagine this scenario: You and your staff have sunk two to three hours a week for the last year building up a strong presence on Facebook. You have nearly 2,000 friends whom you interact with on a daily basis. Your analytics team shares that nearly 25 percent of your website's traffic comes from Facebook, and the catering side of your business collects at least two new leads per week from Facebook as well. So far, so good, right?

Then a problem surfaces. You log in to your account to find out it's been banned! Why? It's not because someone on your staff posted some inappropriate content. The issue is that at the time you created the account to market your food truck business, you created it on a personal profile Facebook page.

Facebook is very clear in its rules of use for personal profiles versus Facebook for Business (you can find this info in the "Registration and Account Security" section at www.facebook.com/terms.php). This section states the following:

> Facebook users provide their real names and information, and we need your help to keep it that way. Here are some commitments you make to us relating to registering and maintaining the security of your account:
>
> You will not provide any false personal information on Facebook, or create an account for anyone other than yourself without permission.

WARNING

What these rules state is that by creating a personal profile using your business name, you're in breach of the user agreement you agreed to when you first created the account, and you risk having your account permanently banned if Facebook finds out. If your account is banned, all the time you've spent building up friends and creating networks is nullified in an instant; you can't retain any of your friends or networks because Facebook doesn't provide any notice to either the profile creator or the creator's friends.

A personal profile within Facebook is all about you, not your business. This profile provides your real name, your likes and dislikes, your location and other various informational items about *you*. This personal profile is the means by which you're able to connect with family, friends, classmates, and co-workers, and these people become your "friends."

A *Facebook Page* is the proper way to promote your mobile food business within Facebook. The Facebook Page looks similar to a personal profile, but it's not the same thing.

TIP

If you need a clear way to distinguish between the two types of pages, look for the Like button at the top of the page. This button is a clear sign that the page is a Facebook Page and not a personal profile page.

If you happen to be one of those business owners who has already created a personal profile page for your food truck business, you still have time to correct this error. Head to Facebook and create your new business page with the guidance I provide in the earlier section "Setting up and using your Facebook Page the right way"; this process should take only a few minutes. After you complete this step, go to your original business page and begin sending out regular messages to your friends with a link to the new page. Hopefully, before Facebook catches on to your previous mistake, you'll be able to convert all your friends into "likes" on your new page. You should also modify the old page to be specifically about you as soon as possible. By following this step in conjunction with creating your new business page, you may be able to avoid being banned altogether.

Determining whether advertising on Facebook is right for your food truck

Facebook is a platform that lets you reach millions of potential customers by creating a free page for your business, but Facebook also offers a paid advertising option in which you promote your food truck's Facebook Page, website, or current promotion to people who match a specific set of demographics you choose.

The cost of Facebook advertising has two forms: either you pay every time someone clicks on your advertisement (CPC) or you pay every time someone sees your ad (CPM). Whichever method you choose, you set a maximum daily budget for your Facebook advertising costs, which you can adjust at any time.

This form of advertising is different from other online advertising because Facebook has the demographic data of its users. Facebook lets you know the age, location, and gender of the people who click on your ads; you can get this detailed feedback for each ad campaign you run. Facebook provides you with current statistics on how many people have either clicked or seen your ad, so you're able to determine whether those people are being converted into added views of your web page or increased customers at your service window. By using Facebook's feedback, you can hone your next campaign to better target new customers.

WARNING

To maximize the effectiveness of any ad campaign, you need to know who your customers are. If you know who your target market is, Facebook provides an excellent platform for advertising to them, however, if you don't have a firm grasp of your customer demographics, using a precise advertising method like Facebook may not work for you. The end result of a poorly targeted ad campaign is that you throw away money that may have been better spent in more traditional advertising mediums. For details on figuring out your target customers, check out Chapter 3.

TIP

If you decide to move forward with Facebook ads, check out www.facebook.com/business/products/ads, and keep the following tips in mind:

>> Include a call to action in your ad; in other words, create a request or direction for the customer to do something. For example, your call to action may be for viewers to go to your website to find out the details of a giveaway or event you're attending or to download a coupon for a discount the next time they visit your truck.

>> Keep your offers up-to-date.

>> Geo-target your campaigns well. If you operate in a small area, don't advertise anywhere outside of that area, because although you may have fans around the country, an ad won't be any good for a fan who isn't able to visit your truck.

TIP

For more info on how to maximize your Facebook marketing efforts, check out the latest edition of *Facebook Marketing For Dummies,* by John Hayden, Paul Dunay, and Richard Krueger (John Wiley & Sons).

Checking In with Foursquare

In 2015, more than 68 percent of people in the United States used smartphones, an increase of 35 percent over 2011. Over 60 million of these phone users are actively using Foursquare, a geo-location application that allows them to *check-in* to businesses around the world, show their friends the places they're visiting, and leave feedback and tips. As a mobile food business owner, you can leverage this social media platform by offering deals to customers who check in.

Although most food trucks don't have physical storefronts, Foursquare is a social media tool that, used properly, can still help you increase your mobile business as well as your profits. Listing your food truck business on Foursquare and using Foursquare successfully are easy processes, which I walk you through in the following sections.

Setting up an account for your food truck

To get started on this task, head over to www.foursquare.com. To create your account, you're given the options to sign up with your Facebook account or with an email address. Because the Facebook option ties your Foursquare account to your business Facebook account, I recommend using a general business email address so other staff members can control the account if you choose not to do it on your own and so your personal information can remain private. From there, fill in your business information to set up your account. (If you already have a personal account, log in and skip to the first step in the following list.) After you've logged in to your account, you need to claim your business and provide relevant information about it. Just follow these steps:

1. **Type your business name into the search field on the top right side of the page. When you see your venue on the list, click on it.**

   If your food truck doesn't show up in the search, you need to add it to the system by searching for your location. You're asked if you want to add the venue; select "yes." Then fill out the business form (business name, mailing address, type of business, and contact information) and submit. When your venue has been created, go on to Step 2.

2. **Click the Claim Here button to claim your mobile food business.**

   Verify the information listed for your business.

3. **Click Continue Claiming this Venue and provide the info requested.**

   You're asked whether your business is a chain; select the relevant answer. Because your food truck is mobile, I suggest you select a Moving Target as a venue. Foursquare has a number of prerequisites that deal specifically with moving targets, but don't worry; your food truck meets them all.

   If you choose not to set up your venue as a moving target, I recommend that when you create the venue, you choose the address where your truck is most often located or where you park your truck (such as at your commercial kitchen), in order to maximize the number of times your truck shows up in the Places tab organically.

After claiming your location, you can log in to see who has checked in at any time, and you can set up deals for Foursquare users who check in at your truck (I cover this topic in detail in the next section).

TIP

After you've claimed your listing, Foursquare will send you a window cling for your service window. Be sure to put it up immediately so that anyone walking by will know you're on Foursquare.

Social media platforms are designed to be tied together. When you decide to utilize a Foursquare special or reward, tweet about it on Twitter and share it on your Facebook Page. The more involved your customers know you are, the more likely they are to track down your truck.

Attract More Business with an Instagram Account

If you haven't created a food truck Instagram account yet, pause your reading and get over there to get that step out of the way and come back to finish this section.

All you will need is a username that ties into your food truck brand (hopefully it matches your Facebook and Twitter user names), and a few photos to get started. One of the things food truck vendors need to understand is that more and more consumers are paying attention to social media while they are outside their homes and offices, so nothing will grab their attention and draw them to your service window than some perfectly timed photos of your business and the food you offer.

Today's social media society thrives on exclusivity. Not only do customers want what everyone else has, but they want it before everyone else.

Followers yearn for VIP treatment and first class service in whatever form we can get it. Those on Instagram are no different. One of the best ways to provide exclusivity to your Instagram followers is posting a special code in the form of a photo and letting your followers share it at your service window to get a discount. Giving them, and only them (don't post it on any other social media platforms), this special attention is what will keep them coming back. Just make sure that posting these types of deals doesn't become an everyday occurrence. Not only is it showing appreciation to your food truck Instagram account followers, but the lines at your food truck should also see a spike in traffic.

Instagram hasn't always been about marketing and advertising for brands. In fact, most people view Instagram as a private place to share photos of themselves, their friends, and family. So make sure your food truck Instagram account isn't strictly setup to sell. Keep in mind that most people following your truck are going to want an insider's view on what's really going on behind the scenes.

Considering Other Social Media Platforms

With every passing day, another software developer seems to come up with a new application to help connect the world. I show you the current major players earlier in this chapter. Other sites you may choose to put into your food truck social media arsenal include the sites in the following sections.

Pinterest

Numerous food truck vendors have joined Pinterest, the popular visual bookmarking tool. Pinterest, which launched in 2010, has grown to more than 100 million users. Every day, people use the website to "pin" images and videos to their personal pin boards so they can save and share the things they love. The site gets social when people follow each other and repin or comment on each other's pins.

The vast majority of Pinterest users are women between the ages of 25 and 34, so it's a natural place for mobile food business to spend time if they want to connect with that target audience. If you are wondering how to use it, it is easy to get creative inspiration by reviewing other food truck pinboards (www.pinterest.com).

Pinterest is a place for storytelling. Help consumers become emotionally connected to your food truck brand by pinning content that reveals more about your brand personality than just your menu items.

This platform is a social destination, so get involved with its community. Find active Pinterest members and build relationships with them by following them, repinning their content and commenting on their pins. The commenting feature in Pinterest is still greatly underutilized, and you can stand out by using it frequently.

The best part of Pinterest is that you don't have to go it alone. Create group pinboards and invite other users to pin content to those boards. For example, ask customers to pin pictures of them before they eat one of your menu items or while they wait in line to give their order. You also could hold a contest to crowdsource pins. Ask customers to review your food on your website and pin a quote from their review to a special contest pinboard. You benefit from more reviews and a pinboard that's filled with testimonials.

Yelp

Yelp (www.yelp.com) is a social networking, user review, and local search website. Yelp had more than 54 million unique monthly visitors as of data from the end of 2010.

Yelp enables you to read and respond to reviews about your food truck business. As a small business owner, you need to understand that — with or without you — conversations will take place about your business. Yelp provides a constructive — and ultimately beneficial — platform for you to receive criticism about your food truck, respond to criticism, and take the appropriate action.

Although Yelp may not be a necessity for every small business owner, I strongly recommend that every food truck business use it. Yelp provides an opportunity to converse with your patrons about your menu or services and improve them if needed. Another perk to being listed on Yelp is that it increases your truck's search engine visibility and encourages people to socialize and recommend your business to their friends.

Although you can read the reviews your customers give without signing up for an account, if you want to interact and respond to their reviews, you need an account. Just go to `www.biz.yelp.com/support` for a walk-through of the process of creating your business listing. If you find your truck is already listed on Yelp, you need to submit a request to Yelp via email to unlock the owner control. After you have access to your account, you can interact with the individuals who write comments (positive or negative) associated with your food truck.

Using Yelp gives you a direct conduit to your customers. It's an open window into your business and to the way you run it. Building a good rapport with the people who comment can lead to readers seeing how you deal with certain situations and help them determine whether they want to do business with you. At the same time, it gives you the chance to mend fences with individuals who may not have been thrilled with your food and service and offer suggestions on how to correct their problems.

Klout

Klout (`www.klout.com`) is a website that provides social media analytics to measure a user's influence across his social network. The analysis is based on data taken from sites such as Twitter, Facebook, Foursquare, and YouTube and measures the size of a person's network, the content created, and how other people interact with that content.

Your daily Klout Score ranges from 1 to 100, with higher scores representing a wider and stronger sphere of influence. Klout uses unpublished variables to measure True Reach, Amplification Probability, and Network Score:

>> **True Reach** represents the size of your engaged audience and is based on your followers and friends who actively listen and react to your messages.

>> **Amplification Probability** is the likelihood that your messages will generate actions (retweets, @messages, "likes," and comments).

>> **Network Score** indicates how influential your engaged audience is.

Your final Klout Score is a representation of how successful you are at engaging your audience and how big an impact your messages have on others. Getting started on Klout is as easy as simply going to www.klout.com and logging in with your Twitter or Facebook account. After you've connected one of those services with your account, Klout does the rest.

Chapter 17

Attracting and Retaining Your Customers

ew things are more satisfying than watching your service window fill with familiar faces. Repeat customers — the kind who keep coming back day after day and week after week — are crucial for the success of any food truck. Although going after new customers is important, building loyalty and gaining return customers are much easier and less expensive. Consider this: If you can get every customer to return once, you'll double your business.

But how do you turn a new customer into a repeat one? In this chapter, I explain how to truly understand your customers and exceed their expectations. I also describe how to improve your service, use email marketing, come up with catchy slogans, and satisfy unhappy customers so they return to your truck.

Getting a Handle on Who Your Customer Really Is

You're a smart and savvy business owner and know everything you need to know about your food truck. You've researched your target audience (see Chapter 3) and developed the proper offline and social media strategies (see Chapters 15 and 16) to get your followers to find your truck. But do you *really* know who your food truck's customer is? And how well should a food truck owner really know his customers anyway?

The truth is that your customers are smart and savvy, too. You can't fool them with common marketing pitches because they know when you're just pitching them. Stop pitching and start focusing on getting to know them, so you can convert them from merely customers to loyal followers.

In the following sections, I list a few important traits of the typical food truck follower, explain the differences between knowing and understanding followers, describe what you can do to observe and listen to them, and provide pointers on walking through a typical customer experience.

Figuring out a few traits of food truck followers

The assimilation of social media as a basis of communication in the mobile food industry has altered the way consumers are able to find their next meal. The once-static food patrons have become dynamic social food truck followers. This new breed of customer shapes the way you market your business, products, and services. Are you aware of the defining characteristics of food truck followers?

>> **They're hyper-connected.** The smartphone is the constant companion of today's food truck fan. The food truck follower treats his smartphone more like a pocket knowledge base than a phone.

>> **They readily reach out to peers and influencers.** Social media has given your customers full access to the opinions and experiences of their family, friends, and the people they trust. People care about what others think and certainly like to draw upon the past experiences of those who may have tried out something before they've had the chance. If three friends tell this individual that they love a particular food truck or a specific item on your menu, he may be a bit more inclined to track you down and make a purchase.

>> **They're constantly researching.** Review sites like Yelp, Foursquare, Google Places, and so on offer customers the opportunity to voice their praises and

complaints about food truck cuisine, service, or even the overall business for future customers to read and evaluate. The good, the bad, and the ugly about past customers' experiences is available for research and review.

>> **They share what they think of you.** It's not uncommon for food truck followers to use the very sites they use to research your food truck to also share their thoughts about your food. The beauty of many of these tools is the fact that you can respond to these questions, comments, and concerns quickly. If one of your food truck followers lodges a complaint through social networks or review sites, you can respond accordingly and much faster than before social media made its way onto the scene.

>> **They expect food trucks to engage them.** Due to the real-time nature of social media and the precedent set by many food truck owners of giving nearly instant response to customer feedback, many food truck followers expect the same of all trucks they visit.

REMEMBER

Don't let this unleashed communication platform get the best of you. Focused research, a strong strategy, and a dedicated effort on your part will help you inter-act with food truck customers and turn them into loyal followers. The way you communicate with current and potential customers has been revolutionized (as you discover in Chapter 16). Your followers are at the wheel, and food truck own-ers need to have their proverbial finger on the pulse of what's driving their audi-ence. The best way to do this is to listen to your customers and observe those who stick around your truck long enough to eat the meal they just purchased (see the later section "Observing and listening to your followers" for more information).

Knowing versus understanding your followers

There's a difference between *knowing* who your customer is and *understanding* your customer. One mistake some truck owners make is that they spend most of their time on the former and too little time on the latter. Ultimately, this strategy results in failure. Why? If you don't understand your customers, you won't have a full understanding of their needs, and if you don't understand their needs, they won't turn into loyal followers.

As a food truck owner, you need to both know and understand your followers:

>> **Knowing your customers** typically entails collecting information by merely watching who walks up to your service window. It means you know who your customers are demographically and what they're ordering.

>> **Understanding your customers** helps you deliver a product and service that meet not only their current needs but also their evolving and future needs.

Do you understand your customers? Ask yourself these questions:

>> **Why are customers interested in my truck?** By understanding what attracts customer to your truck, you can either improve on these specific areas or use the data to change the other aspects of your truck to attract even more paying customers.

>> **Which menu items are commonly overlooked?** If you have menu items that just don't sell, you need to know why they're not being ordered. Is there an ingredient that just doesn't work? Or can you do something different in the preparation of these menu items to improve sales? If improving a menu item still doesn't work, it may be time to pull it from the menu altogether.

>> **Why are customers going to my competitors' trucks in addition to mine? Why are some abandoning my truck altogether?** Do your competitors serve something, such as a dessert, that you could easily add to your menu? Or is one of your competitors just providing a much better product than you are? With this information, you can make educated changes to your menu selection or how you serve your customers.

>> **Why do my customers give word-of-mouth referrals to competitors' trucks but not mine?** Understanding why you aren't getting this type of feedback can help you improve your product and service so your customers spread the word about your business to their friends and family.

>> **How are my customers' behaviors and preferences changing and evolving?** You need to be aware of and listen to your customers so you can stay in front of any type of changes in market preference. Being able to determine whether a particular culinary trend is picking up steam in your market and making changes *before* your competitors keeps you on the leading edge of the industry, which portrays you as a leader and not a follower.

Each of these questions represents an opportunity for you. If you understand your customers' perspective in each instance and offer a solution, you'll be in a position to deliver a valuable, memorable, and referral-worthy meal.

Observing and listening to your guests

To understand your customers (as I recommend in the preceding section), you must know what motivates them to choose your truck over the trucks of your competitors. The best way to find out is to observe and listen to your customers and then analyze this information to assist you in making improvements.

Your food truck's success should be centered on your customers, so think about them, what they need from you, and how you can meet their needs. To improve your service, you need to know what needs improving.

Although you may not have a lot of time to spend outside of your truck, you can learn a great deal from your customers by speaking with them directly or by observing how they act while they're standing in line. You may choose to observe and/or talk to customers from the service window or by walking around the truck and engaging with them directly. Ask your customers questions, such as how they found out about your truck or why they choose your truck over another one parked in the area. These questions can provide helpful information that you can later use to make adjustments to your menu or even your marketing strategy.

As you're observing and interacting with your customers, pay attention to their body language. Do they appear to be agitated? If so, you may find out that they think the wait in line is too long. You can then look for ways to speed up the time it takes your staff to prepare your food or maybe even have a staff member take pre-orders from the people standing in line so you can minimize the unassisted wait a customer has to deal with. Nipping these issues in the bud before they become a real problem can show your customers that you do care about them and that you're willing to make changes to improve your service before they stop coming to your truck altogether.

Walking through a typical customer experience

Because your customers will typically take their meals and leave your truck to eat them, it may be difficult to fully understand and observe their tendencies as you might if you owned a restaurant. To understand what customers see and feel when they walk up to your truck, take the time to do frequent walk-throughs of the area outside your truck from the customers' perspective. In other words, put on "customer eyes." Take the following steps:

1. **Walk up to your truck and pretend you're seeing your truck for the first time.**

   Take a good look at what your customers see:

   - Does the truck's appearance match the concept you're trying to create?

   - Do you have interesting focal points for your customers to see when they're in line?

   - How easy is it for a line to form?

   - Do you have a sensible traffic flow pattern?

   - If you provide service after the sun goes down, is the lighting right for your customers to feel safe? Does it give them the ability to see your menu?

   - Most importantly, is everything clean?

Pay close attention to all the details; your customers certainly will. Something as small as papers taped on the side of your truck can give the impression that you're running an amateur operation, besides the fact that they're a complete eyesore. Change what needs to be changed to create a memorable look and feel for your food truck. Showcase your business personality through its design and make sure your business personality matches that of your customers. (Chapter 7 gives you more information on how to present your vehicle.)

2. **Do a walk-through of a typical customer transaction:**

   - Does someone greet you when you walk up to the truck, even if you aren't in line?

   - Does the staff appear friendly, efficient, and helpful?

   - When you make it up to the front of the line, what happens? Does the server pay attention to you and make eye contact with you?

TIP

Have a friend whom the staff doesn't know do the walk-through for you. Have her play the role of the type of customer you serve and ask for feedback on each step of the experience.

3. **Focus on the areas in which you can improve.**

   Make a list of each item that needs improving and come up with suggestions for improvement. If you can, present the items to your employees in a group meeting and have them brainstorm with you to come up with the best solutions.

   For example: Suppose you notice that things get crowded when customers are waiting for their meal to be served but step out of line so the next customer can place his order. What can you do to change the traffic flow? Is there a city garbage receptacle or bench taking up much-needed standing room?

Setting and Exceeding Expectations

Expectations are the nonverbal agreements you establish with your customers about the food and service you and your staff provide them. These may be things such as the quantity or quality of your food, but they may also include the timing involved in getting an order completed or even the plating and appearance of their meal as you serve it. These expectations are the basis on which your customers evaluate your food truck and measure their satisfaction with it. The more you meet — and even exceed — your customers' expectations, the more likely those folks are to become loyal followers of your food truck. In the following sections, I explain how to set and exceed expectations for your food truck in order to build and retain your following.

Setting expectations for your food truck

Meeting customer expectations is essential for creating repeat customers; if you don't, your customers will seek out an alternative to your truck, no matter how good your food tastes.

REMEMBER

The process of setting customer expectations requires careful attention to the beginning of the initial customer experience. Your job is to describe what you provide, how you prepare it, and what the customer should expect. If you don't make this clear from the start, customers may define their own expectations, which may or may not match the expectations you want them to have.

You can start this process as soon as your service staff greets each new customer. Ask each customer whether she's been to the truck in the past. If she hasn't, explain the style of cuisine, the ingredients, or each menu item and any special cooking techniques used, such as how long your beef brisket is marinated before it ever gets on the truck. If a customer is a regular but you have a new menu item, you can provide her with this same type of information and even compare it to other food she's already had. If you've modified your operations, such as preparing a dish in a new way or a new chef trying a new cooking technique, share this information with your customer so you're able to set her expectations from those she may already have.

Going beyond your customers' expectations

After you set your customers' expectations, set a goal for your staff to exceed them. Exceeding expectations simply means delivering your food on time and as advertised while at the same time providing your customers with excellent service (see the next section for details). This formula leads to long-lasting relationships with the individuals who frequent your food truck.

REMEMBER

You can exceed expectations with simple things, such as giving a first-time customer a sample of a couple of your menu items to help her determine which one she wants to order. Or if a customer orders multiple items off your menu, throw in a free side item or drink. You don't necessarily need to give anything away for free; just add more value or over deliver to each customer. You can do so by something as simple as a smile on a rainy day or a hand-written "thank you" on each receipt. You'll find that using these tactics is a great way to create buzz around your business and to get your customers referring others to your truck.

Consider two food trucks with comparable menus, meals, and prices:

>> One delivers its services strictly to expectations. The service is good but somewhat impersonal. Customers get what they pay for — no more, no less.

>> The second food truck owner has set a different standard for his employees. Returning customers are greeted by name when they step up to the service window. The individual taking the order remembers the menu item the customer ordered and enjoyed on her last visit and suggests another menu item that he feels the customer may like as well. The chef even comes to the service window before the customer leaves to make sure everything is prepared to her satisfaction.

At the first truck, the customers' expectations were met. At the second, the customers' expectations were exceeded because of the way they were treated. It didn't cost any more to provide this extra service, but it did require a customer-focused business owner and staff.

Always Treating Customers the Right Way

If you want customers to return to your service window, you need to offer them the best possible service and products and make them feel respected, welcome, and appreciated. The moment a customer feels uneasy doing business with you or any of your staff is the beginning of the end of your relationship with that customer. Keep your customers happy, and they'll keep coming back — and suggest to others that they check you out, too. Here are some guidelines:

>> **Make a great first impression.** Encourage your employees to approach each interaction with a new customer as they would a job interview; servers need to be helpful and friendly. Explain to your staff that this type of behavior increases the chance that the customer will not only leave a tip but also return to tip again in the future.

REMEMBER

People are more loyal to people than they are to places. This idea, paired with an ongoing server training program, encourages your wait-staff to connect with customers on a personal level, thus building loyalty rather than just serving them a meal.

>> **Recognize that knowledge is power.** Your staff should know your menu backward and forward and be able to not only offer great suggestions but also relay the components of every dish. Nothing is better than a great recommendation from someone on the inside. This advice also applies to selling specials as well as add-ons, such as a side dish, beverage, or dessert. In the end, it all adds up and increases your bottom line.

TIP

Staff should be knowledgeable about other things related to the meal as well (for example, a great wine pairing for the meal a customer plans to take home to eat). Their knowledge adds value, which, in addition to providing great food or service, gives your customers an incentive to come back.

- >> **Connect to every customer's ego.** A knowledgeable staff is important, but one of the best ways to get your customers coming back for more is to make them feel important. Ego is the easiest way to connect with your customer, and it's free! How can you do this? Have your staff learn the names of your customers and use their names throughout their experience at your food truck. There's no better way to make a customer feel important. When customers get to know you and your staff, they connect with more than just the food.

- >> **Set an example.** Keep in mind that your staff is watching you. Whether or not you see them doing it, your staff is looking to you for clues about what's important, what's acceptable, and what won't be tolerated. Just as children imitate their parents, your behavior sets the tone for your entire staff.

- >> **Be consistent.** Despite your best efforts, some customers won't be completely satisfied and will go somewhere else. It's a natural part of doing business, and you need to be able to accept that. Making constant changes to your menu and recipes in an attempt to please everyone only drives away the customers who were happy with your food truck the way it was.

REMEMBER

Keeping things consistent allows happy customers to get the same food and service that brought them back in the first place. If they return to your truck only to find that you've changed things, they may not be as happy, and they may decide to go elsewhere for their next meal.

Establishing Email Lists to Promote Special Deals

REMEMBER

Email marketing is great from a customer retention standpoint, not only because it enables you to include promotional information but also because it helps you develop a more intimate relationship with your customers. Email is personal. When a customer gives you access to his inbox, it's a sign that the customer trusts you and your brand and wants to further the relationship. You can use your email list to update customers on what you're up to, share personal business stories, and include information about promotions and special events you plan to attend or host to bring people back to your service window.

So how do you build an email list? After a customer has finished ordering her meal and is waiting for it, have your staff ask her to provide an email address (or business card) for future correspondence. You can add this information to a paper list that you keep near the cash register and then enter into a computer later, or you can use a point-of-sale (POS) system that allows for this type of data to be manually entered at the time of purchase. There are many Internet email marketing sites you can use to monitor your email lists online. A few options are A Weber www.aweber.com, Constant Contact www.constantcontact.com, and Mail Chimp www.maillchimp.com. Explain that your food truck occasionally offers specials and free meals to its most valued customers and that you'd like to include the customer's email on the list. Most likely, customers will provide their email addresses, which allows you to create a database of information (including email, name, and zip code) about your customers. You can ask for more information, but many customers are leery of providing too much personal information at the point of purchase. If you want to gather this information at a later date, you can request it during an email marketing campaign.

Use this database to distribute special offers to previous customers and drive business to your service window on slow days. For example, if your food truck constantly sells out quickly on the weekends but typically sees little business on Tuesday nights, send out an email on Tuesday morning to invite customers to redeem a gift certificate for a free side dish. Explain that the offer is valid only for that Tuesday evening, and encourage your customers to stop by and redeem the gift. Suddenly, your line will fill up with customers who may have otherwise had dinner at home that Tuesday night. By reaching out to your customers with a few simple emails and giving them a reason to visit you again, you can turn a slow night into a busy one.

The goal of this strategy is to keep your business clearly positioned in the forefront of your customers' minds. Your customers likely won't think of your business unless prompted by an email, advertisement, or special occasion. In fact, they may always think of your truck as their Friday lunch stop unless you give them a reason to track you down on Tuesday night as well. Make it your goal to casually remind them of the fun they had the last time they visited your truck, and invite them to repeat the experience with a special offer. By doing so, you're encouraging repeat business by reaching out to customers who you know already enjoy your services. It sets them apart and lets them see how much you value their loyalty.

Distinguishing Your Food Truck from Your Competitors with a Catchy Line

So your truck is all decked out in a fabulous wrap and has great food and service that exceeds customer expectations, yet the line at the service window is never as long as you think it should be. You've spent all your time creating your concept and menu and still wonder why it's not working for you.

The vast majority of food trucks have good food, good service, and wonderful concepts, so your truck may not be as special in the customers' eyes as you think it is.

Put yourself in the shoes of the individuals who walk up to your truck. Why should they come to your food truck as opposed to the other trucks in your city? The truth is that if you don't stand out from your customers' other options, they probably won't give you a shot, and your chances of building and retaining followers will decrease.

No two food trucks are the same (except in the case of franchises). So what makes your truck special or different from any other in your area? If the lines at your food truck aren't as long as you want, you need to better articulate the essence of your mobile restaurant and your menu so people will have a reason to come to your place instead of your competitors'. You need to create and announce an identity for your food truck that makes it unique.

So how can you do that? Follow these easy steps and you'll be on your way to creating differentiation between your truck and others:

1. **Make a list of the real benefits or advantages that you currently offer to your customers.**

   Think about what's special about your mobile bistro. Is it your food? Your service? Your locations? Your menu selection?

   TIP

   Ask your customers, your staff, and friends and family what makes your truck special or different. Perhaps you have a unique recipe that people really appreciate and come to enjoy, or one of your cooks comes out of the truck and greets the customers in line, or you have bilingual servers who can communicate with some customers in their native languages.

   Following are some aspects that can help you determine your unique selling proposition (USP):

   - A wide variety of dishes on the menu
   - Unique, ethnic meals or menu items
   - Reasonable prices
   - High-quality food
   - The originality of the dishes
   - Fantastic presentation
   - Excellent service
   - Any other distinct advantage that you may have or can provide that your competitors don't.

2. **Make a second list of benefits or special things that your competitors offer but you don't.**

   Do they have a big lot that they park in with permanent seating? Do they offer a location at a popular bar that you don't go to? Do they have a super-chef with a reputation that you can't offer? You can use their perceived advantages to create your own. For example, if your competition regularly parks in a location next to a bar and you don't, you can take advantage of that aspect and market yourself as a family-friendly business.

3. **Compare the two lists you've made and write down the top five advantages and/or differentiators that make your place unique. Then combine them into one short sentence or phrase.**

By doing so, you'll come up with a powerful and memorable tag line or differentiation statement, and you'll be ahead of your competitors who simply advertise their trucks in the most traditional ways.

Consider the tag line from the Cinnamon Snail — a vegan food truck that operates in New Jersey and caters to customers who follow strict vegan diets — whose slogan is "Food to Inspire Peace and Bliss."

REMEMBER

People respond to short, remarkable messages. If you can articulate the essence of your truck in a few precise words and consistently use them in all your marketing materials (business cards, letterhead, email messages, website, and so on) to promote your food truck business, you should be able to stand out from the crowd.

Converting Unsatisfied Guests into Repeat Customers

When you first open your food truck for business, you'll feel that you have to retain every single customer you can, but don't allow yourself and your staff to become a proverbial doormat for customers. Unsatisfied customers are an inevitable consequence of running a food truck, no matter how committed you are to making all your customers happy. Sometimes a customer will be justified in being upset, but other times the situation will be entirely out of your (or your staff's) control. Following are some strategies to assist you in diffusing these situations and making the customer feel better — perhaps even turning her into a repeat customer.

>> **Create written policies.** Before you open your service window for the first time, take the time to create written policies regarding returns or refunds and be sure to place them where customers can see them. If possible, try to include this same information on your receipts. By doing this, you assure that there can be no doubt about your food truck's terms of sale. (Flip to Chapter 12 for more information on handling returns and refunds.)

- » **Communicate in a calm voice.** Customers get irate from time to time, but it's your duty to handle them in a calm, collected fashion. You want to keep the energy level low-key in an effort to diffuse a potentially volatile situation and prevent matters from spinning out of control. Train your employees how to be nonconfrontational with customers and use tact when speaking. A calm demeanor may be all it takes to calm down an irritated customer.

- » **Use empathy.** Showing empathy doesn't necessarily mean agreeing with the unhappy customer. It simply means that you let the customer know you understand she's upset, and you want to calmly gather the information you need to best resolve the situation. By showing that you care about the customer and her feelings, you help the situation to remain calm rather than escalate into angry words. Just stating "I'm sorry that you're having a bad experience" can often diffuse a volatile situation.

- » **Find the problem.** You must identify the true nature of the problem, and you have to ask the customer some questions to do so. Resolution of any problem is only possible when you have a clear understanding of its underlying cause. After the customer has told you what the problem is, repeat it back to her in your own words so you're sure you know what caused the situation.

  For example, you can ask something like, "How was your meal today?"; if the customer responds with "It was cold, and it took ten minutes for me to get it," you can say, "I'm terribly sorry for the long delay and that after waiting so long, the food even came to you cold." You can then work on finding a solution.

- » **Find potential solutions.** If the problem has potential solutions that you can actually offer, relay these solutions to the customer in a calm manner. Maybe the meal can simply be replaced with one that meets her specifications or perhaps a coupon for a free meal on her next visit will suffice. Also ask the customer what she wants you to do, in a nondefensive manner. Often, what will make her happy is less than you may have offered. If you throw in the "something extra" you were prepared to give all along, you may have a customer for life.

- » **Understand that some people just won't be happy.** You must accept that despite your best efforts, some customers will never be happy. If you've exhausted all possible options and the customer remains hostile and unhappy, you just have to accept the fact that this person probably won't be a repeat customer.

REMEMBER

Don't let one bad experience get you or a staff member down. As long as you aren't consistently running into customers you can't solve problems for, you'll be able to attract new customers who will make up for the few who get away. Losing a customer is never a good thing, but sometimes those losses are opportunities to concentrate on growth and staff mentoring and support. Arming new employees with the skills they need to resolve conflict is necessary for your food truck business, because sooner or later, that unhappy customer will walk up to your truck.

IN THIS CHAPTER

Adding a truck to your fleet

Considering catering, franchising, and opening a brick-and-mortar restaurant

Making over your brand if it isn't working

Putting your food truck business up for sell

Chapter 18

What's Next? Determining the Future of Your Food Truck Business

You plan for your vacations, your children's education, and other big events in your life. So why hesitate about planning for the future of your food truck business? Most truck owners rarely put transition planning at the top of their to-do list, until they're forced to do so. Mapping out or projecting the future of your food truck can have an enormous impact on where it heads. Whether you want to expand or sell your business, planning ahead (or at least knowing what options you have) offers you a head start.

Have you been thinking about adding another vehicle to your fleet? How about providing catering or banquet services to expand your reach into feeding your community? Perhaps your food truck brand has grown to the point that you think it may be time to franchise it, or maybe you want to open a brick-and-mortar restaurant based on your truck's brand. I discuss all these options in this chapter, along with the possibilities of rebranding your concept and selling your business.

REMEMBER

The best way to manage your food truck business is to constantly ask yourself, "What's next?" The answer may be a small adjustment in your food truck's operation, an additional sales location, changes to the menu, or a new marketing strategy. Just keep in mind that there'll always be something next.

Expanding Your Fleet

Are you consistently being asked to bring your food truck to more areas of the city that just one can't handle? If so, this is a great sign that you've created a concept and menu that's accepted by your community, who are looking to you to provide this service even more than you already do. The problem with this scenario is that your truck can be in only one place at a time. So how can you remedy this situation? Expansion!

Expanding your food truck business to a second truck (or more!) requires careful planning on your part. A benefit to expanding your fleet is that your business will be able to be in more than one place at a time, which means more sales. The downside to expansion is that you'll be required to invest in another vehicle as well as additional staff to operate it. The decision to extend the scope of your food truck empire should be a result of thoughtful deliberation on various factors, including the financial status of your business, the logistics involved in making a change, and even the state of your emotional readiness. Before you embark on an expansion of your business, you need to consider the items in the following sections.

Evaluating economies of scale

It's a simple fact: Adding a second truck to your business means you'll have to buy more stuff. By increasing your purchasing volume, though, you may be able to get lower prices for everything, including your menu ingredients and your packaging. You may even receive discounts on your commercial kitchen if you need more time to prepare for your expanded services (which comes into play for food truck owners who have a lease agreement based on the number of hours a month they use the kitchen).

Adding a truck can also put you into a better position to defend your business against price-cutting by your competitors. As you branch out to other markets, you may be able to sell more. This growth in sales volume can help you offset lower per-unit profit.

REMEMBER

As your business increases in size, the costs you pay for your food (cost per unit) can fall, thus resulting in your ability to lower prices or increase your profit, or both. This concept is called *economies of scale.* You should only expand if your economies of scale will allow your business to either sell your food at lower prices or take more profit per order. Speak with your suppliers to find out whether they offer discounts on bigger orders to supply additional trucks; if they do, recalculate your food costs (see Chapter 8 for info on calculating food costs and menu prices). Other costs to consider when thinking about expanding your fleet are the increased weekly costs for fueling additional vehicles and extra maintenance costs for those trucks (Chapter 13 covers this topic in detail).

Focusing on financing

You need to carefully study the financial ramifications of any business expansion and whether your cash flow can support the additional investment. Determining where and how you'll get the money to pay for a new truck, additional inventory, and a bigger staff is important. The ideal situation is to expand when your concept has proven (by a fantastic bottom line) that additional demand exists.

REMEMBER

If you need more capital than you have saved up, make sure the expansion will be profitable enough so you can earn enough money to repay any loans you may need to take to acquire this funding. Too many small businesses have met with failure due to overly aggressive growth. Like any other business decision, only expand when you have financial benefits to gain. Check out Chapters 4 and 5 for help with crunching the numbers.

Keeping an eye on the competition

As I mention in Chapter 3, market research plays a key part in your decision to expand your business. With this research, you get important clues about your market and some indication about what your competitors are up to. If your competitors are increasing their operations, it may be because they've seen new, untapped opportunities in the market. If this is the case, you have two options: (1) Wait and see how your competitors do with their expansion, or (2) follow their lead immediately.

>> By waiting for the results of a competitor's speculation into a new area, you can verify for yourself whether a demand actually exists and whether the benefits outweigh the risks involved. If your competitor's expansion proves to be a mistake, though, you can sit back and be thankful that you weren't the one burned by a costly misjudgment.

>> Immediately following another truck's expansion is risky, and I don't suggest you blindly follow another truck's lead to expand until you've done your own research to determine whether expansion fits *your* business model.

Embracing a change in your role

If you're opening a second truck, you'll need additional staff to operate and manage it (unless you've figured out a way to be in two places at the same time). Also, when expanding, you need to be prepared to delegate more responsibilities to others.

Given these new members in your food truck organization, make sure you stay open to new ideas. For example, the manager of your second truck may have suggestions for how to improve various aspects of the business. Be ready to listen and act on these suggestions, even if you're like many food truck owners who think they know their business by heart, and they — and only they — have the monopoly of ideas on how best to run it. Don't hold onto the idea that you can run the business better than anyone else.

Also note that if you're the creative person in your operation, chances are that the task of taking care of business will take you away from some of the creative work in the kitchen. Business growth may force you to let go of the complete culinary control you enjoyed when the company was much smaller, and that isn't an easy adjustment for some. However, don't fret when making this transition. Remember that this is still your business; you're simply stepping away from one role into another for the sole purpose of improving your business. You can't spend all day working on the business side and then expect to be able to find time to also run the kitchen and the truck as efficiently as you did when preparing food in the truck was your main focus.

Providing Catering Services

If you're not ready to add another truck to your fleet (as I describe earlier in this chapter), catering is a great way to expand the reach of your food truck business. According to the estimates from IBISWorld, catering is a $12-billion-a-year industry, and many food truck owners are joining in. Of the food truck owners I've spoken with, those who are focused on catering events, from office parties to weddings, are covering as much as 40 to 75 percent of their business model from catering alone.

Catering can be done either on-site (some commercial kitchens provide a separate dining facility for their renters) or off-site, with your truck pulled outside of the event area. One advantage of expanding your food truck business into catering is that your start-up costs are very low. Because you already have everything set up for your mobile kitchen, the biggest issue you'll have is finding clients who are interested in using your catering services for their event.

To make sure your customers know that you offer catering services, create a special catering flier with a menu, and have your staff mention your catering services to patrons during their visit to your truck.

If you're thinking about delving into the world of food truck catering to supplement the time your truck isn't busy on the streets, you should be aware of some common mistakes beginner caterers have run into over the years. Check out the following guidelines for successfully easing your way into the catering arena:

>> Catering is usually an efficient revenue stream if priced correctly. Study your competitors, including local grocery stores and delis, to find out what items they cater and how much they charge. Make sure you price accordingly, especially if you offer items that are difficult to find anywhere else in the area.

>> Never give anything away for free. If you give something away for free, clients will always expect freebies. Just as you train your food truck staff to behave in a certain manner, you must train your clients to pay for your services and value your talent. You can give a discount for a charitable event, but make sure you cover all your costs and some of your time.

>> Always put in writing what services you're going to provide for a client and what the client is going to do for you. Don't rely on a verbal agreement.

>> To protect your reputation, you have to know your limits. Saying no to a prospective catering job that you aren't equipped to do or turning down an event on a day when you're already booked is better than doing the job poorly.

>> Find staff members who are willing and able to work both in the truck and at catered functions. This way you don't have to double up on the number of employees you have (those for the truck and a completely different staff for catering).

>> Keep your menu simple. Most of your jobs will come from people who have eaten from your truck, so use your current menu as the basis of the meals you cater. If a customer wants you to expand your menu, make sure you discuss the additional items he may want. Having a rotating menu (as I discuss in Chapter 8) comes in handy so you don't have to create items you may not be familiar with.

>> Be careful never to run out of food at a catering event. Some dishes will go more quickly if you're not distributing the portions yourself, so make sure you have enough. These items may include mashed potatoes, soup, salad, and pasta.

Franchising Your Food Truck Business

Do you think your food truck business is unique? Are your friends, family, and, most importantly, your customers telling you that you should franchise your truck?

In general, *franchising* means the opening of additional trucks through the sale of franchise rights to independent investors *(franchisees)* who will use your name and business model. The franchisee pays you (the *franchisor*) an initial franchise fee in return for the rights to open and operate a food truck under your franchise trademark and menu and for training in how to operate the business. After the start-up period, franchisees may also pay you an ongoing royalty fee (4 to 8 percent of sales) for your continued support and training in advertising, marketing, kitchen guidance, and financial and other services.

Although not entirely accepted by many in the food truck industry (because they feel that the mobile food industry is based on single, solo food trucks, each with their own personal branding and concept), some culinary entrepreneurs are finding that franchising is a way to quickly expand their food truck business with minimal capital and risk. Franchising offers you a number of advantages over other expansion strategies in this chapter:

>> Your business expands by using someone else's money; a franchisee furnishes all the capital required to start the business.

>> Franchisees are responsible for all hiring, leasing, and opening expenses, thus reducing your risk.

>> Franchises can open quickly, often getting a new concept out ahead of the competition.

>> A franchisee assumes the risk of ultimately succeeding or failing.

Some of the disadvantages of franchising include the following:

>> Franchising is a regulated industry. You need to develop and operate your franchise system to satisfy federal and state franchise laws.

>> To set up a franchise around your food truck business, you need to invest time and capital, which goes toward regulatory compliance, attorney fees, and the creation of the systems and programs to be provided to franchisees.

>> After you franchise your business, your role changes from *business operator* to *franchisor.* This role change requires the management of your franchise system, respecting franchise sales, advertising, product development, and service development, which takes you away from the day-to-day operations of your own food truck.

To find out more about franchising your business, contact an attorney who specializes in this area. Depending on where your investors plan to operate a franchise, the attorney needs to be knowledgeable of both state and federal guidelines relating to this issue.

Opening a Brick-and-Mortar Restaurant Based on Your Food Truck's Concept

Although the food truck revolution continues to grow throughout the country, it's also making its way indoors. The owners of some of the most successful trucks in cities such as Los Angeles, New York City, and Chicago are using the hard-earned knowledge, fame, and bankability gained from operating their mobile eateries to expand into their own brick-and-mortar restaurants.

The cost of a used food truck can be as little as $50,000, but opening a small restaurant can easily cost $500,000, while larger restaurants can run into the millions. This is (in addition to the fact that loans are now more difficult to get) the primary reason that so many food trucks have opened since 2008. Many food truck owners' primary goal in starting a food truck is to test a concept and menu before taking on the expense of a restaurant. But these trucks become a hit, racking up good reviews and, more importantly, devoted fans. In essence, the owners of these food trucks find that the trucks are an engine for inexpensive validation. In some cases, a truck's popularity can even help persuade potential landlords to sweeten property deals.

Some obvious advantages to expanding your business into a restaurant include the following:

» You'll have additional room for inventory and cooking, which no longer has to be done in a severely cramped kitchen or a rented space shared with others.

» In a restaurant, you have fewer limitations; for example, you can be a little more creative, and you have the ability to serve more people. Also, if you get a liquor license, you open yourself up to an entirely new revenue stream that (at the time of this writing) is something a food truck can't tap into.

» A restaurant's income typically stays steady during extreme weather swings, while the revenue from a truck can drop 25 to 30 percent during winter months.

» You can use the restaurant as a training ground for your new employees, instead of baptizing them in the fire of the hectic food truck world.

REMEMBER

Most brick-and-mortar eateries attract a different kind of customer base than food trucks do. Instead of young people on a budget who don't mind long waits at a truck, restaurants tend to draw families willing to pay more for the convenience of sitting down. Before you invest your time and money into the route of opening a restaurant, make sure you adjust your concept and menu to meet the possibility of a change in customers.

TIP

If expanding your food truck business into a restaurant atmosphere is something you're interested in, check out the latest edition of *Running a Restaurant For Dummies* by Michael Garvey, Heather Dismore, and Andrew G. Dismore (published by John Wiley & Sons).

Rebranding Your Truck If Your Concept Just Isn't Working

You had a great idea for a food truck. You developed a smart concept and built a strong, highly desirable, and well-priced menu. Your staff is experienced in providing high-quality food and great service, but at the end of the day, your business just hasn't become profitable. Things started off a bit slower than you'd hoped, and your lines never got as long as your competitors'. You've tasted their food, and it's no better than yours. So what's the problem?

Ask yourself a few questions. Is your food truck brand too bland? Do you need to discover how to stand out from the rest of the food trucks navigating the streets of your town? If your concept has become tired and uninteresting to your market's consumers, *rebranding* may be the direction you need to take. Rebranding is the process of reinventing your current concept. Your truck needs it when your original concept brand is no longer doing its job. In the following sections, I walk you through the steps of rebranding your truck.

REMEMBER

Get excited about your rebranding and maintain your passion for your business. Nothing is quite like opening your truck's service window with a fresh look and a new beginning. By sticking to the following rebranding guidelines, you can look forward to many more years of success in the food truck industry.

Knowing when you need to rebrand

REMEMBER

A number of reasons may exist for needing to rebrand your food truck, including staying current with menu trends, shedding negative images, and distinguishing yourself from competitors. Even if you have a great reputation for the food you offer, if that experience doesn't have the same power to attract the masses as it once did, tweaking it won't pay off. If your sales locations are still viable and you and your staff have built a good reputation in the market, you may still need to create a new concept that appeals to the changing consumer trends of those who dine at food trucks.

A lot of food truck owners encounter a moment in their food truck's life cycle when something needs to change. Things may not be working like they once did, or maybe they're just bored with their truck's concept. No matter what the reason, if your truck or concept needs an overhaul, rebranding is the answer.

Noting a few considerations before you begin

REMEMBER

A food truck shouldn't be a business that's just "food for the money" but rather the value of the entire customer experience (menu, atmosphere, and service). You need to evaluate each of these factors and then adjust them accordingly. Before jumping into the process of rebranding, though, consider the following guidelines:

>> **Proceed with a clear plan.** Successful rebranding relies on creative strategies that keep everyone focused as the project progresses.

>> **Understand your brand's value to your existing customers.** Consider your food truck's current strengths and keep them so you don't alienate your established customers. Unnecessary changes can damage your rebranding effort.

>> **Walk in your diners' shoes.** Take time to understand the challenges that your customers face when they dine at your food truck or even when they visit your website. (Take note of the feedback customers provide; see Chapter 14 for details.)

>> **Keep in mind that rebranding doesn't have to be expensive.** Creative thoughts don't necessarily equate to exorbitant costs. Effective, innovative ideas can come from you, your staff, or even amateur consultants, such as marketing interns from your local university.

>> **Realize that your business isn't too small to rebrand.** Every food truck eventually needs to be refreshed as the industry evolves. Even if you own a single truck with a small staff, rebranding is a tool that any size of food truck business can use.

Taking action

Sales are down, but why? You need to determine the answer to this question to know how to properly rebrand your food truck business. From your first sale to the time you step away from your business, you must track the factors involved in creating a product and service your customers desire. To find out more on the topic of evaluating your business, flip to Chapter 14.

After putting together the areas you want to correct, study them to determine what adjustments you need to make to solve them. Do you need to rework your menu, or do you need to streamline your operational processes to get your food out faster and in a less expensive way? Analyze what expenses may be involved in implementing any changes. Hone them toward what will save your customers money or offer them best products. Also, identify what improvements are more likely to bring in new customers. Finally, estimate a time line for each of these changes and their execution. While some changes, such as improving your customer service, can be changed immediately, other changes, such as switching up menu items, may take a little more time.

When you've assembled a list of what's wrong, how to fix the problems, and what your time line for carrying out those changes is, the next step is to specify the role of everyone involved in accomplishing those changes. You can do all these things by creating an action plan, such as the following example:

1. **Determine what needs to improve.**

   Improve customer service, relating to menu items.

2. **Find out what activities you need to carry out to achieve the goal.**

   Train service staff to better understand the menu.

3. **Decide what team member is responsible for each part of the change.**

   You (or your truck manager) are responsible for putting together a training program for your service staff and then implementing it.

4. **Set a date when the goal should be achieved.**

   One week to develop training course; one day to walk staff through training and to test each individual.

5. **Measure the progress, checking in weekly with each person involved.**

   Meet with all staff members to find out whether they're able to better explain the preparation and ingredients of each menu item.

   Talk with or survey customers to find out whether they feel that they're being provided more information about the menu.

6. **Evaluate results.**

   If your customers are pleased with the changes, keep this training program for all new hires. If customers don't feel any positive changes have been made, repeat training, reevaluate the training, or create a new training program.

TIP

After you've created an action plan, discuss where team members are, what you got right, and where you need to make adjustments. Track what works and what doesn't, and gather updates at weekly staff meetings to ensure that the team is keeping their eye on the ball.

Staying aware of potential challenges

REMEMBER

Rebranding won't lead to significant changes if it isn't done when needed, even if you follow the same steps in concept development, research, testing, and planning as you did with your brand-new food truck. Unlike setting your original concept in place, you'll face a new set of challenges in the rebranding process.

>> Potentially, the public eye may have a lot of existing perceptions of your business. You'll need to address these perceptions from the top down so the entire staff is on board with your rebranding strategy. If you have an established brand that was built over time, the rebranding process can take several months, and your staff will need to help you make sure it's implemented. It'll take a careful plan and a helpful staff to make sure your rebranding is executed without a hitch.

>> Even if you have a simple rebrand, you'll have to market your new look. You'll need to build awareness and buzz. Your current patrons and email subscribers are the best tools for creating that buzz. If you've decided to go with a new look that requires repainting or rewrapping you truck, before you close your truck, begin a teaser campaign with your current customers. Encourage them to follow you on Twitter and Facebook, subscribe to your email list (if they aren't already), and visit your website. Use your email list to market weeks before starting the project, and plan a reopening event within the first couple weeks of finishing the project.

>> Evolution is inevitable in any growing business, and for a company to need to grow into a new brand is completely natural. Revamping a new look requires thinking beyond what your food truck business is and what it can become. You must be ready and willing to let go of things from the past that you felt were perfect, because there's a good chance they no longer are.

Selling Your Food Truck

For many business owners, the loss of motivation to log in the long hours, take incredible risks, and work for peanuts is simply a sign that it's time to cash out. If your food truck has been a success, you've probably had to pour most of your time, energy, and money into it. You may see your truck as an extension of yourself, and imagining life without it may be nearly impossible.

On the other hand, your food truck business may have been only marginally successful and something you can't wait to get rid of. Or perhaps you entered the mobile food industry with the idea that it would be a short-term opportunity that could culminate in bigger things (that have or haven't occurred).

Whatever your situation, selling your food truck business is one of the most important things you'll ever do, because unlike all the other business decision you've made over the years, you'll do this only once. You get a single chance to put a price tag on it, and when you sign the sales documents, it's over. In the following sections, I list a few signs that you may be ready to sell your truck; I also provide tips on setting a price and finding a broker.

Recognizing that you may be ready to sell

Here are a few indicators that it may be time to sell your food truck:

>> **It's not fun anymore.** Burnout is a very real issue for food truck owners and an entirely legitimate reason to sell.

>> **You aren't willing to invest in future growth.** You may be comfortable with the current size and profitability of your food truck and have no desire to make the capital investment necessary to take it to the next level.

>> **Your management skills are overmatched.** It's not uncommon for mobile food vendors to build their business to a certain point and then realize they lack the skills required to go further.

REMEMBER

Although these are just some of the reasons food truck owners use to determine whether they're ready to sell their business, you can also use these indicators to modify your current business model. Instead of selling, you may decide to change your role or bring in staff or partners to fill the needs of the business to grow.

WARNING

Here's one last consideration: Make sure you're ready to sell, both financially and emotionally, and think about what life will be like after the truck is out of your hands. What will you do, not only for money but also with your time? If you sell your truck before you're actually ready, you can suffer remorse after handing over the keys to the new owner.

Setting your sales price

Selling a business is both art and science, and in no other area is this more evident than in its valuation. If you're considering selling your business, knowing how much it's worth is important. Too many owners have no idea, and while every seller wants to achieve maximum value for their business, setting an asking price that's too high can signal to buyers that you may not be serious about selling. In the following sections, I guide you through the process of setting a price for your truck.

Gathering important documents

The first step is getting your books in order. Not being able to provide accurate financial statements in a timely manner can cause a deal to unravel. Be sure to have the following documents on hand before you actively start selling your business:

>> Last three years' profit-and-loss statements (or as many years as you've been opened if less than three)

>> Last three years' balance sheets

>> Last three years' full tax returns

>> List of equipment

TIP

Estimate the value of the equipment you own. Believe it or not, your truck, stoves, grills, and refrigerators are highly valuable. Look up the price for these items from equipment resellers that sell the same brands or check out a full list of suppliers from Foodservice Equipment Distributors Association (www.feda.com) and estimate their current market value by determining their age and condition.

>> List of inventories

Be ready to furnish other documentation, such as insurance policies, employment agreements, supplier contracts, trademarked or copyrighted recipes used, equipment leases, and bank statements.

Finding a pro to help you

Prospective buyers want to know how much money they can make from their investment. The value of your food truck business is based on its net income as well as its assets and liabilities. A food truck can bring in a lot of revenue without being very profitable. Although daily, weekly, monthly, and annual revenue of your food truck play a critical element in determining the overall worth of your business, you also have other factors to consider. Food trucks are different than most other businesses, which is why determining fair market value is more complex.

REMEMBER

Being fair or neutral as the owner can be difficult when it comes to valuing the reputation of your food truck, which is why obtaining a business evaluation from a professional is so critical. Because a financial analyst isn't vested in your company, he'll be able to provide a realistic valuation that's free from emotional attachments. I suggest you look for an analyst that specializes in evaluating food industry businesses. Due to the short length of the mobile food industry's existence, your best evaluations will probably come from analysts who have experience in evaluating restaurant businesses.

Using a business broker

You're an expert at running your food truck business, not selling it. I'm surprised by how many vendors are hesitant to hire a business broker to help them with the sale of their business. Sure, saving the 10 percent brokerage fee is nice, but in most cases a good broker can make up for his fee by increasing the value of your sales price. Even though you think you'll be able to sell your business yourself, you're better off hiring a broker who will handle the tasks involved, such as preparing documents, marketing, showing your business to potential buyers, and negotiating the deal.

So where can you find these professionals?

>> **Through referrals:** One of the most common ways to find a broker is through local referrals. Find out who's listing food truck businesses in your area (or nationally) and then discreetly verify their qualifications through industry contacts.

>> **From legal and financial professionals:** A good chance exists that your attorney and accountant are in the loop regarding your exit plans (if they're not, they should be). Ask them to help identify sales brokers in your area.

>> **At your local chamber of commerce:** This organization usually possesses current information about local professionals and can help you identify a broker who's most qualified to help sell your mobile food business.

WARNING

After you've hired a broker, don't make the mistake of disengaging from the selling process. Although your broker will work hard to market your business, no one has more motivation to sell (or inside knowledge about the business) than you do.

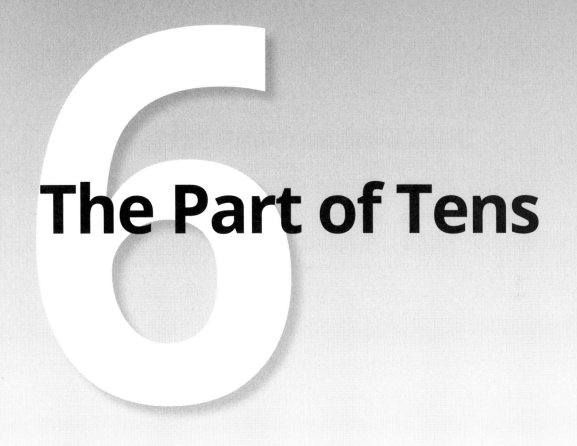

The Part of Tens

Chapter 19

Ten Myths about Food Trucks

O pening a food truck isn't like the movie *Field of Dreams.* If you build it, they may come, or they may just say they'll come. Or they may show up once and never come back.

The mobile food industry is just like any other fledgling industry — it has many success stories, but it also has many stories of failure. Having unrealistic expectations before you make up your mind to open a food truck can give you a false sense of security during the decision-making process. In this chapter, I first dispel some of the most common myths about running a food truck, and then I dispel some myths attributed to the food truck industry.

Running a Food Truck Is Easy

Many people think that running a food truck is a piece of cake because they've seen TV programs such as *The Great Food Truck Race* and *Eat Street* and have watched the operators of those trucks run them (seemingly) quite easily. But beware! To run a food truck, you need to be on the streets six or seven days a week serving lunch and dinner, not to mention the need to be present at any food truck event that pops up. Owning a food truck means working a majority of your waking hours, especially at the start of your business. While your friends and family are out enjoying their holidays, you'll be working. If you aren't out serving your customers, you're shopping for supplies or preparing food. You may be scouting new parking locations or meeting with the city council to make sure a new ordinance that would restrict your business isn't passed.

REMEMBER

Running a food truck involves extremely long hours, no matter how good your staff is. The success of your mobile business relates directly to the amount of time and effort you put into running it. Chapter 1 has full details on determining whether you have what it takes to run a food truck.

I'll Get Rich by Owning a Food Truck

Because the mobile food industry is seeing huge popularity and expansion, some people think that opening a food truck has become the next get-rich-quick business model. As a food truck owner, you're going to experience some good times and some bad. Yes, food trucks can earn a lot of money. However, most of them typically spend almost all they make. Unfortunately, your fixed costs don't change and your bills come due every month. The financing company doesn't reduce your payment just because you have a bad month of sales. Your staff still needs to be paid, too. You must load your truck up with food for every shift, so you must pay for your ingredients, fuel, and insurance. Unless you happen to be independently wealthy and already own your commercial kitchen, you're going to owe rent to your kitchen landlord.

REMEMBER

You can earn a decent living as a food truck owner only if you intend to work in the truck. Many people think they'll open a food truck and draw a paycheck without actually cooking, managing, or working at the service window. Food trucks don't support dead weight for very long. If you don't plan on working, don't plan on getting paid. Do not pass go. Do not collect $200 . . . you have bills to pay.

I Love to Cook, So I Should Open a Food Truck

Sure, your friends and family keep telling you that you should open a food truck because you're such a great cook. They're being nice; that's what friends and families do. They're not the most impartial judges, though. They're happy to get a free meal when they visit your house, but are paying customers going to react the same way if their steak sandwich is overcooked?

TIP

The fastest way to ruin your favorite hobby is to make it your only source of income. Cooking for your friends and family is completely different than cooking for strangers who are paying their hard-earned money for the food you create. Instead of jumping blindly into a large investment of your time and money, try catering a few small parties for individuals who aren't your friends or family. Getting honest opinions of individuals who are paying for your services will tell you very quickly whether you should convert your hobby into your career.

I've Worked in a Food Truck, So I'm Ready to Run the Show

Working in a restaurant or another food truck before owning one gives you a definite advantage over someone starting a truck who has never worked in the mobile food industry. Having previous professional culinary experience, however, doesn't necessarily mean that you're cut out for life as a food truck owner. Being an employee is very different than being the actual employer.

As an employee, you can go home after your shift and not worry about how the next truck payment is going to be made. You aren't concerned about how you're going to be able to pay the commercial kitchen rent if you have another slow week due to the rain that's forecasted. You probably aren't staying up late with your accountant or suppliers to determine ways to trim labor costs or improve the menu.

Owning a food truck is more than a full-time job. It doesn't go away when you park the truck. It's always in the back of your mind. If there's a problem with the truck on your day off, as the owner, you may have to come in and fix it or have it towed to the service shop. The benefits of owning a food truck come with a lot of responsibilities, too.

I'm Going to Be a Celebrity Chef

Everyone dreams of fame and success, and people in food service industries are no different. Why wouldn't you think that if you open a food truck you can become the next Jamie Oliver, Anthony Bourdain, or Bobby Flay? Well, there are tens of thousands of chefs and cooks around the world, and literally thousands of talented and highly trained food truck owners and restaurant chefs who are completely unknown outside of their local area. So how do you think you and your food truck are going to become famous?

Gordon Ramsey, Emeril Lagasse, Wolfgang Puck, and other celebrity chefs seem to be everywhere these days. They have their network cooking shows, fancy cookware lines, and world-renowned restaurants. But they didn't start out famous. They started out with hard work. Although it may be fun to pretend you'll make it big in the entertainment industry, chances are you'll have to settle for being an everyday food truck chef.

Food Trucks Compete Unfairly with Restaurants

One of the most common complaints by disgruntled restaurant owners is that food truck operators' relatively low costs give them an unfair advantage. Before the recent uptick in mobile food vendors across the United States, this occurrence in the restaurant industry was always referred to as a *competitive advantage.* So long as the owner of a competitive advantage was passing the benefit of their "advantage" to their customers in terms of value both economically and in the quality of their cuisine, this has always been looked at as a positive.

The fact that the mobile food industry has changed its perceived limitation as a "food of only convenience" and having a "lack of gourmet flair" is what has shifted consumer perception. The current emphasis on value in the market strongly favors the food truck model, and the value of their gourmet fare is what has attracted many consumers to the new generation of food trucks. However, the bottom line is that if food trucks don't serve quality products, their followers will stop showing up, the same way they stop frequenting restaurants that serve inferior products.

Food Trucks Don't Pay Rent

Food trucks may not have lease or tax payments as high as those of restaurants, but food trucks still have to pay for licenses, permits, food, and staff. In many communities, food trucks also are legally required to pay rent for storage space and the commercial kitchen where they do most of their prep work. The costs can add up!

TECHNICAL STUFF

In cities such as San Francisco, mobile vendors are charged upwards of $10,000 a year to maintain their licenses in certain districts. New York City limits the number of permits it issues to street vendors, which include trucks and carts. Outside of liquor licenses, cities don't limit the number of restaurants that can operate within their city limits.

Food Trucks Go Only to Trendy Areas

Of course food trucks go to trendy areas; food trucks thrive in areas with high foot traffic. In the same way, restaurant owners try to find areas where their business model has the best chance to succeed. Why should food trucks be held down to a foundation or lease when they can simply start up their truck and drive to another area where consumers spend their time?

Some people say that trucks develop followings akin to cults. Food trucks do have followers; the difference lies in their devotion and, as shown to date, food truck followers will follow their food wherever it goes. So if a food truck has a dedicated following, it can go anywhere and operate, thus creating new trendy areas that new restaurateurs can then follow if they choose.

Food Trucks Create More Traffic and Pollution than Restaurants Do

Unhappy restaurant owners who want limiting regulations placed on food truck owners started the myth that food trucks must create additional traffic and pollution to the areas in which they operate based on the fact that food trucks are trucks. Because food trucks spend the majority of their operating time parked in a lot or on the street selling their fare, the point of creating more traffic seems moot. Another way to look at this argument is from the standpoint that food trucks use social media to inform customers of their location from day to day. Much of their sales come from people already in the area, as opposed to many brick-and-mortar establishments, which get people taking taxis or driving themselves to the restaurant's permanent location. Imagine the cuts in deaths due to traffic incidents if people stopped using taxis or personal vehicles to get to their food source.

The longer the food truck industry is popular, the more likely it is that technology will help it to become greener, too. For example, many trucks around the United

States already run their vehicles off the vegetable oil they produce so as to cut down on oil costs for fuel and the emissions their trucks create. Are people as critical of restaurants that generate upwards of 41 percent of their carbon footprint from merely heating and lighting their restaurants? I'd certainly take a food truck that's driving around town on vegetable oil or biodiesel over a restaurant that requires nuclear or coal-based power generation.

The Health Department Doesn't Inspect Food Trucks

One of the more common myths I hear from restaurant owners who aren't fond of the mobile food industry is that food trucks aren't regulated by the same health requirements that they're held to. The idea that food trucks are mobile and thus unable to be tracked by health departments is completely incorrect. For example, the city of Boston requires its food truck operators to install a GPS tracking device before they're even awarded permits to operate, just so the health department can track down their trucks at any time. Other cities require their food trucks to submit weekly truck routes for their review. This procedure gives the health department a way to find any food truck they randomly decide to inspect.

Food trucks follow the same regulations and are required to submit to the same types of inspections as restaurants. Not only that, but in most cities, a food truck is inspected multiple times per year (once before a permit is issued and once again at a random time during the year). Also, the commercial kitchen a food truck is required to prep in must be inspected and maintain health department standards. The grades they receive from health inspectors must be placed in spaces that can be seen by the general public or the truck risks being shut down.

WARNING

As I mentioned in the last section, in addition to standard health inspections of the truck, food truck owners must also be concerned about the inspections that their commercial kitchens receive. If a truck's kitchen receives a failing grade, the truck must either shut down until all the citations are cleared or move to a commercial kitchen that has passed its health department inspection.

Check out Chapters 13 and 21 for additional info on health inspections.

Chapter 20

Ten Tips for Preventing Food Truck Failure

The number of food trucks has been growing exponentially since 2008, yet some food trucks still haven't been able to succeed. In this chapter, you find ten reasons why some food trucks don't survive and tips you can use to avoid these shortfalls.

Develop an Identity and Stick to It

A food truck's success depends on its ability to establish a brand and stick to it, so develop an identity and focus on perfecting it. If your food truck doesn't differentiate itself from the competition, consumer acceptance of your truck's concept is bound to wane quickly after the excitement of a "new kid on the block" attraction fades. Simple, cookie-cutter imitation of an existing concept doesn't have staying power, and most imitations are bound to fail quickly. See Chapter 2 for guidelines on generating a concept for your food truck.

Bringing every customer in your area up to your service window is impossible, so don't spend too much time trying to. Establish your target market (see the next section for details), and then create the style of food and environment that's suitable for that market. Ask yourself, "What experience am I selling from my truck?" Then promote that experience. After you create your identity, make sure it's reflected all of your marketing efforts and in your menu; see Chapter 8 for help.

WARNING

Creating an overreaching menu is one of the most common mistakes a food truck can make. A menu with too much selection tries to do a lot while accomplishing very little. This tactic often sacrifices overall food quality, and it also creates a tremendous amount of waste. Instead, keep your menu simple with no more than four to six items and, ideally, variations on the same thing — chicken, fish, or carne asada tacos, for example. Doing so makes your concept identifiable, brand friendly, and significantly easier to produce.

Analyze Your Market Carefully

As I explain in Chapter 3, market analysis plays a major role in the success or failure of your food truck. Failure to establish that a market for your food truck cuisine exists and failing to stay aware of trends in your local market are two of the biggest mistakes you can make as a food truck operator. These errors are so tragic because they're mistakes that can easily be avoided.

Before opening your food truck business, you need to establish a demand for your cuisine and an ability to capture some market share. After you've opened your service window, you should continue to analyze the direction of consumer demand and make any changes or adjustments as needed. Without this fact-based knowledge of your market, making these informed business changes is near impossible.

TIP

You can perform something as simple as walking your city streets and conducting a survey to establish local consumer likes and dislikes, perceptions, needs, and demands.

TIP

A great way to test your product is to ask an existing food truck operator to do a daily or weekly collaboration. Most operators love to bring something fresh to their customers and having something new onboard often gets customers talking about you. Collaborating with other food truck owners is a terrific way to get your product out there and gain some valuable feedback from real live customers.

Write a Business Plan

A business plan is your written guide of what you want your mobile restaurant to be and how you plan to achieve this goal. It forces you to plan ahead, think about the competition, formulate a marketing strategy, define your management structure, and plan your financing, among other things. It becomes your road map to success.

WARNING

Don't proceed without a solid business plan. Not putting a business plan together doesn't mean that your food truck will fail, but it does mean you'll do the following:

» Spend more money

» Reach fewer of the right customers

» Be less efficient

» Grow your business more slowly, if at all

Think of it this way: If I told you I was going to pay you to drive across the country but that your compensation would be based solely on how quickly you could get there, would you use a map or would you set out on your trip hoping to find a quick route on your own?

The same thinking applies to your food truck's business plan. Could you be successful without one? Sure. But it's going to cost you more and take you longer. So why not just use the map? The old adage "failing to plan is planning to fail" is never more critical than in the mobile food industry. Avoid this mistake and enjoy the fruits of your labor. Chapter 4 has full details on how to create a food truck business plan.

Plan for a Year's Worth of Capital

The mobile food industry is known to have low entry and exit points compared to the restaurant industry (in other words, it doesn't take as much money to start or sell a food truck as it takes to start or sell a restaurant). Thus, most food truck owners try to enter the industry with low capital. As a result, most enter this industry with just enough funding to open the service window but not enough to sustain them in the first few lean months. Unexpected and unforeseen events happen all the time, especially in a food truck business.

REMEMBER

Don't get caught up in the dream of being profitable from Day 1. Plan ahead and make sure you have money left in the bank to help you ride out the difficult days when, say, your truck needs a new generator. A good goal to set for yourself is to allocate enough capital to keep your business afloat for at least 8 to 12 months while you establish yourself in the market. Chapters 4 and 5 provide more info on the financial aspects of starting and running your truck.

Hire and Train Wisely

Bad service will kill your business quickly — it's just that simple. Your food truck has a finite amount of goodwill, and bad staff will use it up all too quickly. Employees are the representatives of your business. Put a substantial amount of time and effort into the hiring process and don't settle for individuals who are less than extraordinary.

Although your team may be very well qualified and your concept may be great, if the concept isn't properly executed, chances are great that your plans will fail. In order to prevent this, it's essential to have proper training manuals/protocols, checklists, goals, and incentives and to make sure they're followed. Flip to Chapter 11 for the full scoop on hiring and training your staff.

TIP

Most food truck owners lack formalized training in procedural and operational processes. If you fit into this category, take the time to learn from an experienced owner or hire a consultant for expert advice.

Have a Grand Opening

"You never get a second chance to make a good first impression" was never truer than in the mobile food industry business. This is why actors rehearse before opening night and why you should, too.

TIP

Hosting a grand opening event is a chance to immediately establish your truck as a member in the local community. Rather than opening your service window and waiting for your guests to arrive, create an event that will lead first-time guests to become your regular customers. Some of the mistakes to sidestep in planning a food truck grand opening are easy to avoid:

>> **Prepare for a crowd.** Many new food truck owners have made the mistake of being too eager to promote opening before they're ready to handle the large crowd it may draw. During a grand opening event, don't hesitate to overstaff

your truck. The first impression you make to the community can be totally altered if you're not ready, regardless of how carefully the actual event has been planned.

>> **Expect the unexpected.** It's the nature of the mobile food industry for things to happen unexpectedly, so it's essential to plan for the things you can control. Address every detail prior to the event so you're able to deal with surprises that may arise — problems like the truck not starting or getting a flat tire on the way to the event. Think about what you'll do if, after you get to the event, your generator fails to start or you run out of propane — or even food. Have a way to correct these (or other) issues before they happen.

>> **Time your event carefully.** Consider other events that may be taking place in the area that could decrease the interest in your grand opening. If it's opening day for your hometown sports team, for example, you may want to consider moving your event up or back a week to avoid the chance that your event won't be attended because everyone will be at the game (or at home watching it).

Ensure Consistency

After you've created an identity for your food truck (which I discuss earlier in this chapter), it's important that you consistently preserve that identity. Every time a customer walks up to your service window, he should experience the same food quality and service. It shouldn't matter which chef is working the kitchen on any given day. This consistency is why McDonald's maintains the number-one sales of any restaurant in the world. No matter where you order a Big Mac, you receive the exact same product. You need to strive for this level of consistency for your food because it's the key to establishing a regular customer base. Managing a customer's expectations is an essential part of running your food truck, and consistently providing the same quality product ultimately can determine its success or failure.

TIP

Your kitchen staff can't maintain consistency without formal recipes. Developing them is critical to controlling costs, curtailing waste, and providing effective staff training. Turn to Chapter 8 to find out more about creating your food truck's menu.

Control Your Food Costs

Outside of the initial capital required to purchase your truck, the cost of food is a mobile bistro's single biggest expense. The ability to manage food costs is one of the most important elements of running a successful food truck.

Determining a proper pricing scheme is the most critical factor in managing food costs. Should you keep your prices lower than those of comparable items at other food trucks or restaurants in your area, or do you make your prices equal to or higher? How should you determine the pricing scheme for your truck? How can you set a price and make it profitable?

The answers to these questions aren't random. Successful food truck owners set the price of a product as a direct relationship to the cost of making that product. Keeping track of how inventory is ordered and minimizing costs so all food that's purchased ends up in a customer's hands can drastically improve your bottom line and provide valuable flexibility in determining your pricing. Be sure to go to Chapter 8 to see how to set your menu pricing.

TIP

Erring on the side of caution and occasionally running out of items on the menu is better than preparing too much food. Running out of items can actually be beneficial to your truck. If a customer orders an item that's sold out, he'll usually order something else gladly and perceive that the sold-out item is popular and of high quality. Thus, he'll be encouraged to visit again in hopes of trying that item. Just make sure that running out of your popular items doesn't become commonplace and part of your customer's perception.

Solicit Opinions Other Than Your Own

When you constrain changes in your business, you automatically prevent ideas that could lead to your success from being found outside of your comfort zone. A shrewd food truck vendor knows it's all about the customer, not your personal tastes and opinions. You must be open to opinions other than your own.

TIP

Strive to maintain a healthy obsession with product and service quality. You must keep a pulse on what your customers like and dislike about your menu and staff. Ask your customers for their complaints or even be so bold as to ask how you can become their favorite food truck. Chapter 14 has details on how to evaluate and use customer feedback.

Be a Present Leader

Don't be an absentee owner. If you want to own a food truck, you must expect to work in it. The only way to maintain familiarity with your business is to spend a significant amount of time there, both physically and mentally. No matter how good your staff is, it's only human nature for them to try to push the boundaries. They may want to do things differently or their own way. It's important to maintain control of your staff and immediately address any problems that arise to ensure that problems don't get out of control. The only way to do this is for you to be there.

WARNING

Don't confuse physical presence with micromanagement. Although your presence is important, it's essential that it doesn't negatively impact the morale of the staff or interfere with their ability to carry out their assigned tasks. Work hard and set an example for your team. If you display dedication and commitment, you may inspire your team to show you the same level of commitment to your mobile food business.

Chapter 21

Ten Tips for Dealing with Food Truck Health Inspections

I t seems to happen regularly. They appear out of nowhere. Unexpected, they arrive just before you're ready to leave the parking lot or right before a busy lunch is about to begin. A clipboard-carrying individual presents you with his credentials and you hope under your breath that everything is ready for his review.

Your friendly neighborhood health inspector has arrived.

Although it may be tempting to put off certain repairs or overlook a few minor health violations in hopes that the health inspector won't pay you a visit in the near future, a better practice is to treat every day as the day an inspector will show up. In this chapter, I provide ten tips to keep that health report spotless and those citation costs to a minimum. (Flip to Chapter 13 for more information on running a safe, clean food truck.)

TECHNICAL STUFF

Although municipalities across the United States are facing budgetary shortfalls, health inspectors are not only a public safety necessity but also a fantastic government profit center. Business owners outside the mobile food industry have noted that visits by health inspectors have been far less frequent since the beginning of the recession in 2008. But with the constant discussion of food trucks from Los Angeles to New York City, local health inspectors seem to be visiting food truck owners on a more consistent basis. Fines for health violations can range from a mere $50 to hundreds of dollars. In Los Angeles, a failing food truck can pay more than $150 for a reinspection and hopefully a better score.

Inspect Your Food Truck Every Month

REMEMBER

The best way for you and your employees to prepare for any inspection is by performing a self-inspection on your food truck every month. The saying "practice makes perfect" fits perfectly into any conversation about the health inspections your food truck receives. When conducting self-inspections, you should take the role of the inspector and have another staff member take your role so your employees know what will be looked at and how they can help maintain your truck with minimal assistance. Here are some tips for conducting monthly truck inspections:

>> *Surprise!* Most routine inspections are unannounced, so pick a random day of the week to surprise your employees with an inspection. This element of surprise keeps them on their toes and encourages them to maintain proper food handling practices daily.

>> **Arm yourself with the right tools.** To provide a thorough inspection, you need to be as prepared to inspect your truck as the health officials are. Some of the more common tools an inspector carries are a thermometer, a flashlight, a clipboard, and inspection forms. Using these tools allows you be as accurate and true to the process as possible.

>> **Use the local inspection sheet.** Using the same sheet as health inspectors allows you to know exactly what they're looking for and the severity of each violation. Most health departments have these forms available online. Health inspectors also have extra forms with them and are more than happy to provide you with a copy for your own inspections.

>> **Start outside.** The first thing an inspector sees when she arrives to perform an inspection is the outside of your truck. For this reason, the exterior cleanliness of the truck is crucial because it offers the inspector that all-important first impression of your mobile food business.

>> **Give your truck the white-glove treatment.** Overinspecting your food truck is a surefire way to pass a future health inspection. Being extremely thorough in your self-inspections keeps you one step ahead of any violations that may be found by a real inspector. Striving for perfection shows your employees and inspectors that you're serious about running a safe and healthy mobile food business.

>> **Ask "why" questions.** During inspections, health officials often ask employees questions about the tasks they're currently performing. The inspector is there not only to ensure proper food-safety practices but also to educate your staff on the prevention of future health violations. In your self-inspections, you must take over this role. Asking workers task-oriented and safety questions during your own inspections keeps the knowledge fresh in their minds and helps you gauge whether your training techniques are effective.

>> **Check your records.** Most health departments require food truck employees to be certified food handlers, which means each employee must receive training and pass a test in safe food-handling practices. Your inspector may ask you for any other critical records that you have (including temperature, employee illness, hand-washing, training, or HACCP [Hazard Analysis & Critical Control Points] records) to ensure that you're properly monitoring state and federal food safety practices. Taking the time to review these records yourself keeps them in order and up-to-date and also ensures that you'll have them on hand when the real inspector shows up. Having these records both on the truck and in your off-truck office prevents an inspector from having to reschedule to a time when you'll have the records present for his review.

>> **Point out the positive as well as the negative.** Positive reinforcement is a proven teaching method, so make sure to point out when an employee is doing something correctly during an inspection. When an employee is performing a task incorrectly, take the time to explain the proper technique so she's less likely to repeat the error.

>> **Review your findings.** Plan a short meeting to go over your inspection findings with your team. Point out the positive and negative findings and spend a little time explaining proper practices that need to be implemented. Providing knowledge of why a certain action is required is more likely to resonate with your employees than just telling them to do something.

TIP

The best rule here is common sense: Would you eat from your food truck? Or better yet, would you feed your loved ones off your food truck? The answer always needs to be YES! If the answer is no, you need to improve things.

Schedule a Mandatory Staff Meeting to Delegate Tasks

Within a day of your monthly self-inspection, or official health department inspection, schedule a staff meeting to go over the findings. Make sure your staff knows this meeting is more official than your regular meetings. Be sure to have an agenda plus a time and action plan, and assign tasks to each employee regarding what needs to be inspected and cleaned in order to comply with health department regulations.

Be sure you give yourself or your truck manager enough time to complete all the assigned tasks before the inspection. Finding out that a task hasn't been completed during a follow-up inspection can leave a bad taste in an inspector's mouth and may give her some pause before rescheduling another inspection to make sure all areas of the truck have been properly cleaned.

Figure Out What to Fix from the Past

Use your previous inspection reports, which the health department provides upon completion of its inspection, as a guide to help you and your staff clean your kitchen, service window area, storage, and cooler areas. Before an inspector shows up, he usually does the same thing and typically makes a point of reexamining these areas to make sure you're keeping them up to snuff. Showing that you've taken care of previous issues tells an inspector that you take his reports seriously. Some health officials even speed up their inspections knowing that you're willing to listen to them and follow their advice.

Ask for an Inspection by an Exterminator

Nothing will shut down a food truck faster than an inspector finding a cockroach or the remains of a little critter. Because rodents, flies, cockroaches, and other pests can contaminate food and food preparation surfaces, any evidence of vermin or insects inside a food truck can cause point deductions. If an active infestation is discovered, the health inspector can shut down the establishment immediately and keep it closed until the problem is resolved.

You or your employees may not see any type of bug in your truck throughout the year, but having an annual inspection done by an exterminator and keeping the records on file will certainly help ease your mind when the health inspector comes calling.

Check Your Refrigeration

You and your employees open and close your food truck refrigerators numerous times throughout the day, causing their internal temperature to rise several degrees. If your refrigerator is set at exactly the minimum required temperature of 41degrees Fahrenheit, the actual temperature may be several degrees higher by the middle of the day. Consistently check the temperature inside the refrigerators to make sure your food is being stored at the proper temperature.

WARNING

If your refrigerator has shelves built into the doors, keep in mind that these shelves are the warmest places in the appliance and aren't the best place to store perishables. Inspectors can't seem to resist the urge to check the temperatures of the foods stored in these shelves. You can safely store fruit drinks, bottled drinks, products in jars, sauces, condiments, and generally products with a longer shelf life on the shelves and in the compartments on the inside of the refrigerator door.

TIP

Often a cooler thermometer will appear to be working properly, but the inspector's digital thermometer will say differently, which may cost you in terms of points and profits. Make sure you or your chef has a meat thermometer at room temperature in the truck. Placing one in the pocket of a chef coat is a great idea.

Another refrigeration area to look at is the drainage. Each week, make sure your drains are flowing freely by pouring boiling water into the bottom of the appliance to find and remove any clogs.

Keep Your Cooler Shelves Clean

TIP

The bottoms of cooler shelves have a tendency to collect grime, dirt, or residue from vegetables, meat, spilled milk, and so on and are regularly missed by cleaners. A health inspector informed me that a lot of fairly new food trucks are found guilty of making this mistake during inspections after their openings. Every week, or as needed, fill a sink with warm soapy water, remove all trays and racks from the inside of the cooler, and wash them in the sink. Wash the inside of the cooler along the sides and bottom with the warm soapy water, too.

Check Your Water Temperature

Over time, the water heaters used in food trucks can fail to reach their maximum water temperature. Although the water may feel hot to your touch, it may not meet your health department's standard. Why risk a mark against you during your inspection — or even a fine — if using a thermometer under your water tap monthly can help you avoid it? If you determine that your water heater isn't producing water at its maximum temperature (check the manufacture's guide for the specific data for your equipment), contact a licensed plumber to repair or replace the unit.

Clean Your Drinking Glasses

Yes, your personal coffee mugs or water cups that you have sitting around while you're busy working the grill can be inspected, too. The problem probably isn't a citable one, but any significant sign of dirt and wear can affect the way the inspector perceives your entire operation. So don't give her any more reason to look deeper into an inspection to find issues you may have missed. An easy way to keep these items in check is to wash them daily as you clean the truck interior and equipment at the end of the workday.

Proactively Make an Appointment for an Inspection

After you and your team have completed a thorough cleaning of the truck (with the help of the preceding sections), call your health inspector and ask him to schedule your vehicle for an inspection. Let him know that you're attempting to achieve a high health department score and that you'd like an inspection in the near future. Due to their tight schedules, many inspectors will fit you in as soon as possible because they know they'll be busy later in the year as new inspections, reinspections, and follow-up inspections are called for. And that way, you'll know that your truck is as clean as possible during the inspection.

Inform Your Staff that the Health Inspector Is Coming — It's Showtime!

Make sure that every one of your employees knows that the inspector may show up. Even if it's a week before the scheduled inspection, make sure your employees are on their toes by monitoring the truck's cleanliness and pointing out issues that need correction immediately.

TIP

Remind everyone to wash their hands frequently, and keep water splashed in the hand sinks. Nothing is worse than having your hand sinks spotless and dry when the inspector shows up.

Index

cost
  of franchises, 36
  of incorporating, 101
  of mobile payment options, 206–207
Cousins Maine Lobsters (website), 37
covering windows, 230
CPA (Certified Public Accountant), 97
craigslist (website), 31, 173
creating
  balance sheets, 75–77
  a competitive analysis, 49–50
  employee schedules, 187–189
  inventory system, 162–167
  logo, 118–120
  menus, 140
  organizations, 102–103
  press releases, 259–261
  repeat customers, 302–303
  supply list, 156–157
  SWOT analysis, 50–51
  vehicles, 30–31
  websites, 261–268
  your marketing message, 254–255
Creative Mobile Systems (website), 31
creativity, motivations for, 40
credit-card payments, 205–206
criticism, of employees, 186
cross-contamination, 214, 215–216
crowds, managing the, 14–15
Cruising Kitchens (website), 31
cuisine
  about, 18–19
  ethnic, 128
  sticking to one basic, 21
Culinary Incubator (website), 145
culinary skills, requirements for, 21
current liabilities, 77
customer base, narrowing concept based on, 22
customer feedback, 243–247
customer indicators, 241
customers
  about, 291

  creating repeat, 302–303
  distinguishing yourself from competitors, 300–302
  engaging in a recipe contest, 273
  establishing email lists with, 299–300
  estimating numbers of, 67
  expectations of, 296–298
  finding customer data from, 48
  identifying and analyzing potential, 42–45
  listening to your, 294–295
  observing your, 294–295
  researching, 292–296
  safety of, 224–229
  talking to face to face, 245
  treating them the right way, 298–299
  typical experience for, 295–296
cuts, 225–226

D

data
  acting on, 52
  finding on competitors, 47–48
date, in press releases, 259
days of operation, on website, 265
D.C. Empanadas (food truck), 38
debt capital
  about, 84, 85
  government assistance, 87–88
  local banks, 85–87
decision-making
  for franchises, 36
  for menu, 128–131
decorating, 120–121
defensive driving, 228
defrosting food, 214
delegating tasks, 337–338
delivery schedule, negotiating with suppliers on, 160
demographic survey, 22
demographics, 42–45, 254
descriptions, on menu board, 138–139

incorporating, 101

Indeed (website), 173

Indian cuisine, 19

indirect competitors, 46

indirect costs, pricing and, 133

industry description and outlook, in market analysis, 61

industry expertise, as a consideration for accountants, 97

injuries, avoiding, 224–228

inspections, health department, 326

inspiration, from others, 21

Instagram, 287

insurance
  about, 107
  additional insured certificates, 109
  as an employee benefit, 190
  basics of, 107–109
  finding providers, 97–98

Insure My Food Trailer (website), 98

Insure My Food Truck (website), 98

insured certificates, 109

internal temperature, 214

interviewing
  employees, 176–178
  suppliers, 159

introduction, in press releases, 259

Intuit GoPayment, 206

inventory
  building a system, 162–167
  defined, 162
  determining level of, 162–163
  taking for commercial kitchens, 146–147

inventory value indicator, 240

investors, compensating, 91

inviting friends on Facebook, 281

IRS
  paperwork for new hires, 178–179
  website, 102, 106

Italian cuisine, 19

item quantity, negotiating with suppliers on, 160

J

Jamie Oliver's Food Revolution, 27

job descriptions
  in job description, 175
  writing, 174–175

job title, in job description, 174

joining franchises, 35–38

K

Kelly, Thomas (business owner), 273

Kent, Peter (author)
  Search Engine Optimization For Dummies, 268

key performance indicators (KPIs)
  about, 238
  most useful, 238–242
  using, 242

keywords, in Twitter bio, 274

Kickstarter.com (website), 91

kitchen. *See* commercial kitchen

kitchen incubator, 144–145

kitchen indicators, 239–240

kitchen workers, 172

Klout, 289–290

knowing your followers, 293–294

Kogi BBQ, 38, 279

KPI Library (website), 238

KPIs. *See* key performance indicators (KPIs)

Krueger, Richard (author)
  Facebook Marketing For Dummies, 285

L

labor hours indicator, 240

lacerations, 225–226

Lacy, Kyle (author)
  Twitter Marketing For Dummies, 272

landfill usage, for "green" kitchens, 151

layout
  for commercial kitchens, 148–149
  of menu board, 138–139

leadership, 332–333

leasing vehicles, 29–30

LEED Green Building Rating System, 151

legal issues
  about, 93–94
  accountants, 96–97
  attorneys, 94–96
  business structures, 99–101
  buying insurance, 107–109
  insurance providers, 97–98
  licenses and permits, 104–107
  local laws, 103–104
  organizations, 102–103

legal knowledge, for truck wrapping, 122

legal professionals, for business brokers, 318

LegalZoom (website), 34, 101, 107

liabilities
  current, 77
  defined, 63, 76
  long-term, 77

license, 104

lighting, 23

limited partnerships, 89, 100

LinkedIn (website), 173, 190

listening, to your customers, 294–295

listeria monocytogenes, 213

local banks, 85–87

local laws, familiarizing yourself with, 103–104

local parks, 116–117

locations
  for commercial office, 198
  considerations for, 21
  for truck, 230

logo, creating your, 118–120

long-term liabilities, 77

M

magazine articles, finding customer data from, 48

Mail Chimp (website), 300

maintenance, regular, 231, 232–233

managed care programs, 190

management powers, in partnerships, 100

management team, in business plan, 58, 64

managers, 171

managing
  food costs, 331–332
  health inspections, 335–340
  refunds, 207–208
  returns, 207–208

map, on website, 264–265

marinating food, 214

market
  about, 39
  analysis tools, 49–52
  analyzing your, 42–45, 328
  competition, 40
  competitive response cycle, 41–42
  identifying potential customers, 42–45
  monitoring your competition, 45–48
  profitability, 41–42

market analysis, in business plan, 61–62

market share, in market analysis, 62

market test results, in market analysis, 62

marketing. *See also* public relations (PR)
  about, 253
  communicating your message with public relations, 256–259
  creating a website, 261–268
  defining your message, 253–255

marketing and public relations (PR) cost indicator, 241

marketing indicators, 241–242

Martindale-Hubbell (website), 95

Martinez, Raul (ice cream vendor), 38

materials, for truck wrapping, 122

meals, free or discounted, 191

mechanics, finding, 233–234

media, in market analysis, 62

Mediterranean cuisine, 19

meet-ups, food truck, 116

menu
  about, 127
  changing, 142

processing credit-card payments, 205–206

Products and Services subsection, in an executive summary, 58

professional support, for franchises, 36

professionalism, for visiting local banks, 87

profit and loss distribution, in partnerships, 100

profitability, relationship with competitive response cycle, 41–42

profits, estimating, 74

projecting cash flow, 74–75

promoting Facebook pages on your website, 282

promotional tweets, 276

Propser.com (website), 90

proximity, determining, 150

PRWeb (website), 259

psychology, applying to pricing, 137

public relations (PR). *See also* marketing

about, 253

communicating your marketing message with, 256–259

defined, 256

press releases, 259–261

puncture wounds, 225–226

purchasing vehicles, 30–32

Q

QSR Magazine (website), 173

qualifications, in job description, 175

R

raising capital, 101

rebranding, 312–315

reducing waste, 166–167

references

asking for, 234

for attorneys, 96

referrals, for business brokers, 318

refrigeration

checking, 338–339

of food, 215

inventory for, 147

refrigeration unit, 230

refunds, handling, 207–208

registering names, 34–35

reheating food, 215

Remember icon, 3

renting

about, 324–325

commercial kitchens from restaurants, 152

repair shop, 234

repeat customers, creating, 302–303

requirements, in job description, 175

research firms, 44–45

researching

customers, 292–296

names, 34–35

relying on, 113

target customers, 254

resources

atmosphere, 23

for franchises, 37

in market analysis, 62

response rates indicator, 241

restaurant industry trade shows, 158

restaurants, renting commercial kitchens from, 152

retaining employees, 189–193

retirement plans, as an employee benefit, 190–191

retrofitting, 25

returns, handling, 207–208

retweet, 272

Rickshaw Dumpling Truck (website), 275

Risk Strategies Company (website), 98

Road Stoves

as a leasing company, 29

website, 31

role changes, 308

royalties, 37, 310

rules, for franchises, 36

Running a Restaurant For Dummies (Garvey, Dismore and Dismore), 312

S

safety
  about, 211–212
  cross-contamination, 214, 215–216
  of customers, 224–229
  of employees, 224–229
  food, 212–217
  fuel costs, 231–232
  hand-washing, 216–217
  temperature, 229–230
sales
  forecasting, 66–69
  tracking, 202–203
  under-ringing, 165
sales for the year, estimating, 68–69
Sales Forecast subsection, in an executive
    summary, 58
sales indicators, 239–240
sales inquiry conversion rate indicator, 241
sales per head indicator, 239
salmonella, 213
savings, personal, 82–83
savory foods, 18–19
SBA (Small Business Administration), 87–88, 191
SBDC (Small Business Development Center),
    43–44
Scan/US (website), 113
schedules, creating for employees, 187–189
Schillace, David (business owner), 273
schools, 153, 173
Sea Birds Truck (website), 274
search engine optimization (SEO), 266–268
Search Engine Optimization For Dummies (Kent), 268
security, 201
seed capital, 80
self-reliance, 12
selling your food truck business, 316–318
sending tweets, 275–278
SEO (search engine optimization), 266–268
service mark, 34
service window attendants, 171

ServSafe Certification (website), 172
setting
  expectations, 297
  sales price for your business, 317–318
setup
  Facebook page, 280–282
  Foursquare account, 286–287
  mobile phone on Facebook, 282
  office, 196–199
shared-use commercial kitchen, 144–145
shigella, 213
silent partners, 89
simplicity, for logo, 119
Simply Hired (website), 190
size
  of commercial kitchen, 149–150
  of commercial office, 198
  of firm, as a consideration for accountants, 97
  of logo, 119
slips, 226–227
Small Business Administration (SBA), 87–88, 191
small business associations, 43–44
Small Business Development Center (SBDC),
    43–44
SoCalMFVA (Southern California Mobile Food
    Vendors Association), 38
social clubs, 153
social media
  about, 269
  Facebook, 279–285
  finding customer data from, 47–48
  Foursquare, 285–287
  importance of, 269–270
  Instagram, 287
  Klout, 289–290
  Pinterest, 288
  Twitter, 270–279
  Yelp, 288–289
software, 200–201
sole proprietorships, as a business structure, 99
soliciting opinions, 332

Notes

Notes

About the Author

Richard Myrick is one of the foremost thought leaders on the mobile food industry. To service the needs of individuals and food truck owners, Richard founded the Mobile Cuisine website (www.mobile-cuisine.com) in 2010 to fill an information void he found when he began researching how to start a mobile hot dog cart in Chicago. Richard found that no central repository of mobile street food information was available anywhere on the Internet, and with that, the idea for Mobile Cuisine was born.

Richard is an architect by degree (Lawrence Technological University, Southfield, Michigan) and began his career in real estate development and architectural planning after spending 12 years in the United States Air Force. During his time working for mall developers across the Midwest, Richard assisted in the build-out of more than 100 restaurants, varying in size from small food kiosks to stand-alone fine-dining facilities.

Shortly after the original publishing of this book, Richard received a culinary scholarship through Food Network's *The Great Food Truck Race* to the Illinois Institute of Art – Chicago. This experience gave him a unique perspective on the food service industry, which he shares with Mobile Cuisine's readers daily.

Richard, a Michigan native, currently resides outside of Detroit, Michigan, with his wife, Hannah. He is the father of three beautiful and intelligent girls: Erica, Ally, and Tessa.

For more information, please contact Richard at rmyrick@mobile-cusine.com; you can also read his articles at www.mobile-cuisine.com.

Authors' Acknowledgments

I have to thank Tracy Boggier, the acquisitions editor for this book, for your confidence in me, for your encouragement, and for keeping me on track. Thank you for the opportunity to work with the best in the business.

A special thank you to my wife, Hannah, who has put up with all the late nights and early mornings to write this book on time (okay, maybe not all on time).

And finally, I want to thank everyone who has ever wanted to join or is currently in the mobile food industry. Without you, I would have never had a reason to start up Mobile Cuisine and write this book. Your dedication and desire to create mobile culinary delights is an inspiration, and I will always try to help promote the industry to the people you serve.

Dedication

This book is dedicated to all my friends and family who have been so supportive throughout my life. Most of all, it's dedicated to my wife, Hannah, and children, Erica, Ally, and Tessa, who are my inspiration in everything I do and every choice I make.

Publisher's Acknowledgments

Acquisitions Editor: Tracy Boggier

Project Editor: Tim Gallan

Technical Reviewer: Scott Cramer

Art Coordinator: Alicia B. South

Production Editor: Vasanth Koilraj

Cover Image: © Falasophy™; (Branding & Food Truck Design) Design Womb; (Mobile Food & Food Truck Photography) Michelle Edmunds Photography; (Photo Imaging & Retouching) Core Group Studio

Apple & Mac

iPad For Dummies,
6th Edition
978-1-118-72306-7

iPhone For Dummies,
7th Edition
978-1-118-69083-3

Macs All-in-One
For Dummies, 4th Edition
978-1-118-82210-4

OS X Mavericks
For Dummies
978-1-118-69188-5

Blogging & Social Media

Facebook For Dummies,
5th Edition
978-1-118-63312-0

Social Media Engagement
For Dummies
978-1-118-53019-1

WordPress For Dummies,
6th Edition
978-1-118-79161-5

Business

Stock Investing
For Dummies, 4th Edition
978-1-118-37678-2

Investing For Dummies,
6th Edition
978-0-470-90545-6

Personal Finance

Personal Finance
For Dummies, 7th Edition
978-1-118-11785-9

QuickBooks 2014
For Dummies
978-1-118-72005-9

Small Business Marketing
Kit For Dummies,
3rd Edition
978-1-118-31183-7

Careers

Job Interviews
For Dummies, 4th Edition
978-1-118-11290-8

Job Searching with Social
Media For Dummies,
2nd Edition
978-1-118-67856-5

Personal Branding
For Dummies
978-1-118-11792-7

Resumes For Dummies,
6th Edition
978-0-470-87361-8

Starting an Etsy Business
For Dummies, 2nd Edition
978-1-118-59024-9

Diet & Nutrition

Belly Fat Diet For Dummies
978-1-118-34585-6

Mediterranean Diet
For Dummies
978-1-118-71525-3

Nutrition For Dummies,
5th Edition
978-0-470-93231-5

Digital Photography

Digital SLR Photography
All-in-One For Dummies,
2nd Edition
978-1-118-59082-9

Digital SLR Video &
Filmmaking For Dummies
978-1-118-36598-4

Photoshop Elements 12
For Dummies
978-1-118-72714-0

Gardening

Herb Gardening
For Dummies, 2nd Edition
978-0-470-61778-6

Gardening with Free-Range
Chickens For Dummies
978-1-118-54754-0

Health

Boosting Your Immunity
For Dummies
978-1-118-40200-9

Diabetes For Dummies,
4th Edition
978-1-118-29447-5

Living Paleo For Dummies
978-1-118-29405-5

Big Data

Big Data For Dummies
978-1-118-50422-2

Data Visualization
For Dummies
978-1-118-50289-1

Hadoop For Dummies
978-1-118-60755-8

Language &
Foreign Language

500 Spanish Verbs
For Dummies
978-1-118-02382-2

English Grammar
For Dummies, 2nd Edition
978-0-470-54664-2

French All-in-One
For Dummies
978-1-118-22815-9

German Essentials
For Dummies
978-1-118-18422-6

Italian For Dummies,
2nd Edition
978-1-118-00465-4

Available in print and e-book formats.

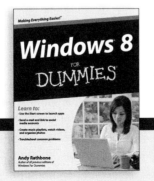

Available wherever books are sold. **For more information or to order direct visit www.dummies.com**

Math & Science

Algebra I For Dummies,
2nd Edition
978-0-470-55964-2

Anatomy and Physiology
For Dummies, 2nd Edition
978-0-470-92326-9

Astronomy For Dummies,
3rd Edition
978-1-118-37697-3

Biology For Dummies,
2nd Edition
978-0-470-59875-7

Chemistry For Dummies,
2nd Edition
978-1-118-00730-3

1001 Algebra II Practice
Problems For Dummies
978-1-118-44662-1

Microsoft Office

Excel 2013 For Dummies
978-1-118-51012-4

Office 2013 All-in-One
For Dummies
978-1-118-51636-2

PowerPoint 2013
For Dummies
978-1-118-50253-2

Word 2013 For Dummies
978-1-118-49123-2

Music

Blues Harmonica
For Dummies
978-1-118-25269-7

Guitar For Dummies,
3rd Edition
978-1-118-11554-1

iPod & iTunes
For Dummies, 10th Edition
978-1-118-50864-0

Programming

Beginning Programming
with C For Dummies
978-1-118-73763-7

Excel VBA Programming
For Dummies, 3rd Edition
978-1-118-49037-2

Java For Dummies,
6th Edition
978-1-118-40780-6

Religion & Inspiration

The Bible For Dummies
978-0-7645-5296-0

Buddhism For Dummies,
2nd Edition
978-1-118-02379-2

Catholicism For Dummies,
2nd Edition
978-1-118-07778-8

Self-Help & Relationships

Beating Sugar Addiction
For Dummies
978-1-118-54645-1

Meditation For Dummies,
3rd Edition
978-1-118-29144-3

Seniors

Laptops For Seniors
For Dummies, 3rd Edition
978-1-118-71105-7

Computers For Seniors
For Dummies, 3rd Edition
978-1-118-11553-4

iPad For Seniors
For Dummies, 6th Edition
978-1-118-72826-0

Social Security
For Dummies
978-1-118-20573-0

Smartphones & Tablets

Android Phones
For Dummies, 2nd Edition
978-1-118-72030-1

Nexus Tablets
For Dummies
978-1-118-77243-0

Samsung Galaxy S 4
For Dummies
978-1-118-64222-1

Samsung Galaxy Tabs
For Dummies
978-1-118-77294-2

Test Prep

ACT For Dummies,
5th Edition
978-1-118-01259-8

ASVAB For Dummies,
3rd Edition
978-0-470-63760-9

GRE For Dummies,
7th Edition
978-0-470-88921-3

Officer Candidate Tests
For Dummies
978-0-470-59876-4

Physician's Assistant Exam
For Dummies
978-1-118-11556-5

Series 7 Exam For Dummie
978-0-470-09932-2

Windows 8

Windows 8.1 All-in-One
For Dummies
978-1-118-82087-2

Windows 8.1 For Dummies
978-1-118-82121-3

Windows 8.1 For Dummies,
Book + DVD Bundle
978-1-118-82107-7

⟨e⟩ Available in print and e-book formats.

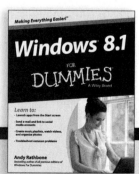

Available wherever books are sold. **For more information or to order direct visit www.dummies.com**

Take Dummies with you everywhere you go!

Whether you are excited about e-books, want more from the web, must have your mobile apps, or are swept up in social media, Dummies makes everything easier.

...age the Power

For Dummies is the global leader in the reference category and one of the most trusted and highly regarded brands in the world. No longer just focused on books, customers now have access to the For Dummies content they need in the format they want. Let us help you develop a solution that will fit your brand and help you connect with your customers.

Advertising & Sponsorships

Connect with an engaged audience on a powerful multimedia site, and position your message alongside expert how-to content.

Targeted ads • Video • Email marketing • Microsites • Sweepstakes sponsorship